*John Persico Jr., PhD*
*Patricia Rouner Morris*

# The New Business Values for Success in the Twenty-First Century
### *Improvement, Innovation, Inclusion, Incentives, Information*

"**I**n this latest book, John Persico and Patricia Rouner Morris set out to reframe crucial values for an interdependent world. They examine the need for individuals and organizations to consider the next wave of value change. This wave will be more appropriate for the common good and can lead to the transformation that TQM and the Quality Movement foreshadowed. Indeed, the era of TQM, according to the authors, may have been just the first phase of a longer wave of deep changes for our government, organization, and businesses.

The book cites five new values and links them to quality, strategy, roles, incentives, and measurement. The authors' early experiences with the Q movement have clearly influenced their outlook. They address all the right concepts to bring about significant change.

In the discussion of deeper organizations in Chapter 10, we begin to see the emergent theme of the responsibility of society as a whole. The notion of including long-term value for stockholders, employees, customers, and society as a whole is a powerful one. Linking strength to learning and to caring on the corporate level is a critical element of this book. The notion of a personal quality journal is fresh and attractive. The 12-step program is practical and innovative.

The discussion of new style incentives is one of the most valuable and thought-provoking of the entire book. The authors have rejected the old notion of performance appraisal and competition. Here a good discussion of the other possibilities comes forth. The authors outline many possibilities linking their argument to the history of the Q movement and to the recent changes in organizations like Sony.

This book offers new intellectual tools to better deal with and understand values in the shaping of the future."

**Gail R. Dimitroff**
*Managing Director,*
*Gail Dimitroff and Associates,*
*La Mesa, CA*

"**T**he unbounded prosperity of certain business ventures at times appears independent of management. Other ventures are not so fortunate. As a manager who has struggled with the task of building a business in a difficult market, I am always on the look-out for resources that will help me achieve my goals. This book is one such resource, and a wonderful one at that.

I have many university textbooks on my shelf that I once studied relentlessly and now rarely open. On the other hand, I have a few excellent handbooks acquired intermittently during my professional career that I refer to regularly. Most of these handbooks are published by well-established companies that produce a product tempered by challenging applications and persistent competition. They are concise, practical texts based on years of collective experience. They teach me things that I never learned in school but use every day. *New Business Values* is a handbook of this stature. It is a workbook that you read, put on your desk, and then revisit again and again.

For me, the endearing aspect of this book is the practical wisdom of the authors that allows them to address the soul of a business as opposed to the mechanics of a business. They remind us in numerous ways that the health of a business is related to the health of the individuals who make up the business. Their holistic approach leads us, as managers, to look at ourselves. And not just at our skills, but at our hearts."

**Dennis D. Chilcote, PhD**
*Director of Engineering,*
*BioTrol,*
*Eden Prairie, MN*

The Haworth Press, Inc.

## NOTES FOR PROFESSIONAL LIBRARIANS AND LIBRARY USERS

This is an original book title published by The Haworth Press, Inc. Unless otherwise noted in specific chapters with attribution, materials in this book have not been previously published elsewhere in any format or language.

## CONSERVATION AND PRESERVATION NOTES

All books published by The Haworth Press, Inc. and its imprints are printed on certified ph neutral, acid free book grade paper. This paper meets the minimum requirements of American National Standard for Information Sciences–Permanence of Paper for Printed Material, ANSI Z39.48-1984.

# The New Business Values
## for Success
## in the Twenty-First Century
### *Improvement, Innovation, Inclusion, Incentives, Information*

# *HAWORTH* Marketing Resources
## Innovations in Practice & Professional Services
### William J. Winston, Senior Editor

New, Recent, and Forthcoming Titles:

# The New Business Values for Success in the Twenty-First Century

## Improvement, Innovation, Inclusion, Incentives, Information

John Persico Jr., PhD
Patricia Rouner Morris

The Haworth Press
New York • London

The Haworth Press, Inc., 10 Alice Street, Binghamton, NY 13904-1580

Cover design by Monica Seifert.

**Library of Congress Cataloging-in-Publication Data**

Persico, John.
    The new business values for success in the twenty-first century : improvement, innovation, inclusion, incentives, information / John Persico Jr., Patricia Rouner Morris.
        p.   cm.
    Includes bibliographical references (p.   ) and index.
    ISBN 0-7890-0155-1
    1. Industrial management. 2. Success in business. I. Morris, Patricia Rouner. II. Title.
HD31.P382  1997
650—DC21
                                                                96-51808
                                                                    CIP

# CONTENTS

# ABOUT THE AUTHORS

**John Persico Jr., PhD,** is the president of Strategy 1000, an independent consulting and training firm. As an independent consultant, he helps managers to rethink how they do business and helps leaders develop strategies for long-term success. From 1986 to 1993, he was a member of Process Management International in Minnesota. His clients have included well-known organizations, such as Chevron Corporation, the U.S. Navy, the U.S. Department of Defense, International Nickel Corporation, the Pillsbury Corporation, and Fletcher Challenge Corporation. In 1989, he was selected as a member of an Executive Study Mission to Japan. With a group of twenty other managers from four different countries, he spent two weeks studying some of the leading organizations in Japan. Dr. Persico is currently writing a book on strategy which will expand on some of the insights that he has gained into the strategic thinking and planning process during the last few years. Dr. Persico lives in St. Paul, Minnesota, and can be reached by telephone at (612) 426-4563 or by e-mail at johntwice@msn.com.

**Patricia Rouner Morris** has more than fifteen years of experience as a writer and editor, including seven years in the quality arena. She is the owner of The Compleat Editor, where she helps her clients to say what they mean to say in a way that reaches their intended audience. She is also a partner in a training firm that helps executives and others improve their communication skills through small group and one-on-one consulting. Her role in *The New Business Values* was to edit, rewrite, consult, comment, criticize, nag, argue, and continually question. These are skills she claims she has sharpened as the mother of two teenage children.

# Acknowledgments

This book was written over a period of several years and changed several different times as new ideas and examples were added to our store of knowledge and wisdom. It would be impossible to identify, much less thank, all of the different people who have helped shape our thinking or who helped with this manuscript. Nevertheless, there are those who stand out because of their special and unique contributions. First are our spouses, Karen and Steve, without whose support we could never have taken the time and loss of income to spend on this effort. Pat would also like to thank her children, Stephanie and Patrick, and especially her uncle Merle Miller, for his example of what a manager should be.

Over the years, Dr. W. Edwards Deming, Dr. Noriaki Kano, Dr. Gary N. McLean, Dr. Kevin Dooley, and numerous colleagues at Process Management International helped shape our ideas and theories and mold them into tactics and strategies that work in the real world. Beth Propst, Gail Dimitroff, Paul Fjelsta, Joel Finlay, Bud Gooch, Nancy Hoy, Jason Jones, Mike Kenfield, Karen Lindberg, Sharon Loubert, Marilyn Monda, Sam P.W., Robert Reber, Lou Schultz, Keith Setterholm, Darrell Schroeder, Lori Silverman, Hana Tomasek, Michael Tveite, John Vollum, Ward Warkenton, and James York all taught us much about business and consulting. Many of our clients and colleagues taught us by giving us real-world problems and examples of practice: Lynda Laskow of Allina Medical; William Dobson, Lorne Ames, and James Ashcroft of INCO Ltd.; Jacquie Daniel of Chevron; David Johnson of Blandin Paper Company; Karen Larson of Partnership for Excellence; Lynn Moline of Lynn Moline Associates; Frank Rechek of McGill-Jensen; Cyndi Wilke of North Memorial Medical Center; Dave Tuckwell and Doug Witt of Gardewine Trucking; and Gerry Damon of Pearl Harbor Naval Shipyard. They were and are wonderful people to work with who have helped us with their knowledge and ability to apply the tools and techniques described in this book.

Although they are seldom acknowledged, we believe that we owe some of our knowledge and wisdom to the wonderful professional societies that exist to help managers, consultants, and others develop more effective ways to be successful. Over the years, we have learned much from the American Society for Quality Control, the American Society for Training and Development, the International Society for Performance Improvement, the Minnesota Council for Quality, the Organizational Development Network, and the Strategic Leadership Forum. Such organizations are generally run locally by loyal, dedicated volunteers who give tirelessly and usually receive not one penny for their efforts. It is because of such organizations that many American businesses are now healthy and profitable.

To those we have forgotten to name, we offer our apologies. Finally, any errors within this book are the sole responsibility of the authors.

# PART I:
# INTRODUCTION

Managers are inundated with advice and ideas on how to become successful. Every guru and would-be guru is selling his or her secret or "key" to success. In just the last few years, managers have been told that they would not be successful, would probably not even survive, unless they understood and embraced the following ideas:

- You must thrive on chaos, expect no going back to stability.
- Intelligence, not information, is the road to success.
- Information technology is the key to overcoming hypercompetition.
- Employees must be empowered; hierarchical management is obsolete.
- Continuous quality improvement is the essential foundation for success.
- Business process reengineering is the only way to leap-frog your competition.
- Organizations must become holonic (i.e., think systematically and view the organization as a whole entity) and virtual to compete successfully.
- Innovation and creativity are the most important factors for success.
- Chaos theory is essential to the long-term survival of organizations.
- You will perish unless you recognize your strategic intent and core competencies and build barriers to encroachment.
- Strategic thinking and strategic planning are oxymorons and waste valuable time and resources that should be channeled elsewhere.

- Only learning organizations will survive into the twenty-first century.
- Right-sizing, outsourcing, and subcontracting are the keys to success.
- Union-management cooperation is the wave of the future.
- Entrepreneurship is the only way to be successful. All employees must act and be treated as entrepreneurs.
- The Internet is the cornerstone of business in the twenty-first century.

We pity the poor managers and employees who are confronted by this typhoon of advice. Imagine being hit by not just one typhoon, but by a succession of typhoons. That is what this advice represents to many leaders. How do they know which is right? How do they have time to digest and understand one before the next one comes along? Which ideas are the most important for their organizations?

Few managers have the time, patience, and wisdom to sort out all of these answers. Thus, it seems to many critics that managers merely jump from one fad to the next–onto one bandwagon and parade for a few months, then off to the next bandwagon and parade. Over and over again we hear managers criticized for adopting the program of the month, or the "program du jour" as it has been labeled. So why or how is this book any different? Why read yet another book that purports to tell you how to find the keys to the kingdom, the secrets to where the treasure is hidden, or the success principles for longevity? What makes this book any different or any better?

There are three reasons for spending your time reading this book. The following are three core ideas we want you to come away with and that we hope will make your job somewhat easier.

## *MANAGERS ARE REALLY PRAGMATISTS,*
## *NOT "FADDISTS"*

If we were going to criticize anyone, it would be the academicians, consultants, and gurus who each act as though his/her key is the only key necessary for success. Many of these experts act as though they and they alone have the necessary wisdom to ensure long-term survival and prosperity. The shortsightedness (some might say greediness) of those whom business relies upon for a condensed version of knowledge and wisdom is appalling. Managers work in real time, as their emphasis is front-line expediency to get the product or service delivered and the customer satisfied. Most managers did not sign on with the expectation that they would be business geniuses who would be able to deliver cutting-edge theories and strategies that would help them to leapfrog the competition. Thus, in some respects (wisely or not), they rely on a host of others to provide leading-edge ideas. The more condensed and pragmatic such ideas are, the better. One would think that in the competitive marketplace, the better ideas would win and the chaff would be winnowed out. Unfortunately for managers, the system does not work that well. Gurus whose ideas win out often seem to develop a "messiah" complex and start speaking and acting as though their ideas are the only ones that are essential for survival. Furthermore, there is little acknowledgment that the ideas that do win out are not necessarily right for everyone. However, the most important fact that should temper any wholesale rush to adopt new business practices should be the realization that once any strategy becomes public domain, it begins to lose its value as a means of competitive advantage.

Many gurus either do not want to see the forest or are not able to see the forest. It is very intoxicating to have a great idea and to think that your idea could be the key or secret ingredient for business success. But many academicians and consultants have never managed a business, much less run a large company or started a business from scratch. It is safe to say that (not counting Tom Peters) most consultants and academicians are not entrepreneurs or successful business capitalists. Some of the most outstanding business experts may be excellent business authors and writers, but many write from theory and ideology rather than from a great deal of frontline experience. This does not mean that their ideas cannot be useful. However, it does mean that managers should exhibit a great deal more caution and curiosity than they usually do before embracing as "gospel" many of the ideas in the marketplace. It is a major mistake to assume that the ideas in the leading business books will guarantee you business success.

What many criticize as managers' jumping from one fad to the next is actually a form of pragmatic strategy. It is a trial and error method that helps them to select new ideas to help their businesses become more successful. This method takes many managers down dead ends, but also rewards many others with methods that give them a competitive business advantage. For the busy manager, the adoption of new programs recommended by leading management theorists makes a great deal of sense. But it can be dangerous if managers buy into all of the hype that usually attends the emergence of each new "secret" to success. This book will look at many different ideas and strategies for success and will attempt to challenge your thinking at a conceptual level, yet still provide some pragmatic ideas for the busy manager.

## *THERE IS NO SUCH THING AS ONE TIMELESS SECRET TO SUCCESS*

If you have ever read any of the biographies of the superrich or successful (William Gates, Sam Walton, Lee Iacocca, John D. Rockefeller, Andrew Carnegie, etc.), you will be struck by several facts. First, no secrets to making instant money jump out of these biographies. Second, these highly successful men have led very different lifestyles and had very different business backgrounds. Indeed, it is hard to find any common secrets to success that would help you to make millions or to build a multimillion dollar corporation. The most common facts that seem to emerge from such books are the following:

- Success comes from hard work.
- Failure seems to be a necessary precursor to success.
- Highly successful people have high aspirations and are driven to succeed.
- Highly successful people are focused on their goals.
- Serendipity (but not luck) plays a role in all success.
- Highly successful people are risk takers, but are not reckless.
- Highly successful people are bright, but not necessarily geniuses.

- Highly successful people derive their success from a business that they know well.

These insights come from dozens of biographies that have been published over the last thirty years or so. It is interesting that these insights are very different from "programs" such as Business Process Reengineering (BPR) or Total Quality Management (TQM). The nature of programs seems to be at a different conceptual level than risk taking and hard work. Programs such as BPR and TQM are more tangible and more prescriptive. Perhaps this is why they offer such appeal to busy managers who are looking for that "secret" to success.

Many insights can be learned from the history of highly successful businesspeople, but perhaps the two most important lessons are that success is difficult to define and that it is multifaceted. It is easy to leave out the contradictions that generally abound in reality and that make prescriptions for success so much more problematic. For instance, perhaps we have overlooked the fact that many highly successful people are very lazy at times or that many of them have long periods of being unfocused and non-goal-oriented. It is all too easy to select aspects of history that conform to our biases or preconceptions of what is right and what is wrong. If others look at the same records, they will often find many discrepancies to the "secrets" that we have found.

This does not make our insights any less valid; it merely points out that life is a great deal more complicated than can be grasped by human intellect alone. If the collective wisdom of mankind was so great, we should long ago have discovered the secret of life, the beginning of the universe, the day life will end, and what happens when we all die.

Instead, the reality is that we can't find a cure for the common cold, we don't fully understand just how or why many types of drugs (including aspirin) work, we are not sure what magnetism is, and we can't even reliably tell whether or not it will rain tomorrow. Life is infinitely complex and in our efforts to understand it, we carelessly and shortsightedly have a tendency to oversimplify it and to select those "facts" that conform to our reality. Perhaps what is most important, though, is that we keep trying to understand how and why things work.

This book will not pretend to provide the "secret" to success. However, we believe that the values we discuss are critical to success and will be among the prime factors that will govern success in the next century. If the Pareto Principle holds true here, we like to think that the five key values we describe provide 80 percent of the bang for 20 percent of the buck. Thus, focusing on these five new business values will not guarantee success, but you will have the foundation to guide all your other corporate efforts.

## MANY PROGRAMS ARE LIKE TREES, BUT ARE NOT THE FOREST

There are three levels from which to view business ideas. The first level is the most superficial, and represents the "one tree at a time" level. Thus, BPR is different from Statistical Process Control (SPC), which is different from TQM. At this level, every program is unique and distinct.

The second level with which to view business ideas looks at a bunch of trees together. It is deeper conceptually than looking at mere programs and techniques and is generally much less prescriptive. For instance, ideas for creating organizations such as the learning organization, the holonic organization, and the networked organization represent entire schema for how organizations should be or how they should conduct business. Such ideas are a great deal more complex and difficult to enact than merely instituting an SPC program. How does one become a learning or holonic organization? It is not easy to answer such questions, even for the gurus who promote these ideas. The effort for transforming organizations to these ideas is much more of a process than a task. It is a task to start an SPC program or a BPR program. It is a process to transform an organization into a learning organization.

The third level is the deepest level. At this level, we are looking at the entire forest, not just the trees. We are seeing the fundamental nature of the entire enterprise, not merely each individual part. Ideas at this level are so conceptual and fundamental that we have to call them "values." A value is something that is almost timeless, something that drives all of our actions and behaviors. It is a part of our goal system that we rarely ever think about on a day-to-day basis. Yet, whether we think about it or not, it guides the many decisions we make, the actions we take, the programs we adopt, and the goals we are directed to. Many programs and ideas are embraced and endorsed because they conform to our basic business values. Our business values dictate our needs and our tastes. Values do not change overnight. When they do change, it is generally because of unpredictable and unprecedented changes in the larger world.

This book will help you to understand that many programs and ideas are simply tools and techniques that speak to one or more of the new business values. Each program is like a tree in the forest. Only by understanding all of the values that drive your goals can you understand what the forest really looks like. Once you have this perspective, it is extremely powerful. You will then have the insight to put all of the management fads and programs into a broader, more comprehensive perspective. You will see the big picture and how all of these business ideas fit into it. Only when such a sense is gained will you be able to understand the forces that drive success and how each program and new idea can help you achieve success. You will be able to distinguish between worthwhile and worthless ideas, between ideas that are right for your organization and ideas that may be better left to other organizations.

In Part I, Chapter 1 looks at the new business values and why they have replaced the old business values. Chapter 2 demonstrates a model for integrating these new business values into your organization. These two chapters form the foundation for the rest of the book.

Part II examines the new business value of Improvement. Chapter 3 talks about how to start an improvement effort. Chapter 4 describes the role of customer service in an organization. Chapter 5 presents a model that will help any organization to better understand how to create added value for the customer. The fundamentals of a high quality training program will be described in Chapter 6. Chapter 7 discusses the issue of sustainability and its role in continuous improvement. Each of these chapters deals with a theme or topic generally associated with the issue of continuous improvement or Total Quality Management.

Part III examines the new business value of Innovation. Each chapter in this section relates to a program or issue on sustaining creativity and innovation in organizations. Chapter 8 takes a look at Business Process Reengineering and creativity. Chapter 9 suggests several ways that strategic planning/thinking can be improved. Chapter 10 presents a model for creating the organization of the twenty-first century and beyond. This will entail some wild and radical ideas for creating a truly innovative organization. Chapter 11 analyzes the relationship between crime and quality. The key concept of interpreting a system through the use of a different metaphor is also illustrated in this chapter.

Part IV examines the business value of Inclusion. Chapter 12 describes the new value of Inclusion and shows how it enables strategies for harnessing the power of teams and people working together for the good of the organization. Chapter 13 concerns how to become a person who is able to function at a higher level and bring more focused effort to the job and society, while adding more value to everything and everyone you touch. Chapter 14 looks at the role of the organizational leader in bringing about workplace change and in providing a role model for others in the organization who want or need to change.

Part V demonstrates different perspectives on the new value of Incentives in the workplace. Chapter 15 addresses the "What's in it for me?" question—why should anyone change or embrace a new set of business objectives? Chapter 16 looks at the roles of the old suggestion box and the new suggestion systems as they increasingly become a means for obtaining the opinions of all employees. Chapter 17 examines a series of issues and perspectives that face managers who want to create incentives that motivate and not demotivate.

Part VI examines the new value of Information. The role of information in business success is examined, and strategies for changing data into information, information into knowledge, knowledge into intelligence and intelligence into wisdom is discussed in Chapters 18, 19, and 20. The emphasis in these chapters is on understanding fundamental concepts linked to information and how these concepts can be used to create competitive advantage.

# Chapter 1

# The New Organizational Values for Success

While consultants, business gurus, and academicians talk about the need to change and the need of a new paradigm for doing business, businesses all over the country are slowly but consistently migrating to a new set of business values. It is instinctive, like the migration of birds toward their nesting grounds. However, it is an instinct for survival. Intuitively, organizations understand that they must change the way they have conducted business or they will not survive. The change that is needed is so fundamental that new concepts are being invented daily to describe it. The learning organization, reinventing government, the holonic organization, virtual organizations, cluster organizations, chaos organizations, inclusive organizations, networked organizations, etc., are all attempts to describe the emerging state of the twenty-first-century organization. The problem all the experts share is that the new organizational state is still developing and evolving. The descriptions many gurus paint are either underdeveloped or incomplete. Each guru wants to be the first to claim that his or her picture of the new organization is the correct one. But the pictures are those of a developing child. The embryo does not look anything like the adult.

One thing is now clear: the first phase of the "quality revolution" is over in American industry. The intrepid organizations that were the initial pioneers in the quality movement are enshrined in the folklore of quality. Organizations such as Xerox, Ford, Harley-Davidson, Corning Glass, AT&T, and Motorola have become synonymous with the concept of "Total Quality." When any list of companies is compiled to prove that quality really does work, you will usually find one or more of the above-named organizations on the list. These pioneers in the quality movement created a religious fervor for change in American business and industry. The motivation was provided by the success of the Japanese encroachments into the American marketplace. The "sermon on the mount" was preached to the masses at hundreds of seminars led by W. Edwards Deming, Joseph Juran, and other would-be gurus who had saved Japan. Evangelical CEOs such as Robert W. Galvin, David Kearns, James Houghton, and Donald Peterson led from the executive suites. The organizations that had such charismatic leadership shone like supernovas on the quality horizon. Their successes in improving quality, lowering costs, and regaining market share and profits led American managers into frantic efforts to get "Quality" into their organizations.

From about 1982 to 1995, the number of quality consultants grew exponentially, along with the number of organizations that had received the gospel. What did not grow exponentially was the number of organizations that felt Total Quality had worked for them. By the middle 1990s, most organizations had some type of a quality effort in place. Some were pursuing TQM, others were working toward ISO 9000 certifications, and still others were jumping onto the reengineering bandwagon. Nevertheless, fewer than one in a thousand organizations achieved the type of success that characterized Xerox, Ford, Motorola, and Harley-Davidson. Numerous consultants, academicians, and researchers advanced theories to demonstrate why Quality doesn't work or why Quality fails,[1] usually while also explaining why their brand of Quality is the "real" thing.

It should have been obvious from the start that organizations led by CEOs who were going to eat, drink, and sleep Quality were going to make more headway than those with more average leadership. It should also have been apparent that organizations in industries in which the Japanese were a real threat would approach Quality Improvement with more zeal. Most organizations proceeded along the path of change at a pace dictated by crisis, commitment, and urgency. The fewer the problems with customers, the less competition, and the better the bottom line, the slower the pace of change. Too many managers say, "We are growing too fast to worry about Total Quality. Why should we change the way we do business?" Few leaders or organizations are enlightened enough to pursue change with any real commitment when their industry is not facing extinction or drastic competition from some outside source.

In reality, what many have reported as the "failure" of Total Quality may only mark the end of the first phase of an emerging new management paradigm. The pseudoreligious phase of Quality that has dominated American industry for the past fifteen or so years probably marks the first phase of a new organizational paradigm that is replacing the old Taylor paradigm of business. It represents the emergence of a new set of business values that will ultimately displace the old values. Unfortunately, phase one has been characterized by an almost evangelical zeal for such programs as Total Quality, Reengineering, Statistical Process Control, etc.

If the religious or evangelical phase (phase one) of change is over, or at least is moving to a more studied approach, what is next? Will we see the demise of quality improvement efforts in organizations? Will the fervor for teams and process improvement activities go away? Could a new program be in the wings that will displace Total Quality and Reengineering? Such questions presume that managers could return to the past or that businesses could survive by going back to the values that drove success in the United States from 1900 to the 1960s. This is no more possible than it would be for the military to try to return to the methods of Alexander the Great or Julius Caesar.

Much of Total Quality Management embodies the new values that will drive the twenty-first-century organization. Many of the other current practices and programs being espoused also reflect a new set of values for American business and management. The Total Quality paradigm is still in its infancy. The number of programs, acronyms, synonyms, and consultants is testimony to the growth and evolution of a new management paradigm. This is how paradigms evolve. Thomas Kuhn[2] has said,

> The transition from a paradigm in crisis to a new one from which a new tradition of normal science can emerge is far from a cumulative process, one achieved by articulation or extension of the old paradigm. Rather, it is a reconstruction of the field from new fundamentals, a reconstruction that changes some of the field's most elementary theoretical generalizations as well

as many of its paradigmatic methods and applications. During the transition period, there will be a large but never complete overlap between the problems that can be solved by the old and the new paradigms. But there will also be a decisive difference in the modes of solution. When the transition is complete, the profession will have changed its view of the field, its methods, and its goals.

The Taylor paradigm is the paradigm in crisis. It can no longer explain how we should conduct business or how we should manage a business. The business values implicit in the Taylor paradigm have become prescriptions for organizational failure, and those who have inherited Taylorism in their organizations are slowly being drawn into the new management paradigm. However, the new management paradigm requires managers to reject those elementary theoretical generalizations that were part of the old paradigm. Most managers have a very difficult time discarding these old generalizations and accepting the new values for organizational success.

"If it ain't broke don't fix it" was one of the mantras of the old paradigm, reflecting the value of constancy and control. In the new paradigm, continually asking, "How can I improve it?" reflects the value of change and innovation. Rejection of the old values and beliefs will take a very long time, and those who think that a new paradigm is right around the corner will have a long wait. Inevitably, another paradigm will replace the emerging paradigm, but not in the immediate future and at least not until the new paradigm has reached its full development, becoming the normal way of doing business.

Phase one was characterized by an almost religious zeal for quality. In phase two, organizations will pursue many different options to assimilate the new values. There will be less of the bandwagon and "the one best way" approach. Total Quality is one of the cornerstones of phase two of the new paradigm. A continuous improvement process is slowly and irrevocably replacing the Taylor value of control and stability.

The characteristics of phase two will probably be very distinct from those in phase one. Organizations are maturing in their understanding of the new management paradigm. In phase one, many organizations felt the need to adopt a guru. Thus, some organizations were "Demingized," others were Juran followers, and still others were Crosby organizations. In phase two, organizations will pick and choose from among many different concepts and theories to find the ones that best fit their organizational cultures and particular situations.

While there is no one "right way" that dictates how organizations will adopt the new values, it is highly likely that if they don't adopt the new values, they will not be in business much longer. In phase two, organizations will find their own strategies for adopting the new management paradigm. However, the most significant difference between phase two and phase one will be found in terms of an organization's understanding about the role of the new values versus the role of the old values from its old management paradigm. Organizations will need to be able to understand the implicit and explicit role that values play in their survival. Without such an understanding, they can only respond to instinctive impulses that are very effective in some cases, but may lead to shallow solutions in others.

For example, in phase one, Total Quality was seen as an end in itself. The concept of value or of new values was seldom mentioned except in association with costs. Total Quality was defined as satisfying the customers. This was the ultimate goal. After World War II, American managers had lost sight of the customer as an essential factor for business success. In many businesses and government offices, the customer was considered a necessary nuisance. The first phase of the new emerging business paradigm has been characterized by all-out efforts to identify customers and to redefine the needs of customers in the organization. Some organizations have become obsessed with customer satisfaction surveys and distinguishing between the needs of internal and external customers. Few organizations remember that Deming often said that the customers will often not know what they want or need. When service industries climbed aboard the Quality bandwagon, they became equally religious about identifying the needs of their customers and making those needs the dominant drivers of their business strategy. Many service programs decided that what they were doing was different from Quality in manufacturing. Service organizations called their Total Quality efforts by such names as Total Quality Service, Continuous Quality Improvement, and Total Customer Service. Still, the fundamental fact is that service organizations are also moving toward a new set of values to drive their organizations and management style.

As organizations have matured in their quality programs, they have begun to realize that merely satisfying the needs of their customers is not enough to be successful. It is a necessary but not a sufficient condition. The process of pursuing quality is not the end, it is only the means. Since quality is always relative and always moving, it must be a never-ending process. While an organization must have a Quality process in place to stay even with its competition, the true success driver is the value on continuous improvement. Total Quality is one way to foster continuous improvement.

In phase two, continuous improvement becomes part of the table stakes. It takes more for an organization to be successful than just having a TQM program. There are other values that are essential for organizational success in the twenty-first century. The ultimate benchmark for an organization's success is defined by the value that the organization provides for its stakeholders and customers, both long- and short-term. The ultimate organizational goal is to provide value to someone or something.

There are many different definitions of the term "value." *Webster's Seventh New Collegiate Dictionary* defines "value" as (1) a fair return or equivalent in goods, services or money for something exchanged; (2) the monetary worth of something; (3) a relative worth, utility or importance. A common pragmatic business definition of value is "meeting the needs of customers at an acceptable cost," or sometimes, "cost plus quality." This definition looks at "value" as a singular term. The plural of the term is quite different, and is most often associated with ethical behavior or a set of actions. One organization defined "values" as the way things are done, the significant meanings, concepts, or ideas that individuals hold in an organization that particular ways of doing things are preferable to their opposite.[3] Such values are honesty, truth, equity, etc. In the new emerging business paradigm, values and value are critical. They are both the bedrock upon which the new paradigm will be built. However, from a business point of view, several distinctions must be made in order to understand their roles. The first distinction is between "value" and "values." Both will be different in the new paradigm.

In the new paradigm, "value" will need to be defined from both the perspective of the stakeholder as well as the customer. In the old management paradigm, all too often value was defined by the stakeholder. Usually this was a simple matter of how much the stock price had increased or the size of the dividend payment. The stakeholders' views and the customers' views of value are not always the same. Donald Berwick, in his book *Curing Health Care,*[4] defines customers as "those whose needs we serve or who depend upon us . . . " and stakeholders as "those who have a vested interest in the organization." "Vested" generally implies that some financial interest is at stake in the organization. Employees, owners, managers, stockholders, and investors are all stakeholders in an organization. The government, unions, and suppliers might also be considered as another group of stakeholders. Customers can be stakeholders as, of course, stakeholders can also be customers. However, it is possible for the needs of one group to conflict with those of the other group. For instance, customers like low costs; investors and owners like high profit margins, and employees and unions like high wages and benefits.

The concept of "Total Value" reflects what will be a driving force in phase two of the new management paradigm. "Total Value" can be defined as "value to the stakeholders plus value to the customers." Few managers have recognized the need to provide for, and balance, value, both to the stakeholders and to the customers. In the West, we have erred on the side of the stakeholder, tending to forget about the value to the customer. Furthermore, we compounded the problem since the needs of all stakeholders were not equally balanced. By and large, the needs of stockholders and owners far outranked and obscured the needs of employees, unions, and other stakeholders.

A good improvement process provides a way to meet the needs of the customer. Customer Service Quality, Continuous Quality Improvement, Supplier Partnerships, Statistical Process Control, Labor-Management Cooperation, and World Class Manufacturing are all important elements of a Continuous Improvement effort. Today, Total Quality and Continuous Quality Improvement are seen as key management strategies for eliminating deficiencies in all areas of an organization and in all types of organizations. In education, government, the military, health care, and private industry, there are numerous examples of Continuous Improvement efforts being undertaken and managers struggling with the paradigm changes that are involved. Continuous Improvement is not just viewed as a production program, but as a means of adding value to every process in an organization. The emphasis on Continuous Improvement has provided a way for managers and employees to work smarter and to use the brainpower of everyone in the organization. Many see such programs as the best way to align the mission and vision of the organization with the needs and wants of their customers and stakeholders.

However, a serious flaw in the approach to change was characteristic of many organizational efforts in phase one. Edward de Bono, in his book *Sur Petition*,[5] noted that putting all the emphasis on pursuing incremental improvements may prevent more needed change. This has been called the "rearranging deck chairs on the Titanic" syndrome. Or, as I* have often noted in my seminars, the last buggy whip company to go out of business probably had the highest quality and lowest costs.

Organizations in phase one have been almost frenetic in their approaches to continuous improvement, pursuing tools and techniques as though each new method, from benchmarking to quality function deployment to hoshin planning and statistical process control, would be the secret that would help them leapfrog over the competition.

There has been little understanding of the role that values play in the new paradigm and of the emerging values that form the core of the new management paradigm. These values shape the programs, structures, strategies, goals, and objectives of the organization, both explicitly and implicitly. They shape it almost instinctively, as managers search for the "right" tools and programs to help them survive in the marketplace. The search is often random and idiosyncratic, a constant embracing and throwing out of techniques and concepts.

There are many good tools and programs in the global marketplace. There is certainly no lack of philosophies, theories, and techniques. From Crosby to Deming to Juran to Hammer and Hamel,

---

All references to "I" within this book refer to the opinions and experiences of John Persico.

and in each new issue of *Harvard Business Review*, managers are exposed to numerous consultants and academicians telling them what they need to do and how to do it. Unfortunately, what has been missing from phase one is the concept of integration and the requirement that Continuous Improvement be treated as part of a total value system, not just a series of isolated tools, techniques, and strategies to reduce variation and eliminate waste and rework. Furthermore, the definition of Continuous Improvement that was held by many managers in phase one is narrow and limiting. Many managers believed that Continuous Quality Improvement was just a program to reduce waste and rework, to "get it done right the first time." Contrast this definition with Genichi Taguchi's definition of quality: "The loss imparted to society from the time a product is shipped." Taguchi defines quality as the loss to society, the business, and the customer for any deviation from ideal in terms of the way the product should perform. Taguchi's definition puts Quality and Continuous Improvement into the realm of a value. It becomes more than just a program or tool; Taguchi understands that continuous improvement can reduce such standard wastes as disposal costs, waste costs, rework costs, warranty costs, failure costs, etc., as well as such wastes as environmental costs, disposal costs, obsolescence costs, replacement costs, substitution costs, and even opportunity costs that are not traditionally accounted for by Western management accounting systems.[6]

Taguchi has given us a definition of Total Quality which includes value to the stakeholders, value to the customer, and value to society. When a product or service fails, it is not only the customer who loses; a great many more stakeholders lose as well. There is systemic, holistic thinking involved in such a concept. Taguchi is viewing the organization, products, customers, stakeholders, and society as part of one integrated system. Much like John Donne's famous poem that says, "Any man's death diminishes me, because I am involved in Mankind; And therefore never send to know for whom the bell tolls; it tolls for thee," we all suffer from the loss of quality and value in our society. For this reason, we must move beyond the narrow definition of quality that characterized phase one of the emerging management paradigm and try to gain a deeper understanding of the new values and the impact they will have on the twenty-first-century organization.

The New Business Values can help to put all of the various concepts, tools, techniques, and methodologies into focus. They provide a powerful way to look at what an organization does and must do to be successful. Reducing waste and rework is not enough. It isn't enough to have SPC programs, JIT programs, or supplier partnership programs. Nor will labor-management cooperation, employee empowerment, or customer satisfaction programs be enough. Each of these efforts addresses only part of the system while ignoring the whole. In fact, in many cases, such efforts lead to suboptimization of the organization. As each function in the organization attempts to do its own thing, there are losses to other parts of the organization. The net result is that the gain to the organization is often exceeded by the overall losses from the suboptimization. Continuous Improvement can only be effective and long lasting when the organization is seen as a system, and when it is understood that what is done in purchasing affects production, what is done in human resources affects sales, that SPC changes the accounting system, and reengineering will affect employee morale.

The New Business Values can help to understand these problems by forcing us to identify and balance the needs of all stakeholders as well as the needs of both internal and external customers. However, the New Business Values are more than just the means to help us integrate Continuous Improvement into our organizations. Just as Continuous Improvement has political implications for an organization (although seldom discussed because it is expected to be a rational process), so too do the New Business Values hold many political implications for organizations and society. The values affect the decisions and actions made in our organizations.

It is important to distinguish between ethical values and business values. Ethical values are generally explicit in an organization. They may be incorporated in a business statement or business philosophy. Ethical values such as honesty, truth, and fairness are fundamental to the practices and behaviors that govern interchanges between people in a democratic society. However, such values are actually incomplete. In reality, they are supplemented by a second set of values: business values. This second set is generally implicit and unspoken, and is often unrecognized. Nevertheless, business values generally have a much greater impact and influence on organizational decisions, policies, procedures, structure, and strategy than do ethical values. For instance, the value on command and control implicit in the old-styled Taylor paradigm of organizations has done more to shape how employees are treated and how business is transacted in most American organizations than any single set of ethical values. While the necessity for an explicit set of ethical values is recognized for organizations, we believe organizations can benefit from recognizing and understanding the implicit, or business, values that drive value in the organization, both for customers and for stakeholders. Furthermore, it is the business values that have guided American organizations for the past 100 years that are most in need of change. Ethical values may be as close to timeless and enduring as any set of concepts presently understood. This is a question beyond the scope of this book. However, it is clear that business values are undergoing profound changes and it is these changes which will comprise the focus of this book.

Herve De Jordy maintains that both left-wing liberal positions and right-wing conservative positions are dead or dying because of their failure to understand the role that value and values play in the new economic era. According to De Jordy, politicians and managers do not understand the implication of this role in either business or politics. For instance, right-wing political economic theory argues that capital is the most important factor in production. Most business philosophies and Western economies have been built upon this value and its interpretation. Indeed, most of the laws that affect business and industry are based on the belief in this value. On the other hand, left-wing and liberal economics argues that labor is the most important factor in production. Most socialist economics and much of Western labor law and policy were formulated with the assumption that this value is paramount.

However, these values will no longer sustain organizations and the political decisions needed in the global economy of the twenty-first century. De Jordy[7] argues,

> Capital and labor are presently being replaced by a new economic theory of Value. This new theory is the "Innovation

Theory of Value" whereby capital and labor are seen as resources required to advance innovation. It is not merely enough to make the same old things faster, we must use information and knowledge to make new things better. Knowledge must now be added to capital and labor as a fundamental source of value and productivity. It is through new knowledge that new things add value to the lives of people and create more productive societies. In the twenty-first century, the Total Value created by an organization will be its primary measure of success. However, Total Value cannot be measured by today's simplistic accounting procedures. We need more than profit-and-loss statements to determine the total value that an organization contributes to stakeholders and customers.

Total Value must account for the value of knowledge and intellectual capital as well as factoring costs to society, the global environment, and even to future generations. The total value added by our entire economic system will determine our nation's success or failure in the global marketplace. Since only total value creates wealth and leads to greater productivity, it is likely that twenty-first-century economics will be built upon this concept. This will lead to major changes in the laws and policies that surround business, industry, labor, education, and government. Part of the redefining process will mean that each of these institutions must fundamentally challenge their basic business values. This will entail more than just reinventing government or reengineering the corporation. It is going to take an ongoing reevaluation of the role that the New Business Values have in the organization and the realization that these values also impact stakeholders, customers, and ultimately the entire system. Change to any part of the system must be done within a systemic framework of values that looks at the interrelationships and interdependencies of all values in the entire system.

This book will help those managers and organizational leaders move into and through the second phase of the emerging management paradigm. It is structured around five new values. Each value is essential, but no one value is sufficient to achieve total value. The five values will also be referred to as value drivers because they are the primary impelling forces that enable an organization to provide total value for its stakeholders, customers, and society. These five values are Innovation, Improvement, Incentives, Information, and Inclusion. They are replacing the old business values of command, control, motivate, exclude, and isolate.

In each section of this book, strategies and tactics will be described that can be used to help optimize these value drivers. Each of the five values can be addressed with an infinite number of strategies and methodologies. However, an organization's overall success will be dictated by two factors. The first is how adequately the organization addresses each of the value drivers. This can be measured by an analysis of the organization's stakeholders and customers in terms of their satisfaction and the level of value they feel is provided. Second is how well the organization integrates the five value drivers. The value drivers cannot be treated as independent or separate from one another. The interplay of efforts to foster improvements will impact innovation and will lead to the need to address incentives that change information structures and impel the organization to adopt strategies to make the organization more inclusive.

The five new values and their fit in the new emerging management paradigm will be described in the next chapter. In each of the following sections, one of the five value drivers will be discussed along with some tools, strategies, and methods to help optimize the driver. These are not new tools that have not already been touted in the marketplace. However, we will examine many new concepts and ideas about these tools from a systematic and holistic perspective.

## REFERENCE NOTES

1. Howe, R.J., Gaeddert, D., and Howe, M.A. *Quality on Trial.* St. Paul, MN: West Publishing Co., 1993.

2. Kuhn, T.S. *The Structure of Scientific Revolutions.* Chicago: University of Chicago Press, 1962.

3. Fairview Values Project Task Force. "Identifying and integrating organization values for Fairview Hospitals and Healthcare Services." Unpublished report. The Fairview Values Project Task Force, Minneapolis, MN: September, 1992.

4. Berwick, D.M., Godfrey, A.B., and Roessner, J. *Curing Health Care.* San Francisco: Jossey-Bass, Inc., 1990.

5. de Bono, E. *Sur Petition.* New York: HarperCollins Publishers, Inc., 1992.

6. Munro-Faure, L. and Munro-Faure, M. *Implementing Total Quality Management.* London: Pitman Publishing, 1992.

7. De Jordy, H. *Blueprint for a Country Turnaround.* Toronto: CdC International Press Ltd., 1992

# Chapter 2

# A New Model for Organizations

No organization can grow or change unless its form fits its function. While it has often been noted that form follows function, it is equally true that when an organization changes in any fundamental way, it must fundamentally alter its basic form. Failure to achieve such redesign has been one of the primary reasons organizations such as IBM and General Motors have struggled in the 1990s. The concept of organizational form is analogous to the shell that surrounds the chambered nautilus. As the creature grows, it must continually add to and enlarge its surrounding structure. In organizations, the surrounding structure is made up of the people, technology, methods, processes, information, and procedures that govern day-to-day operations. These parts of the organizational structure are perhaps more appropriately referred to as the "architecture" of the organization. The concept of organization architecture has been defined by Nadler, Gerstein, Shaw, and Associates in their book, *Organizational Architecture*: "By architecture we mean a more inclusive view of the elements of design of the social and work systems that make up a large organization. . . . Architecture encourages us to think about the process of building organizations, not just designing them."[1] We have used this concept to develop a blueprint for organizations that are interested in providing long-term value for their stakeholders, customers, and employees.

The blueprint comes from observations, experiences, and research concerning the emerging values that are needed for success in the twenty-first-century organization. The five values that are at the core of the new emerging paradigm for business form a model for the way business needs to be conducted.

There have been many "models" describing the "right" way to run an organization or what it takes to have an effective organization. These include such models as Likert's System 4 model, Ouchi's Theory Z, Blake and Mouton's Grid Management, McKinsey's Seven S model, and of course, Taylor's Scientific Management. Each of these models were useful in their time. Dr. George Box from the University of Wisconsin has noted, "All models are wrong, some are useful."[2]

The inevitability of change and new events renders all models obsolete at some point. The cry for organizations to vertically integrate inevitably changes to a cry for diversification, which eventually succumbs to cries to develop core competencies. Each successive strategy or technique is seen as a replacement or new innovation, rather than a refinement or addition to what went before. In most cases, the strategy or program is merely a new way to address one of the core underlying values that drive organizational actions and ideas. Organizations often pursue one new program after another without understanding how they fit together or why the programs are really needed. Many employees are bewildered and wonder why management ricochets from one program to another. There is no understanding of the underlying dynamics which are acting as pressure points on the organization.

Thus, Process Management, Total Quality, Statistical Process Control, Continuous Quality Improvement, Flexible Manufacturing, Just-In-Time systems, Cellular Manufacturing, and High Performance Management systems are all simply variations on a theme for addressing the emerging value of Improvement. Continuous Improvement has become a requirement for organizational success. Business Process Engineering, Quality Function Deployment, redesign, reinvention, new product development, creativity, and diversity programs are all variations on a theme for addressing the emerging value of Innovation. Organizations need new products and services as well as improved products and services.

New-style performance measures, pay for knowledge, profit sharing, gain sharing, competency-based compensation, and reward management are varieties on a theme for addressing the need for new incentive systems for organizations–incentives that are more consistent with people in the twenty-first century than with people earlier in the twentieth century. Incentives are a key value in the new emerging management paradigm. The learning organization, the reflective organization, the seven management and planning tools, strategic thinking, Hoshin planning, chaos theory, benchmarking, and advanced management information systems are all strategies for enhancing the use of information in organizations. Information is one of the new values for the twenty-first-century organization. In the past, information was haphazardly collected and then restricted to a privileged few on a "need to know" basis. Successful organizations will seek to maximize the amount of information they can assimilate, and assure its distribution to the greatest number of people and points in the organization.

Finally, team building, collaboration, cross-functional management, self-managed work teams, consensus modeling, group vision and mission sessions, open communication, and empowerment of employees reflect the growing value and belief in inclusion rather than exclusion. Organizations with different fiefdoms and kingdoms, where no one can help anyone else because it is "not my job" will soon become extinct. The ninth point of Dr. W. E. Deming's 14 Points concerned the need for creating teamwork in organizations and removing barriers that prevent people from working together. Organizations structured along the Taylor principle of exclusion, stratification, and classification of jobs and functions will lack the flexibility to survive in a competitive marketplace.

Our model, which integrates the five New Business Values for the twenty-first-century organization, will eventually be replaced by a more inclusive model or a model that better meets the needs of some future marketplace. Indeed, some might already want to argue that the model should include several more value drivers. Surely some of you are asking, "Where is the customer in your model?" The answer is that the customers and stakeholders must be the magnetic north for all five values; the needs of the stakeholders and customers must be aligned with your organization's core values.

The simplicity of focusing on a few key value drivers can be extraordinarily beneficial, particularly if those five value drivers provide the majority of the value for your customers and stakeholders. Simply focusing on these five value drivers will help ensure that your organization remains successful and competitive and will help you to understand the role of the many different programs and strategies that are being continually introduced to the marketplace.

The pace of such new concepts and tools is unlikely to diminish. Focusing on the five primary business values will help you to pick and choose among the different tools and to only select those that are consistent with your organization's overall business strategy.

To use these five values as drivers, the following rules must be followed:

### 1. You cannot copy; you must understand why something works. (W. E. Deming)

An organization cannot succeed in a knowledge-based economy if it does not value information and know how to create knowledge from data. In an information-based or knowledge-based organization, managers must be open to continuous education and learning. Such openness transcends mere copying or parroting what others think and feel. It must be based on a genuine willingness to study, challenge, and critically appraise new ideas and concepts. The five value drivers must be driven down into the very fabric and marrow of the organization by continuous study, development, and refinement of the concepts themselves.

### 2. Transforming an organization is an exercise in creativity; a linear or a cookbook approach to organizational change will not work.

The change in management paradigms and the transformation to an organization that will be competitive in the twenty-first century must be based on both intuition and a structured, systematic approach to change. This is a paradox which must be understood and managed. Some aspects of creativity are set free by having clearly defined guidelines, while other aspects are enslaved by such proscriptions. Organizations must learn how to balance between the two extremes. On one extreme is chaos and on the other is stultifying bureaucracy. Chaos theory[3] is being espoused today as a liberating element in organizations, and perhaps a little chaos is what many bureaucratic organizations need. Nevertheless, organizations that strike a positive balance between the two extremes will be more successful in the long run.

### 3. You must study the past, or be condemned to repeat it.

The great philosopher G. Santayana said, "Those who cannot remember the past are doomed to repeat it." Since many managers are loath to study something as "useless" as history, many organizations will travel the same road to oblivion as their predecessors. History is full of lessons for organizations, but most "business history" is dominated by historians. There are very few businesspeople who study history. What a tragic waste of experience and knowledge! There are thousands of lessons in the past that could help organizations remain competitive for more than 1,000 years. For instance, in studying long-lived organizations such as the Catholic Church and the Roman Empire, we have found many useful ideas that would benefit modern organizations. These ideas might be called "the success habits of the highly successful Romans."

### 4. You cannot change an organization without changing yourself. Do not challenge the organization if you are not willing to challenge yourself.

An organization is composed of people and, like a chain, it is only as strong as its weakest link. It is foolish to think that everything around you needs to change except yourself. Such a belief shows a fundamental ignorance of systems theory principles. In systems theory, if one element of a system is changed, it requires a dynamic realignment of all other elements. If management style changes in an organization, it is imperative that reward and recognition systems change. If leadership styles change, it is inevitable that "followership" styles will need to change. If change is going on everywhere around you, you had better think about the changes that you will need to undertake. Inability to make personal changes is one of the major reasons for the failure of many organizational change efforts.

### 5. Change is a process. You must apply the Plan, Do, Study, Act (PDSA) Cycle to all change efforts.

One of the defining characteristics of what is described as "old-style management" is the inability to see things as a process. For example, such processes as training, human resource development, leadership, and research are seen by many managers as functions that are independent or autonomous from the real work of the organization. Instead of viewing such processes as embedded in a flow of time and events that are interdependent, they are seen and treated as largely autonomous elements that can be activated when necessary and then put back on the shelf. Then, typically when times get rough, training and research are the first processes to get cut. Eventually, if things are going well again, training and research will be restored to their former positions. This sequence represents an example of the failure to see training and research as indispensable processes that contribute to the success of an organization. Fundamentally, it is the failure of organizations to apply the Plan, Do, Study, Act (PDSA) Cycle to all processes in an organization and to think in terms of inclusion rather than exclusion.

The PDSA Cycle, which was first described by Walter Shewhart, represents a basic commitment to both continuous learning and improvement. The PDSA Cycle is needed to help ensure that all processes in an organization add value to the organization. Without applying the PDSA Cycle to processes such as training and research, the danger exists that the processes will become independent kingdoms within the larger organizational empire, perpetuating the belief that they are superfluous to the real work of the organization. If the training manager and research director see their work as a series of events rather than as part of a larger process, they will fail to serve the organization as they need to. The PDSA Cycle is the antidote to this happening for all functions and organizational processes.

Values are fundamental principles that help guide our actions and behaviors. The five most important business values for the twenty-first-century organization—Improvement, Innovation, Inclusion, Incentives, and Information—are not necessarily the most important values for an organization. Ethical values such as truth, justice, freedom, and equality are also important.

Business values are those values which guide the economic actions and organizational norms that add value for organizational stakeholders and customers. Truth, justice, and freedom are wonderful values, but they do not drive the economic functions in an organization. Innovation and improvement contribute a great deal more to customer value in most organizations than do loyalty and helpfulness. This is not to argue that loyalty, justice, etc., are not equally important. Indeed, taken together,* ethical values and business values are the most important elements in any organization and, in myriad ways, contribute to the long-term success of the organization. However, ethical values are more subtle and indirect.

Some might argue that we are merely splitting hairs and that the five Business Values are really just an addition to the traditional organizational values. But they are, in fact, different and unique. Ethical values play more of a role in determining what we are and how we choose to live, while the business values of an organization more directly impact customer and stakeholder value, but may not necessarily translate into a more just or equitable society. In terms of fundamental contributions to the well-being of society, there are no substitutes for the ethical values that guide individual behavior. Business values can be linked to successful economic activity, but this is only one element in a free and successful democratic society.

The five New Business Values that will determine the economic success or failure of the twenty-first century—Inclusion, Improvement, Innovation, Incentives, and Information—are "superordinate concepts" in that most, if not all, of what an organization needs to do in terms of structure, policies, and procedures can fit under one or more of the five values. An organization can use the five value drivers as organizing principles or as themes to guide the transformation. These five values can become the focal points for all of the organization's economic activities.

An organization must have a clear focus and purpose to be successful. Together with the vision, mission, and ethical values of the organization, the five New Business Values provide the necessary focus, alignment, and integration for organizations that want to be successful in the twenty-first century. The meaning and relevance of

---

*In practice, ethical values and business values often conflict. There needs to be congruence between the two. This will never happen until organizations are ready to identify both value sets and admit that business values often take precedence over the ethical values espoused.

each of the five New Business Values will be described, beginning with Inclusion.

## *INCLUSION*

In 1787, the U.S. Constitution set up a representative democracy. At that time, most people were largely uneducated, and the means of communication to provide knowledge and learning were virtually nonexistent. It made sense to elect the best and brightest and send them off to some faraway place to confront issues and make decisions that most of the electorate would have been unable to understand. In many respects, the two underlying factors—ignorance and lack of information—determined not only how our government would be run but also (somewhat later, with the emergence of the industrial era) how our businesses would be run. Frederick Taylor's Scientific Management was based on the assumption that workers were both stupid and uninformed. In the Taylor paradigm, this led to a value of exclusion. Workers would do what they were told and would work only on very narrow parts of the process. There would be little or no need to work cooperatively with other employees or management.

Today, neither of these factors is true. Modern means of communication and information transfer make it possible for nearly anyone with a library card or Internet access to build an atom bomb—if that person had the desire to do so. Information is more readily available than at any time in history. Thus, the two key principles upon which our government and industry were built are today invalid. When they were valid, it might have made sense to exclude people from decision making. Basically, this is what representative democracy did in government and the division of employees into managers and nonmanagers did in industry. Just as the majority of the American population were "excluded" from political and policy decisions, the majority of hourly employees were similarly excluded from deciding on basic work force policies and procedures.

Today, the principle of exclusion is dead or dying. Everywhere we look, we can see evidence of this fact. Calls for referendums, electronic voting, and "town meetings" are evidence of people's increasing desire to be more involved in political decisions. In businesses all over the country, people are forming self-managed work teams, developing flatter organizations and opting to create environments wherein they have more control over their work. The fastest growing segment of the economy is the home-based business where people have near total control over their schedules and work choices. We must face the fact that there has been a fundamental change in the values upon which we created both business and government. People will no longer tolerate being excluded from the fundamental decisions and choices that affect their lives.

The value of exclusion must be replaced by the value of Inclusion. In business, worker empowerment, labor-management cooperation, and self-managed work teams are all forms of the inclusion value in action. These practices indicate that people want to be involved in decisions affecting their lives. Companies (as well as governments) that adhere to the exclusion principle will become obsolete or impediments to progress. We may soon need to rebuild our government with one built upon the value of inclusion. This will mean moving toward the type of participatory democracy envisioned by H. Ross Perot and others.

In business, managers must build structures that facilitate the ability of people to be included in all aspects of the operations and management of the organization. An inclusive organization will not only extend the principle to employees but also to its other stakeholders. This will mean that the organization will form supplier partnership programs to include suppliers in decision making. It will form strategic alliances with competitors to better enable each organization to learn and provide value to society. It will form customer partnerships to bring them into the design and development of new products and services. It will form partnerships with the union or unions to ensure that it is addressing the needs of all employees and the quality of work life as well as the quality of work. The union will continue to have a role to ensure that balance is kept between the quality of work life and the quality of work as well as continuing its role as champion of the worker. The organization will foster teamwork between employees and managers in the daily operation and improvement of the organization. It will become an organization where employees are free to take risks and where creativity and idea sharing between all functions and areas are the norm.

Improved communication and information networks will be essential to the process of creating an inclusive organization. Some of this is already happening in organizations where employees are regarded as associates or where employees are seen as internal customers. These organizations often establish profit sharing and other programs to give employees equity in the organization. There will be more employee-owned organizations in the future, and the distinctions between hourly and salaried workers will eventually be discarded. These are only some of the ways some organizations are beginning to invoke the value of inclusion. But even these organizations have a long way to go. The value of inclusion should be a foundation and a basic metric for all organizational decisions and restructuring.

## IMPROVEMENT AND INNOVATION

There is no good definition to distinguish between improvement and innovation. It is all a matter of perspective. Edward de Bono[4] makes a distinction between lateral thinking and vertical thinking, which helps to provide a better understanding of these two values. Drilling for oil deeper and deeper in the same old hole is an example of vertical thinking. This is somewhat analogous to organizational improvement or being more efficient. In quality improvement, we are concerned with eliminating waste, with doing things right the first time. We hammer away at the same problems until we come to the root causes or find the source of the problem and eliminate it.

Moving to a new oil field to drill is an example of lateral thinking. This is analogous to innovation and effectiveness. Organizations need to ask, "Are we doing the right things? Do we have the right products or services?" If you are drilling for oil, the key question is how to balance drilling deeper with drilling new wells. For an organization to be efficient and effective, it must balance lateral thinking with vertical thinking. In other words, it must balance improvement with innovation.

The United States prides itself on being the most innovative nation in the world. In the past, our obsession with breakthroughs and leapfrogging the competition led us to ignore the more mundane task of continuous improvement. With the introduction of Total

Quality Management, the obsession became finding Kaizen-type ("Kaizen" is a Japanese term which means small continuous improvement) improvements. Small incremental improvements in process were compared to base hits which, when added together, will equal home runs. However, perhaps the pendulum has swung too far in the direction of improvement, since we are now witnessing a flock of gurus who promise that "redesign" and "reengineering" will give organizations "quantum" leaps over continuous quality improvement. It is, unfortunately, much easier to copy others' programs and recipes than to work out creative solutions and innovations. It is inevitable, then, that many "reengineered" organizations will no doubt look much like their competitors.

The twenty-first-century organization must balance innovation with improvement. It will look at all areas of the organization to continually improve its products, processes, and services. It will have processes and systems in place to foster creativity and breakthroughs in areas that need innovation, and will also have systems and processes in place to foster those small, never-ending incremental improvements of processes. These twin value drivers will need to be harmonized so the organization can obtain maximum value from efforts directed at both innovation and improvement. The success of the American economy has shown the value of constant innovation, while the success of the Japanese economy has shown the value of constant incremental improvement. Continuous improvement of processes means a never-ending search to improve people, equipment, materials, methods, and the environment. The concepts of continuous improvement and continuous innovation must become key value drivers for all activities and efforts in the organization.

Many organizations misunderstand the need for continuous innovation as it relates to being an inclusive activity. Organizations think that they are innovative because they have a research and development (R&D) department, because they have a large R&D budget, or because they send selected employees to a program on creativity. Reengineering and redesign gurus, while offering a technology that is important, fail to understand the deeper implications of innovation and its role in organizational success. It might help if someone came up with a program for "Continuous Quality Innovation" or "Total Quality Innovation"–a program to help make innovation an organization-wide value. It would not be limited to R&D people or so-called "creative" types, and would balance technical innovation (development of new technology) with conceptual innovation (development of new ideas). Everybody in the organization would be taught how to contribute to this effort. Such an organization would be very close to what Peter Senge has described in his book, *The Fifth Discipline*,[5] as a "learning" organization. However, there would be some key differences. Whereas Senge and Deming talk about the importance of knowledge, a truly innovative organization will be more concerned with wisdom. To do this, the twenty-first-century organization will need to balance knowledge with caring.

Peter Senge once commented that the most important value added to an organization is the knowledge that employees bring to their jobs. This is only half true. All the knowledge in the world is not worth one cent if people do not care enough about their organization, its purpose, or its customers to share their knowledge. Deming talked a great deal about "Profound Knowledge," but seldom touched on the importance of caring. Innovation in service is just as likely to come from employees who care as from employees who have "Profound Knowledge." People who genuinely care about their customers will go the extra mile to help see that they are satisfied and that their needs are met.


## *INCENTIVES*

Incentives are a key value for organizational success. In a sense, they help to demonstrate that the organization is "walking its talk." Incentives can be financial or nonfinancial, and can address either extrinsic or intrinsic motivational factors. The organization must seek to find a balance between these factors. In the Taylor paradigm of management, incentives were only deemed necessary because employees were considered either unmotivated or stupid. Most managers no longer believe either of these things about their employees. Nevertheless, senior managers often ask if incentives should be financial. Seldom do these same managers ask if their own yearly bonuses should be financial.

Psychologist Abraham Maslow developed a pyramid of human needs. Organizations that want to develop effective incentive programs must address all elements of Maslow's Hierarchy. Maslow's hierarchy describes a set of ascending human needs or drives which the "self-actualizing" individual moves toward. At the most elemental level, the individual attempts to fulfill his/her needs for food and water. As these needs are fulfilled, the individual moves on to try to fulfill such needs as safety, security, belonging, self-esteem, and self-actualization. If basic needs such as food and water suddenly become unavailable, the individual "descends" the pyramid to take care of these basic needs first. The individual cannot ascend to a higher step until each of the preceding "lower" needs are fulfilled. An individual's need for incentives will directly relate to the level that an individual is at. Thus, an individual who is at the level of food and basic survival needs will probably not view a personally autographed picture of the company president with much affection. Such an incentive will have a great deal more meaning to the person who is at the level of "self-esteem." An individual who is at the level of "belonging" will view the opportunity to take part on some type of a team problem-solving effort as a very strong incentive. Maslow's hierarchy suggests that the type of incentive that will be rewarding and motivating to an individual will be directly related to the individual's unique position within this hierarchy. It will be different for each person in the organization, but many similarities will exist between people who are at the same place in Maslow's hierarchy.

Incentives are a form of investment. They are an investment in the people that form the organization. In the Taylor school of management, employees were viewed as a liability. The best jobs required minimum labor input. Thus, the best thing that managers could do to optimize the organization was to simplify tasks and eliminate as much of the manual work as possible. The dramatic increase in recent years in the number of organizations using "downsizing" as a strategy is evidence that many managers still subscribe to the values in the Taylor paradigm of management.

Organizations need to spend more time studying "disincentives." If you believe that most people want to do a good job and are smart enough to do it, then the key question is, "Why don't they?" The answer is that most of the time (as Deming remonstrated), the problems are in the system. But what about those times when it is clearly a "motivational" issue? Then look at both your incentives and your disincentives. In many organizations, the list of disincentives is unbelievable in scope and scale, including such conditions as separate cafeterias for managers and nonmanagers, privileged parking spaces, special furniture and office spaces, casual time and dress for some and not others, gate inspections for only hourly employees, exempt versus nonexempt classifications, bonuses, perks, time cards, salary differentials, differential firing practices, break privileges, time-off privileges, and even different methods of providing paychecks. These are all exclusionary practices, or disincentives.

## *INFORMATION*

One quality improvement slogan that is often repeated is, "In God we trust, everyone else must have data." It has often been said that knowledge is power. Academicians make a distinction between data, information, and knowledge. We would include the ethical value of "caring" in this cornucopia. Caring is a form of information. It is conveyed through feelings and emotions, not through the rational cognitive brain. Feelings let us know how we are reacting to external stimuli minutes and perhaps even hours before our brain recognizes that a problem exists. Employees are well able to understand which managers care about them and which organizations truly demonstrate that they value their employees.

To care, you must recognize how you feel. Those who care, and value caring, are in touch with a different kind of information than are those who only value thinking. Many times, caring is a much more powerful type of information. Someone who can only think rationally often overlooks the power of caring. The rational, logical person thinks that caring people are being overly emotional. The rational person does not understand that the caring person is actually privy to a different type of knowledge and information.

Historically, the world has had little respect for caring people. Most caring people were in occupations such as nurse, teacher, minister, and social worker. As we emerge in a global interconnected society, the ability to establish rapport and empathy with others has begun to take on new meaning. Increasingly, organizations ask for team players as opposed to independent players. Team players, by definition, must care about the welfare of the other team members. The organization in an interconnected global economy must care about its customer, its stakeholders, and society. Caring is an ethical value that is fundamental to how the organization handles the five New Business Values. Without the value of caring, the organization can only be driven by the metrics of earnings, quarterly reports, and stock prices. Individuals who lack the capacity to care, or who are driven only by financial results and numerical data, will be at a severe disadvantage in the new global economy.

We are continually processing data from such sources as books, TV, radio, newspapers, electronic data processors, the Internet, experiences, feelings, and other people. Driven by our experiences in real time, we incorporate new data. Consciously or unconsciously, we attempt to convert this data to something meaningful. When it becomes meaningful, it is information. Information that is useful then becomes knowledge. If we add a measure of caring to the knowledge, we may end up creating wisdom. Wisdom transcends mere knowledge in that it implies the ability to make correct decisions based on an appreciation of complexities that knowledge alone cannot convey or bestow. One would much rather be wise than pedantic.

The successful organization will focus on the continuous pursuit of a wide range of information sources, constantly scanning the environment for new and unique information. Its ability to seek and assimilate information will demonstrate the value of information. Furthermore, it will understand the difference between reams of data and useful information. Knowledge must ultimately be only applied to those goals and tasks that the organization really cares about and that are worth caring about in terms of organizational priorities and needs.

Everyone in the successful organization will be involved in the search for knowledge, and the organization will provide incentives for pursuing and using such information. The information will be used for continuous quality improvement and ongoing innovation. In this way, each of the business values are linked and interdependent. You cannot be successful by only focusing on one of the elements. And, of course, it goes without saying that the focus for all of these five value drivers must be the customers (internal and external) and stakeholders. Without this focus, these concepts have no true meaning. Only the customer and stakeholders can define the relevance and meaning for each of the five New Business Values.

If you are looking for a prescription wherein you can forgo thinking, if you are not willing to follow the PDSA cycle, if you want to minimize creativity and innovation, or if you are not willing to have your ideas challenged and to challenge the ideas of others, then this model will probably not help your organization. But it can help those organizations which accept the challenge of applying these new values and are willing to make the changes in their organizations that this will entail.

## REFERENCE NOTES

1. Nadler, D.A., Gerstein, M.S., Shaw, R.B., and Associates. *Organizational Architecture*. San Francisco: Jossey-Bass Publishers, 1992.

2. Box, G.E.P., Hunter, W.G., and Stewart, J.S. *Statistics for Experimenters: An Introduction to Design, Data Analysis, and Model Building*. New York: John Wiley and Sons, 1978.

3. Priestmeyer, H.R. *Organizations and Chaos*. Westport, CT: Quorum Books, 1992.

4. de Bono, E. *Serious Creativity*. New York: Harper Business, 1992.

5. Senge, P. *The Fifth Discipline*. New York: Doubleday, 1990.

# PART II:
# IMPROVEMENT

Improvement has become one of the cornerstones for a successful organization. Organizations may call it different names, but Total Quality Management, Continuous Quality Improvement, Total Quality Leadership, Total Quality Control, and Statistical Quality Programs are all simply reflections of the underlying drive and value that is now being placed on continually finding better and better ways to do things. Many people call it working smarter rather than working harder. Others call it doing more with less. Whatever it is called, it reflects a fundamental shift in the way that most business has been practiced since the late nineteenth century.

If the new value is improvement, the old value was maintenance. Once a product or service was created, the maxim was, "If it ain't broke, don't fix it." Woe to anyone who wanted to change or improve something that already worked. It did not matter if many employees had ideas to make it better. It did not matter if the product could be made even more cheaply with higher quality. It did not matter if the product could be changed to increase customer satisfaction. It did not even matter if the customers had problems with the product, as long as they kept buying it. As long as the customer was buying, you did not touch the product. Contrast this attitude with the comment, "Even if it ain't broke, you should break it and find a better way to build it." This comment is the epitome of the new value that is placed on ever and ever more improvement.

In the past, one often heard the comment, "There is always time to do it over, but never time to do it right in the first place." Today, we increasingly hear of organizations whose slogan is "Do it right the first time." Managers, traditionally below the level of CEO, have been firefighters, not strategic planners or thinkers; but increasingly, we hear that the new role of managers is to think long-term and to plan for the future. Firefighting has become a dirty word in many organizations and a practice to be avoided.

What has caused this shift in business values? We all know the answer because it is self-evident; we have heard it so many times that we are tired of hearing it: global competition. Or, as W. E. Deming said, "We are in a new economic marketplace." Today, products are made in many different parts of the world, assembled in other parts, and delivered to still other parts. The customer could be German, French, Indian, Chinese, or Malaysian. The supplier could be American, Canadian, Japanese, Korean, or Swedish. The standard of living worldwide is rising; the pursuit of high standards drives the fierce competition for high productivity and high leverage of resources. Customers want more and more value for their money and providers need to deliver this value or lose market share. Losing market share now may mean losing your standard of living on a national and societal level. Thus, what is good enough today cannot be good enough tomorrow.

This "hypercompetition" drives a never-ending search for newer and better ways of doing things. Any organization that tries to maintain the status quo is doomed to failure. Rapid obsolescence is replaced by self-obsolescence as organizations compete with themselves to deliberately make their own products obsolete. Even as the marketing hype for Microsoft Windows 95 was just beginning, you can be sure Bill Gates was working on its successor. It would be a prescription for failure if he was not.

This section will describe some of the strategies and ideas that you can use in your organization to create a greater emphasis on improvement. Each of these ideas is like a tree in the forest. No one idea will guarantee you success. Even improvement as a whole will not guarantee you success, since it is only one of several fundamental new values that must be embraced for success. However, without a commitment to the value of Improvement, you will have a much more difficult time finding success in the ever-expanding global marketplace. It seems fairly evident that organizations that are not committed to continually improving their products and services will only have a chance at short-term economic success. The second generation of anything produced today must be better than the first. If you can't make it better, it is almost guaranteed that someone else will.

# Chapter 3

# Creating the Organization
# of Your Dreams

One of the most powerful tools that a business can use to ensure success is the Plan-Do-Check-Act (PDCA) Cycle, developed by Walter Shewhart and made famous by Dr. W. E. Deming. In fact, in Japan it is known as the Deming Cycle. It infuses all of the thinking and planning that the Japanese do about quality. Fundamentally, it is a conceptual tool that integrates theory with experience and experience with theory in a never-ending cycle of planning, doing, checking, and refining. It is the embodiment of the scientific method applied to business systems. In later years, Deming began to refer to it as the P-D-S-A Cycle, substituting the word "Study" for "Check." Deming felt that the word "Study" denoted more serious consideration of the system than merely "checking" the results.

Many businesses seem to work on the "Ready, Fire, Aim" principle. This philosophy is a recipe for "firefighting." One client summed it up aptly when he admitted, "In our company, we always have time to do it over, but never time to do it right." It has often been noted that American managers seem to have an aversion to planning and a propensity for action. This leads them into putting the cart before the horse. One client told me that some of the managers would start fires deliberately. I was dumbfounded by this comment, but it made sense (in a sort of crazy logic) when it was explained that because managers were rewarded for putting out "fires," they could increase the number of possible awards (raises, promotions, etc.) by starting "fires."

Many enlightened business leaders think that all they have to do is change from "Ready, Fire, Aim" to "Ready, Aim, Fire" and they will have it right. This will not work because they are still missing the

"Check." The following example will show how the PDCA Cycle works and why the "Check" step is critical. I often use the example of target shooting in my teaching and illustrate with a target or bull's-eye. It is very effective because many people can identify with some form of aiming at a target, whether it's with a firearm, a dart board, bowling pins, or a golf cup. This example can be used with any of these experiences or any experience with a clearly defined goal.

Pretend you are going target shooting. First, you will "Plan" what to bring, where you will go, who you will go with, when and how long you will be gone, the distance you will shoot, the number of rounds you will shoot, the caliber and type of weapon you will fire, how long you will practice, etc. Then, you "Do." You go to the firing range, set up your target, and shoot. No doubt, you would use good firing technique—squeeze the trigger, hold your breath, etc. What would you do next? Would you adjust your sights? Would you change your hold on the weapon? No, of course not. You would not change anything until you looked to see where your shots went. You would "Check" or "Study" the target. Only after studying the target would you take "Action" to adjust the process. It is essential to include the "Check" step because your adjustments would depend on where your shots went or, in other words, what the data showed. To take action without a "Check" would not make sense. It would amount to random tampering with the process.

Nevertheless, many businesses run without a "check" in their effort. Indeed, many businesses do not even have a target. How could they improve? Could anyone improve without some method to check their actions? Of course not. But the traditional American business is established on the principle of "If it ain't broke, don't fix it." Within this paradigm, you don't need to check or study anything. You just leave things alone. This old paradigm is a recipe for failure in the new competitive global economy. Organizations that intend to stay in business must adopt the concept of Continuous Improvement or, "If it ain't broke, you'd better break it and figure out how to make it better." This kind of thinking underlies the new business value paradigm. You cannot be successful without understanding and utilizing the PDCA Cycle.

Any business can use the PDCA Cycle to be effective. Both large and small businesses can add greater value from practicing the

PDCA discipline. The PDCA Cycle can be used with any effort that you begin in an organization. You do not have to be a big organization with a separate quality department or human resources department to use the PDCA Cycle. Even organizations that have been involved with continuous improvement or quality programs for several years can benefit by revisiting the fundamentals of PDCA.

### *GETTING STARTED*

Many organizations ask how they can get their continuous improvement effort started or how to begin their transformation effort. They are often looking for a formula or recipe for success. There are no such recipes. The PDCA Cycle is a process that can be used, but following it is hard work and requires risk taking. You can start anywhere in the cycle, but you must eventually hit all the steps. Where you start in the cycle depends upon your organization, its present energies, and its disposition.

If you start with the "Plan" step, you need to establish an overall strategic plan for quality improvement and specific goals and objectives that you would like to achieve. This step could take from a few weeks to several months. While this seems like a logical place to start, many organizations don't seem to have the time or inclination to start with the "Plan" Step. Perhaps they have a crisis underway or lack the commitment necessary for an overall top-level plan. They may not be ready for the "Plan" Step but they may want to take the "Do" Step.

Starting with the "Do" step usually means starting with small-scale pilot efforts in several different areas of the organization. Select those areas that are most receptive to the effort and where there is the greatest chance of success. Successful completion of the "Do" step often serves as a means for gaining the commitment of the entire organization and persuading the skeptics of the benefits of the new improvement effort. Nevertheless, this step is not for every organization.

In some organizations, it is possible to start with the "Check" step. A quality audit or a quality assessment can be conducted to determine how the organization's present systems are doing in terms of quality and how "ready" the organization is for a new effort or direction. Often, organizations that have been involved with quality for a number of years, and have hit a ceiling or plateau, find it very useful to start with the "Check" step. Strong assessment data helps organizations mobilize the energy for a breakthrough by identifying potential strengths and weaknesses in their system and focusing on what needs to be done.

The "Action" step is for those who "don't want to reinvent the wheel." Many companies and organizations are content to buy an "off-the-shelf quality model." They may adopt the Deming Prize criteria, the Malcolm Baldrige National Quality Award criteria, or the ISO 9000 criteria as a starting point for their quality efforts. There is nothing wrong with this strategy; indeed, it has many advantages. The criteria for these systems are well documented and come with proven strategies for success. Furthermore, there are many role models and resources available for organizations that want to adopt an off-the-shelf approach.

Regardless of which step an organization begins with, it cannot end with that step. A Total Quality Effort, a Lean Production system, a Just-In-Time system, or a value-added program cannot be developed without progressing around the PDCA Cycle. More than anything, the PDCA Cycle is a means to gain knowledge about a system and its processes as well as its underlying strengths and weaknesses. Unless you understand your system, whether it is the entire organization or a process within the organization, and its interactions, you cannot achieve more than merely copying what others have done before you.

The concept of continuous improvement is predicated on the basis of an open system that is continually interacting and learning from its environment. When an organization fails to take a step in the PDCA Cycle, or when it doesn't continue around the cycle, the learning process is effectively destroyed. From a learning or epistemological point of view, the PDCA Cycle represents the integration of deductive and inductive thinking. For years, philosophers argued whether inductive or deductive logic was the path to true knowledge. C. I. Lewis, in his book *Mind and the World Order*,[1] established that both types of logic were essential to the acquisition of true knowledge. This book heavily influenced the thinking of Dr. Deming who often cited it in his seminars and publications.

In the following analysis, we will use the PDCA Cycle to help focus these issues and demonstrate the power of PDCA thinking. We will lay out a complete improvement process for an organization that knows little or nothing about continuous improvement. By following these steps, the organization can begin its effort, and by going through a second cycle, it can refine and improve its effort. Organizations that have already started an improvement effort can also use this process to assess the effectiveness and progress of their effort.

## *ACTION*

We shall start in the "Action" step, assuming that your business has not yet begun a systematic, continuous improvement or quality effort. The benefits of continuous quality improvement are well documented and proven by the data that will be described. In a sense, many previous "Check" steps have already given us facts to document the benefits of Quality Improvement. If your organization has not yet begun a systematic improvement effort or your senior executives are not yet on board the effort, the following ten key facts should provide strong evidence that can be used to persuade your organization of the benefits of such efforts.

### *1. Stock value of TQM companies does substantially better than average.*

Spurred on by a comment made by Joseph Juran, stock market analysts compared the stock value of Malcolm Baldrige National Quality Award finalists to the market as a whole. The stock value of Baldrige Award finalists showed a much greater value increase than did a comparable set of stocks from nonfinalists.

### *2. PIMS (Profit Impact of Marketing Strategies) studies.*

Sponsored by the Strategic Planning Institute, this database of strategic and marketing data from over 3,000 business units has conclusively demonstrated that quality and profitability are strongly related.

### 3. Quality is a worldwide phenomenon.

Just because everyone is doing something doesn't make it right, but one must wonder when the Japanese, Europeans, Canadians, and several South American countries all have a National Quality Day with specific awards to spur organizational improvement in quality and productivity.

### 4. The rise of ISO 9000.

ISO 9000 provides a starting point for a quality program. It has gained worldwide acceptance and is fast becoming a requirement and benchmark for organizations that want to do business in the global market.

### 5. Speed is of the utmost importance.

Cycle times for product throughput, new product development, and delivery times are falling everywhere. Increasingly, the organization that is the fastest is the most successful. To compete, every company must do it faster and faster with, of course, no reduction in quality.

### 6. Customers are more demanding.

Government regulations, lawyers, guarantees, warranties, more choice, and an increased awareness of quality are making consumers more demanding and more likely to go elsewhere when their demands are not met.

### 7. The concept of a commodity business is dead or dying.

Ted Levitt, the dean of marketers, has said, "There is no such thing as a commodity business, there is only failure to differentiate your product." In traditional commodity businesses such as steel, mining, paper, pulp, oil, and gas, managers are finding that by adding more value than their competition, they can gain market share and profits.

### 8. Waste and rework eats up 20 percent of sales.

Estimates range from 10 percent to 50 percent (Deming), but most experts agree that in organizations without an effective continuous improvement effort, the amount of waste and rework is equal to approximately 20 percent of sales. There is very little that an organization can do that can exceed the return on investment from a Total Quality effort.

### 9. Competition is global.

Not only do we have to compete with the Japanese, Europeans, and Asians, but Brazil, Argentina, Mexico, and some African countries are providing new and emerging technologies aimed at getting their share of the world market.

### 10. People, not machines, add value.

Everybody can buy the newest technology, machines, and equipment. The key factor for success is the ability, knowledge, and skills of your workforce. If you do not have a plan to ensure that you are "Best in Class" in this area, you will not survive. Your people must also be continuously improving.

### *CHECK*

Some organizations start their improvement efforts at the "Check" or "Study" step. The following ten key questions will help you to "Check" your organization. You can use the following questions as a means of assessing your present system and identifying its strengths and weaknesses. Logically, you want to build on what you do well and eliminate what you do poorly.

### 1. How good is morale?

If your employees are your key value drivers, then it makes sense that the first area to assess is the morale of your employees. How committed are they to the organization? How committed is the organization to them?

### 2. How does product service quality compare to your competitors'?

Do you use benchmarking, market studies, comparative shopping, and/or customer surveys to determine why your customers come to you and why they go elsewhere? What are your strengths relative to your competition?

### 3. Are your operating costs lower than your competition's operating costs?

If your operating costs are not lower than your competition's, how will you be able to afford training, education, and development of employees? Furthermore, if your costs are not continually being driven down, how will you match your competition in the future when their costs are even lower?

### 4. Are all your key processes documented, in control, and capable?

You need to understand your processes in order to continually improve them. You should focus on the 80/20 rule and select those areas that will give you the biggest bang for the buck. You will need to use statistical tools to establish and document how well your processes are performing.

### 5. Are you empowering your employees?

Are you training managers to work as coaches and facilitators? Are you giving employees responsibilities and training to make changes that will improve their processes? Are you eliminating bureaucracy and paperwork? Actually, even though it may be the most-used buzzword of the 1990s, you cannot empower employees but you can "disempower" them. What policies and procedure do you have that "disempower" employees?

### 6. How much hierarchy do you have?

It is one thing to talk about empowerment, but if you still have five or more layers of management, chances are that all you are doing is talking. Layers of management who check and make sure others are doing their jobs is an expense that progressive organizations can no longer afford. It adds no value.

### 7. Are you inspecting product or service quality?

Inspection is too late and represents no added value for the customer. Organizations must eliminate inspection and replace it with process control and upstream improvements to ensure that the job is done right the first time.

### 8. Are your customers delighted?

Customer surveys will only tell you if your customers are satisfied. A satisfied customer will switch. You must make extraordinary efforts to convert satisfied customers to delighted, loyal customers. Are you studying your customers and how they perceive your organization? Are you continuously finding ways to add more value for your customers or to reduce product costs?

### 9. Have you balanced growth and development?

Success is not assured by just getting bigger and bigger. Success can only be assured by getting better and better. Many organizations define success as growth and revenue increases. Look at the many organizations that are no longer on the *Fortune 500* list of fastest growing companies. Many of these organizations are now in trouble. Organizations must balance growth with development in order to assure long-term success.

### 10. Are you getting more profitable?

Profitability is still an excellent measure of organizational performance. How does your profitability compare to your competitors'? Why are you more profitable? Less profitable?

## *PLAN*

Once you have made an attempt to answer each of the key questions asked above, you are now ready to move into the "Plan" step. There are ten key myths that often inhibit or create barriers for organizations intent on beginning a continuous improvement or value-added effort.

### *Myth #1. Everybody must be committed for the effort to be successful.*

Nonsense! You will never have 100 percent of your people committed, and it won't matter anyway. Remember, it took only one-third of the early settlers to decide to secede from King George. They began the United States of America, the greatest experiment in democracy the world had ever seen.

### *Myth #2. It takes ten years to see results.*

While it does take many years to change from one paradigm to another, a total paradigm shift is not necessary to obtain or see results from a Total Quality effort. Many organizations have had outstanding success in a matter of a few months and, in some cases, just weeks.

### *Myth #3. You must have a culture change to get results.*

People don't change overnight, neither do organizations. The pundits still are arguing about what "culture" really is and means anyway. The only things you need to change to see results are the attitudes of a few key people. If you want to call this a culture change, great. We merely see it as people being able to change their minds and learn new skills and abilities.

### *Myth #4. You can delegate the leadership of the effort.*

You want to hire a quality manager or TQM coordinator? Wonderful. However, unless you provide the leadership for the effort, it will not work. Leadership is not the same as management and requires a different set of skills. These will be explained in Chapter 13.

### *Myth #5. Quality is free.*

Nothing that requires hard work is free. "Quality" requires an investment of time and money in training, teamwork, and process management. The results will more than pay for themselves, but it certainly is not free.

### *Myth #6. Statistical process control will solve all of your quality problems.*

Statistics are a key tool for understanding variation. However, not all quality problems can be solved simply by understanding variation. Deming defined four types of knowledge needed to successfully manage an organization. He called his four components "A System of Profound Knowledge." Knowledge of Variation was only one of the four elements. The others were Theory of Knowledge, Psychology or Knowledge of People, and Knowledge of Systems. All are essential for problem solving.

### *Myth #7. Total quality management will solve all of your quality problems.*

The Malcolm Baldrige National Quality Award, the Deming Prize, the European Quality Award, etc., do not say anything about knowledge or continuous learning. No system is perfect, and every system must continually be adapting, growing, and changing. The only way this can be done is when everyone understands and can apply Deming's concept of Profound Knowledge.

### *Myth #8. Quality can be a second priority.*

Many organizations practice a "Production first" and "Quality second" system. As someone once stated, "In our organization, we preach quality three weeks a month. Then, as production targets loom during the last week of the month, we shift priorities to get the darn stuff out the door." Quality leads to higher productivity and lower costs. However, quality must come first. If it is a second priority, then you do not understand the essence of quality improvement.

### Myth #9. Everybody must change but me.

You say you believe in the fundamental principles of Total Quality, but when it comes to practicing them, do you act like it is everyone else's job? If so, you are playing a version of "I'm okay, but everyone else isn't." We don't know any managers who are really acting like "new-style" leaders. But we do see a lot of "old-style" leaders making a determined effort to change their attitudes, knowledge, and skills. If you don't think that you need to change, then you must think that you are perfect. This is just another version of the "If it ain't broke, don't fix it" paradigm. We all must be continually improving.

### Myth #10. A little fear is good.

There's no question about it. Fear is a motivator. We will not argue that point. We will argue, however, that no one likes to be motivated by fear and that there are generally repercussions from such motivation. Perhaps the most important thing that managers can do is identify sources of fear in their organizations and remove them. Fear is always counterproductive in the long run.

### DO

If you have gone through each of the above steps and have identified answers or positions to the issues described, then you are ready for the "Do" step. Keep in mind that the PDCA Cycle is a never-ending cycle. Once you have completed the cycle the first time, go back and start over . . . and over . . . and over. The cycle is the heart of continuous improvement. Only by continuously repeating the cycle can you ensure that your organization, process, or system is continually improving.

There are ten key steps that any organization must do to get started in a continuous improvement effort. These ten steps were the highest rated items from a list of over 300 possible action items rated by forty independent consultants. They represent the ten most important first steps to be taken in the first year of your continuous improvement effort.

### 1. Assign your best person 100 percent of the time to coordinate the change effort.

This does not mean that you are delegating leadership of the effort. It does mean that it will be high profile, and shows a willingness to dedicate considerable resources to ensure its success. This person should report directly to the CEO or organizational leader.

### 2. Do set aside 2 to 4 percent of the payroll budget for continuous improvement training and 5 to 10 percent of work time for training.

Education and training are the beginning and ending of Total Quality, according to Dr. Kaoru Ishikawa. Deming devoted two of his fourteen principles to training and education. Training and education are the fuels for the quality engine. To cut these off or skimp on them will choke your effort to death.

### 3. Establish a high-level steering committee. Include the union.

The major leaders of all stakeholders, departments, areas, etc., should be involved to ensure that the organization is working as a team on the effort. At the beginning, you may not have the hearts and souls of all these people, but you will at least have their bodies and their attention. Part of the steering team role is education and part is to ensure commitment and involvement of all key organizational leaders.

### 4. Create an initial plan or roadmap for the effort.

Identify the key objectives and goals of the effort. Begin a planning process that will be subject to continuous improvement. Establish accountability for what will be done and when.

### 5. Merge the business and improvement plans.

The improvement plan must be incorporated into the overall planning process of the organization. This includes, at minimum, a merger with the business plan, but it should also include integration with the strategic plan, the HRD (Human Resources Development) plan, the research and development plan, the quality plan, and the marketing plan. You don't have any of these plans? To learn how a quality planning process works, read Yoji Akao's book on Hoshin Planning.[2]

### 6. Create employee incentives.

It is essential to create a climate where people are committed to the organization and vice versa. This means giving employees incentives for such commitment. Incentives might be in the form of employment security, increased recognition, profit sharing, or a new style of reward system. However you do it, the goal should be to create a sense of equity and fairness. In other words, we are all in this together, and we will all share the rewards of hard work and dedication.

### 7. Flatten the organization and increase responsibilities.

The many layers of management that can be found in large organizations serve little or no purpose. Much of what such managers do could be more easily and efficiently done by computers. Such hierarchical systems derive from a military chain of command protocol where no one was trusted and someone had to be assigned to watch everyone. It was also a system where no one was allowed, much less required, to think for himself/herself. Indeed, it was considered counterproductive for soldiers to think for themselves. Such a system is a major impediment to any organization that wants to compete in the global economy.

### 8. Build open information systems.

Give everyone in the organization access to all information about the organization. Eliminate the "need to know" mentality developed from the military model. Only with an open information system can an organization develop the type of learning system culture needed for continuous improvement. It is impossible to develop such a system when you have people in the role of "information monitors." This is a role much like that of the thought monitors in Orwell's book, *1984.*

### 9. Go for rapid and continuous improvement.

In every organization, there will be some low-hanging fruit that can provide some short-term nourishment while the organization builds the scaffolding needed to systematically cull the rest of the fruit. Don't overlook the value of such nourishment, but don't confuse these short-term gains with the success that will come from the long-term effort. Many organizations plateau because they get complacent with the gains and successes they have achieved from these initial efforts.

### 10. Involve all stakeholders in the effort.

A stakeholder is someone with a vested interest in your organization or process. A customer is someone whose needs you serve or who depends on you to do his/her job. Success in a continuous improvement effort comes from meeting the needs of both customers and stakeholders. Many organizations have too narrow a focus, either disregarding the needs of their customers (typical in American industries) or disregarding the needs of their stakeholders (typical in Japanese industries). Either extreme is a prescription for failure. True success means meeting the needs of both stakeholders and customers.

The PDCA Cycle can be a useful tool for beginning any new improvement effort. For organizations that are already well into such efforts, the PDCA Cycle should provide the foundation for ongoing success. Its use should be evident in all work that is undertaken in the organization. Such organizations should be asked if they have a process to measure how deep their understanding of this cycle is and how much it truly penetrates the work they do. The

Japanese understand that only a thorough understanding and utilization of the PDCA Cycle can provide the momentum and direction for a continuous improvement effort. It is a simple concept, but one that brings together the power of theory and experience.

## REFERENCE NOTES

1. Lewis, C.I. *Mind and the New World Order.* Dover, England: Scribners, 1929.

2. Akao, Y. *Hoshin Kanri.* Cambridge, MA: Productivity Press, 1991

# Chapter 4

# Ten Principles for Creating Loyal, Devoted Customers

One cornerstone of any continuous improvement effort must be a process for the continuous improvement of customer service. Merely meeting the needs of the customer will not provide a competitive edge. Simply giving customers what they want will only create "satisfied" customers. To create a loyal customer, one who will brag about your products and services, it is necessary to ensure the quality of service as well as the quality of the product. When delivering a service, the "how" of service delivery is every bit as important as the "what." To create "extraordinary" customer satisfaction, you must understand and respond to several fundamental principles of "quality" customer service. This chapter will examine some of these basic principles and show how they can be used to create a competitive advantage.

One technique that I have used in customer service training is to ask participants to share their real-life customer service "horror" stories with a team of five or six other participants. (There is never a shortage of such stories.) Following the stories, the team analyzes the various incidents and identifies the factors that led to the customer being dissatisfied. Once each team has done this, I ask them to try to use this "data" and their experience to compile a set of principles for quality customer service. Over the years, I have seen the same principles identified time and time again. The following are ten of the most fundamental and important principles of customer service for any organization. This list will provide an excellent starting point to begin a systematic effort to improve customer satisfaction and service in your organization. Once your organization has a process in place for ensuring consistent reliable action on these principles, it is in a position to begin to understand how to consistently exceed the criteria for customer satisfaction.

### *1. Integrity means that you must attempt to balance customer needs and wants. Needs and wants are not necessarily the same.*

Many years before the quality movement declared that the customer must be the focus for all of our efforts, there was a slogan that stated, "The customer is King." Employees were often told, "The customer is always right." This slogan was seldom heeded, sometimes for good. This may sound like heresy to those in the quality movement, but it is often true that customers do not always know or want what is good for them. This does not mean that we cannot discuss their concerns, desires, or feelings. However, it does mean that if we only address what customers say they want, we may miss addressing what, in the long run, may be more important to them.

The dilemma of balancing needs and wants produces two dangers for an organization. One danger involves the possibility of being seen as arrogant and treating the customer somewhat condescendingly or paternally. The other danger involves pandering to customers and being seen as sleazy, shiftless, and willing to sell anyone anything to make a buck. These are tricky shoals to navigate through. Mark Le Blanc, a Minnesota-based marketing consultant, said that the trick is to "give customers what they need, but package it so that they want it."

Honesty and integrity are essential to handling this problem. Lou Schultz, the CEO of Process Management International, was once conducting a training session on Deming's 14 Points for a large organization. Midway through the first day of the four-day training program, the president of the client organization took Lou aside and said that he really didn't think that the training was very useful and could Lou shorten the course by a couple of days? Lou thought about it and replied, "No, I think you need to hear the whole message and I would be doing you a disservice if I abbreviated the course. If you are not happy when I am done, I will refund your money for the entire training program." The client agreed to this arrangement. At the end of the four days of training, the client personally thanked Lou for standing his ground, saying that it was the best training session that he had ever attended.

There is no substitute for being honest with all customers. Clients must have some degree of trust in the relationship in order for business to occur. We have to make it safe for them to trust us. Lou made it safer by offering a money back guarantee. However, the client still had the risk of his/her time involved which probably far exceeded the cost of the course. It is impossible to entirely eliminate any downside risk in a business transaction. This is why honesty is so important. Without honesty, there can be no long-term trust. Yes, you may sell someone something that he/she doesn't need or that isn't right for him/her, but as soon as the client realizes it, he/she will be hurt and resentful. One way or another, this hurt and resentment will come back to your organization. It may be in the form of lost business or even a lawsuit, but as the saying goes, "What goes around, comes around." One of the most memorable stories for most of us comes from the movie *Miracle on Thirty-Fourth Street*. In the movie, the Macy's Santa Claus sends a customer to Macy's arch rival, Gimbel's. The short-term result was one lost customer. The long-term result was an avalanche of free publicity and good-will for Macy's. Wouldn't you like to be remembered as the organization that "really cared about its customers?"

## 2. Do not assume that you know what the customer wants or needs.

In too many situations, the vendor assumes or takes for granted that he/she knows what the customer needs or wants. A manager at Tectronics Corporation once told me that the company was the king of the hill for so long, it assumed that whatever the company did was right. Tectronics Corporation felt it knew what the customers really wanted better than its customers. The corporation did not understand the danger of this thinking until it began to lose significant market share. By the time Tectronics realized what the solutions were, it had already lost nearly 40 percent of its market to competitors who were more sensitive to customers.

It might be okay to assume that you know what the customer wants if the customer is a static, unchanging element, if you have absolutely no competition, or if you have a totally unchanging business environment. However, even if the second possibility were valid, the first one is never valid. People are always changing. Whatever they want today, they want more, better, or different tomorrow. As they satisfy one set of needs, another set of needs emerges. People are totally dynamic and ever evolving in their needs, wants, and expectations. The greatest danger for any business is to assume that it knows what its customers want. Even if it happens to be true today, it may not be true tomorrow.

It is essential to continuously check out our assumptions in respect to the needs and wants of our customers. If we want excited customers, we must keep up with their changing expectations by setting up a process that can help us to keep in touch with their evolving needs and wants. For instance, astute companies are anticipating the changes in the lives of the baby boomers over time by conducting market and demographic studies that evaluate the impact that lifestyle and aging will have on their consumer preferences and needs. Those organizations that can make correct assumptions from the data will prosper. They will lead their competitors in providing products and services that satisfy the needs and wants of consumers, not only today, but also tomorrow. The front-running organizations are planning to satisfy those needs and wants that today's customers don't even know they have.

### 3. Market research is only one element in identifying customers' needs and wants.

Market research is good for identifying what Dr. Kano calls the "expected dimension" of customer satisfaction. However, there is also the "exciting dimension" (that which delights the customer, but which they cannot verbalize or identify on a survey) and the "assumed dimension." The assumed dimension refers to those quality characteristics that the customer takes for granted. For example, surveys of customer satisfaction with airlines do not usually state pilot training as a satisfier. However, you can bet that if it is not there, the customer will be highly dissatisfied.

It is possible to assess the expected dimension of customer satisfaction through surveys and focus groups. However, surveys will not help to identify the exciting dimension or the assumed dimension. Soichiro Honda did not do any market studies before introducing his motorcycles to the United States. Honda noted that if he had conducted research, it would probably have told him that only hoodlums and punks rode motorcycles. The image one had of a motorcyclist was forever etched in the mind as Marlon Brando from the movie *The Wild One.* Motorcyclists were people who terrorized towns and used illicit drugs. Because of this image, 1956 motorcycle marketing wisdom was that the motorcycle market would never grow beyond 400,000 units per year (the number sold in 1956). Within ten years, the motorcycle market was at nearly five million units per year sold, and Honda had 70 percent of this market.

You need to identify customers' needs/wants by a variety of methods designed to address all three (expected, exciting, and assumed) dimensions. Many businesses limit themselves to rational or left-brain-type consumer analyses. Strategic planning, for example, is generally a left-brain exercise. Left-brain analyses include customer surveys, trend analysis, market research, Gallup surveys, customer needs assessments, and many other methods that are logical, empirical, and analytical. Such methods can be very powerful; however, they are not enough to ensure organizational success. To ensure success means to be able to anticipate the future; this often requires a break with the past. Such breaks can only come about through creative and innovative thinking which draws on right-brain thinking. From Edward de Bono's creativity methods to Roger Von Oech's *Creative Whack Pack,* there are many tools available for organizations that want to tap into the power of right-brain thinking. Unfortunately, most organizations are led by left-brain rational thinkers who usually do not put a high value on pure creativity and play.

While rational thinking is essential for planning and control, it will never be enough to ensure that organizations remain vital and dynamic. Many would argue that the decline and bureaucratization of organizations such as IBM and General Motors came about because of the absence of visionary leaders such as Tom Watson and Alfred Sloan. These were leaders who did not merely manage, but who were creative and dynamic. Similarly, the decline of Disney, Inc., can be associated with the death of Walt Disney, one of the most creative and imaginative leaders ever, while its subsequent revitalization took place because of the creative visionary leadership of Michael Eisner. It is time for businesses to understand the necessity of both right- and left-brain thinking to better help them identify their customers' needs and wants.

### 4. Poor customer service is often the result of a poorly organized business structure.

Barriers between departments (Deming Principle #9) create barriers for your customers. If you are going to redesign or reengineer your organization, the first point of reference for any such effort should be your customers. We have all seen countless examples of businesses that seem designed to avoid or ignore customers rather than to help them. Many companies and government agencies are now using voice mail systems that would try the patience of a saint. I recently called a mail-order company to place an order and was told by a voice mail machine that the company only accepted orders between 9 a.m. and 3:30 p.m. EST. I was calling at 10:30 a.m. EST! Recently, I tried to use Dun & Bradstreet's international database to conduct some research on European organizations. I called its London office for help, and was told to call Texas because I was calling from the United States and the London office did not want to "step on anyone's toes over here." When I called the Texas office, I was told that I should have called Dun & Bradstreet's New Jersey office. After spending two hours trying to contact this office, I finally found that I had been given the wrong number. It was a different Dun & Bradstreet business unit, but at least the people there gave me the correct number and two names. Of course, both these people whose names I was given were out, so I left messages on their voice mail systems. It is still unknown whether they will be able to help me or not.

These stories are not unique. It is a sad commentary that all too many of us can tell similar or worse stories. Most such stories are very benign and, outside of some inconvenience, do not really hurt anyone else. However, there is a dark side to the inefficiency and structural barriers that plague many organizations. From Bhopal to Chernobyl to the Challenger Space Shuttle disaster to the Exxon Valdez, one can find a common line of organizational bureaucracy and ignorance, caused at least in part by systems and structures, that did not facilitate adequate communication between internal customers and external customers. Organizations need to be continually thinking and rethinking basic concepts concerning organizational design and structure. Too many organizations grow and grow, forgetting that structures unattended to can end up dictating strategy.

### 5. Driving fear into the workplace will drive fear into your customers.

Do you use arbitrary numerical goals and objectives to spur productivity? Are your workers on a piecework system to increase output? Do you use "positive" discipline to ensure that employees are behaving the way you want them to? Do you rank and reward employees by conducting annual performance appraisals? Many such practices create a hostile working environment. Poor customer service is often a reflection of how employees are being treated by the management of an organization. If employees are treated as numbers, it should be no surprise that customers get treated as numbers. If employees have little time to be creative or innovative, it should be no surprise that customer service is perfunctory and unimaginative. If workers feel disrespected and threatened, they are not likely to treat customers with respect. If performance is judged by how much gets done rather than how well it gets done, or if goals are jeopardized by taking time to deal with a customer, it should be no surprise when customers complain about the level of service they receive. In many organizations, one hears the complaint, "Making the numbers is the only thing that counts around here." It should be no surprise that there is little time for customer service in such organizations.

At one of his four-day conferences, Dr. Deming was once asked by a telephone company employee what he thought about the company's quota system. Employees of the telephone company were only allowed so much time to answer any particular customer inquiry, and they were expected to answer a certain number per hour. Deming asked what the employee's biggest problem was, and to no one's surprise was told, "Many callers get irate because I don't have enough time to help them or answer their questions." Sadly, some phone companies' solution to this has been to institute random screening of phone calls to determine if operators are dealing with customers courteously and respectfully, putting even more pressure on employees. Pity the employee who cannot spend enough time to satisfy the customer but is expected to be courteous and charming, albeit in a very expeditious manner.

Organizations must clearly establish customer service as a corporate goal and set up the policies and procedures to support this goal. Policies and procedures that are counterproductive must be eliminated. For many organizations, this will mean breaking down sacred cows and traditional ways of doing things. MBO (management by objective) and quota systems are considered by many traditional organizations as prerequisites for doing business. Innovative organizations are beginning to see that such procedures do more harm than good. An organization that wants its customers to feel trusted and respected must also treat its employees the same way. Systems based on distrust and lack of respect for employees are barriers to customer service and must be eliminated.

Today, many organizations are "complying" with diversity criteria merely because it is required by law or seen as the thing to do. Few organizations realize that having a diverse workforce is a better way to meet the needs of a diverse customer population. For instance, many women prefer to see a female gynecologist. Indeed, many women are making this choice. A medical clinic that does not have access to female medical doctors will lose clients to clinics that do. In an increasingly heterogeneous world, the organization with the greatest ability to manage heterogeneity will be most likely to survive and prosper.

### 6. Your corporate policies and procedures are irrelevant to your customers.

A client had a long-term customer whose account was a significant portion of the client's total sales. One day, a vice president at the customer company called in to place a rush order and requested that it be shipped ASAP. The clerk taking the order replied that he would send it out as soon as the paperwork was received. The customer explained again that it was an emergency and asked if the company could just take her verbal order followed by a fax copy. The clerk refused, citing company policy. In fact, it was against company policy; the clerk was just doing his job. The angry customer called the company president, read him the riot act, and canceled half of her purchases for the next year. When the president mentioned this situation to me, I reported other transactions of this type that had come to my attention. He realized that this was no "special cause" but instead was part of the common cause system created by his company's policies and procedures. How many times have you been told that something is against company policy?

You can have the greatest policies and procedures manual in the world. All of your processes may be standardized, flowcharted, and certified to ISO 9001, but none of this will mean a thing to your customer if your processes do not provide value to your customer. A friend once tried to order some merchandise from a catalog and was told by the dealer to call back in a week since the dealer was closed for inventory control. Can you imagine a mail-order company that shuts down for a week to count its inventory? The friend supposed (as he called another company) that this was a "traditional" practice at this organization.

Many organizations set up their policies with no thought of their customers in mind. Bank hours were once an ongoing joke among consumers. Difficulty getting auto parts was well known among those who worked on their cars on weekends. Most auto part dealers were either closed or would close by noon on Saturdays. It is still difficult to locate a tailor that is open during evening and weekend hours. Some of these problems have been resolved in recent times, as banks and most retail stores have seen the light and offered extended hours. Nevertheless, there are countless other examples of organizational policies and procedures that work against quality customer service. We are all familiar with the government office that is closed at noontime, the only time that many of us can get away from work.

### 7. Customers need data and information to make a good decision.

We have probably all seen signs that proclaim, "The customer is always right." We do not believe this. Customers are often misinformed or have poor data with which they make decisions. However, this does not mean that you can then proceed to discount or ignore what customers are telling you. There are many who say, "We must educate our customers." This strikes us as condescending and patronizing. Organizations that say this are not sincere nor approaching the problem from the correct angle.

Customers don't need to be educated, but rather businesses need to understand the reality that their customers perceive. Businesses need to understand that the customers' perceptions are their realities. If your customers are perceiving things differently than you do, then you need to show them how this difference will impact their choices as consumers. How you do this will impact whether or not you keep their business. If you are really concerned about them, they will appreciate being shown why you think the way you do. However, if you are trying to show them how stupid they are and that they are wrong while you are right, you will undoubtedly lose their business. Customers have a sixth sense when it comes to telling who is really concerned about their needs and wants and who is only out to make the sale. To paraphrase Lincoln: "You can fool some of your customers some of the time. . . ." Organizations would do better to spend less money on advertising and more money on efforts to retain customers by providing outstanding customer service. It has consistently been demonstrated that it costs a great deal less to retain a customer than to find a new one. Too many organizations act as though customers are expendable.

### 8. A customer responsibility is a lost opportunity.

How often have you heard a manager say, "But that's the customer's responsibility, it's not our fault"? Many times, such remarks are made in respect to warranty claims, product usage, product maintenance, or some form of damage claim. For instance, "Well, you know it says here that you must oil it every 2,000 hours or the warranty is null and void." Okay, no question that many customers do not read or pay attention to product usage information. Furthermore, there is little doubt that many customers misuse or abuse products. Legally and ethically, producers cannot be held (although sometimes they are) responsible for such abuse. However, most customers do not conduct such abuse intentionally, and that is the secret to unparalleled opportunities to unlock a virtually unlimited number of chances to improve customer satisfaction.

If customers are unintentionally misusing the product, it means that either by improving some feature or performance aspect, you can add more value for the customer. Furthermore, your warranties and customer responsibilities are opportunities just crying out to be exploited. This will not only improve customer satisfaction, it will also help you by reducing claims and increasing the perception of quality associated with the product or service. Customers do not want a product to break down so they can run back to the store to return it. These problems can present wonderful opportunities for the astute.

How many of you wait too long before bringing your car in for an oil change? You know it needs to be changed but it either skips your mind or you just don't have the time. I often wait too long before bringing my car in for an oil change or lube job because I forget about the date or I don't take the time to schedule my next appointment. I mentioned this problem to the service manager at a Rapid Oil Change, and asked if he could call me or drop a postcard every so often to remind me to bring my car in. I was told very firmly, "No, that is your responsibility. We can't be baby-sitting our customers." Think of the opportunity here. What would it take to send a simple postcard to people like me? If each postcard generated an extra forty dollars in sales, it would certainly pay for the time and energy. There are millions of opportunities for the individual who sees responsibilities as situations just crying out to be turned into new sales of products and services.

### 9. Everyone better have a customer and it had better be the next process down the line.

Do people in your organization know who their customers are? If your employees do not have contact with external customers, do they know who their internal customers are? If employees in your organization define their bosses as their primary customer, you are in trouble. You are also in trouble if people in your organization have no sense of themselves as customers or no idea of what their internal customers need and want. Professor Kaoru Ishikawa, a Japanese consultant, created the concept of the "internal customer." He defined customers as "the next process down the line." Ishikawa created this concept because he realized that many employees in organizations would never see their external customers. The external customer was merely a symbol who held little or no meaning to them. Ishikawa wanted to create a means to help align organizations along business processes wherein the end or final focus would be the external customer. However, the alignment mechanism needed to keep people focused on this goal while providing an internal incentive for continual improvement. His creation of the concept of internal customer was a major breakthrough in organizational thinking. It provided a mechanism to help ensure that each employee in the organization would be able to focus on those things that really mattered to the external customer. Furthermore, it provided a focal point for his/her efforts that was not just a symbol, but was a living, breathing person. That person was his/her internal customer.

Customers have to be defined in relation to a process. At various stages in a process, an employee may be a customer or a supplier. Furthermore, someone who is a supplier today may be a customer tomorrow. Nevertheless, the only way that the process can be optimized rather than suboptimized (the way it's done in most traditional organizations) is when everyone and each step in the process is harmonized through the meeting of needs and wants at each stage of the process. This can be done if employees treat internal customers the same way that they would treat external customers. Each employee has one or more customers who must be satisfied and provided optimum quality service and products. As in the analogy about links in a chain, the chain of value to the customer consists of the value added at each step in the production or service process. Each step becomes a microcosm of the final transaction between the organization and the external customer. As in the chain, the overall process will only be as strong as its weakest part.

### 10. Everyone is in the customer service business.

Many organizations have still not put everyone to work in terms of customer service, marketing, and sales. Rather, employees are divided into areas of specialization. Some people do production, some do marketing, some do training, and some do customer service. This seems very shortsighted. If we all have customers, then we are all in the customer service business. Furthermore, if we all have customers, we all had better know how to do sales, marketing, and new product/service development. Why have only a part of the organization labeled with such responsibilities and ignore the inputs and insights of the vast majority of employees in the organization? Just as computers are more powerful when networked and linked together, we need to create systems that link employees in virtual networks of customer service, new product development, research and design, and organizational innovation and improvement.

Creating such an organization will not only overcome the communication problems that are epidemic in most companies, it will also create a system for harnessing the brainpower of all employees. This is the most effective way to help employees improve their jobs and the organization. We must create structures, policies, procedures, reward systems, etc., that allow everyone in the organization to be linked together in a search for the never-ending improvement of products, processes, and services. If satisfying the customer is the most important thing that any of us can do, then it surely makes sense to put the entire organization to work on this effort. As Dr. Deming's point number fourteen says, "Involve everyone in the transformation."

# Chapter 5

# The Three Dimensions of Quality and Performance

There is a good deal of research which shows that a "satisfied" customer will switch. In fact, the research shows that there is not a great deal of difference between a satisfied customer and a dissatisfied customer. Only a small quantitative difference separates satisfied from dissatisfied customers. The really noticeable difference is between satisfied customers and "devoted" customers. Research shows a qualitative difference between satisfied customers and "devoted" customers. Devoted customers do not switch. Devoted customers cannot even be talked into looking at other suppliers. For the devoted customer, the risk of switching far outweighs any foreseeable gain. This is the exact opposite situation that exists for both the satisfied and dissatisfied customer.

Here is an example to demonstrate the difference between being "devoted" and merely satisfied. I deal with L.L. Bean, the Maine-based catalog company, on a regular basis. I am so happy with the basic elements of its operation (service, call-in availability, shipping, etc.) that L.L. Bean is always my first choice for outdoor apparel. I don't look elsewhere because I can't imagine any greater quality in another operation. I don't even want to talk to another company about what it has to offer as long as L.L. Bean keeps up its current level of service.

On the other hand, I am merely satisfied with my present dry cleaners. They are as good as most in my area, but that is not saying much. When I find another dry cleaner nearby or when another one opens, I usually try it out. I have switched dry cleaners about three times in the last five years. Trying to find quality in a dry cleaning service is similar to looking for the Holy Grail. The prevailing attitude among dry cleaners seems to be: "We must be doing something right because we have customers." This is a far cry from "How can we continually improve service and quality?" Have you ever received a customer survey from a dry cleaner or heard of a dry cleaning operation that held customer focus groups? I am merely satisfied with my present dry cleaner and would switch for any number of reasons. For instance, if a new one opened closer to my business or if one advertised lower prices, I would switch, at least temporarily. When levels of service or quality are mediocre, it doesn't take much to lose a "satisfied" customer.

The ability to create "devoted" customers starts with an attitude. You have to believe that it is your major job to continually find ways to improve quality for your customers. Without this fundamental attitude, all of the surveys and market research are a waste of time and money.

One Sunday, Karen (my spouse) and I went out for breakfast to a restaurant that we had patronized for many years because of its good food and good service. The restaurant had recently experienced a surge in popularity, resulting in a long wait for customers to be seated. In fact, twice before, the wait was so long that I walked out. This time again, there were at least sixteen people ahead of me. No one from the restaurant greeted me, nor did I see anyone with a list of names. I went back to the car where Karen had waited, anticipating this result, and angrily declared that I would never go back to that restaurant because its employees didn't care about their customers. Karen asked how I knew they didn't care about their customers. I argued that if they cared, they would see to it that they didn't lose customers because those customers couldn't get in to eat. She countered with the question, "How could they help it if they have more customers than space or staff to handle them?" My answer was that there is always a solution if you care about your customers. Karen challenged me on this premise because she felt that there were often restraints over what a business could or could not do. We ended the discussion by making a wager. She would state four restraints concerning what could or could not be done with the business, and with those restraints in mind, I would find a reasonable solution as to what the restaurant owners could do to keep my business and perhaps even make me a devoted customer. The wager was Sunday breakfast.

She issued the following restraints:

1. They can't move into a larger facility.
2. They can't ask employees to work faster.
3. They can't add more tables.
4. They can't ask us to come back later.

I accepted the four conditions, and asked for some time to think about it. In the meantime, I drove around looking for an alternative place for breakfast. We found a little cafe that had recently opened and we had an excellent breakfast. The little cafe had excellent food, good service, and no waiting time. We will probably never go back to the old breakfast place. We are a lost customer as far as the old breakfast place is concerned, but there is little chance that it keeps track of lost customers. According to a recent study[1] by the REL Consultancy Group, only 17 percent of organizations are trying to reduce customer losses as a way to increase profitability.

I kept thinking about the bet and, as we ordered breakfast, I said to my wife, "I've got it. I have thought of a simple but reasonable solution. And I've got at least six more ideas." She said, "Okay, let's hear it, but I'll be the judge of how 'reasonable' it is." "Do you remember when we went to Scotland five years ago?" I asked. She replied, "Of course, but what has that got to do with this?" "Remember the custom over there in the restaurants? When there were no seats available, the restaurant employees would seat you with someone else. The solution is simple. There are almost always tables for two with only one person at them, tables for four with two people at them, and tables for six with four or fewer people at them. All they need to do is ask customers if they would mind sitting with someone else. They could have a section of tables just for people who do not mind sitting with strangers." I listed several other ideas which Karen agreed all met the previously specified conditions. For instance, the restaurant could simplify the menu so people could order quicker; it could use a buzzer or light on the tables for people who wanted to get their checks in a hurry and leave; employees could precook certain foods that were in high demand so that they could serve customers quicker; they could serve coffee to people who were waiting so that those customers did not get frustrated and leave; the restaurant could have a table with coffee prepared so that customers could serve themselves and get their own refills. Karen got into the game adding several ideas of her own. I was really pleased when she said, "I see what you mean; you really do have to have a different attitude to have devoted customers."

Attitude is the start of customer quality. But there is more to it than that. Deming would have said, "You must have knowledge." For organizations that want to create devoted customers, the knowledge is out there. Dr. Noriaki Kano has created a model (see Figure 5.1) of customer quality that provides a theory to guide organizations in finding ways to create devoted customers. This is the best model that we know of for explaining how to achieve devoted customers.

The model involves three dimensions or aspects of quality which are essential for creating devoted customers. Each of these is a necessary, but not a sufficient, factor for "devoted" customers. Figure 5.2 illustrates that the three dimensions each contribute some portion to the whole. Though they are shown in approximately equal proportions (since the exact proportion each contributes is unknown), the proportions are probably not identical. Each aspect of the model and how the model can be used to create "devoted" customers will be explained.

## DEMANDED QUALITY

Demanded quality is also known as "expected quality." It is drawn as a straight line in Figure 5.1 and is labeled "Dimension Two. " It is drawn as a straight line since there is a linear relationship between what the customer wants and how satisfied the customer is. The more the customer gets what he/she wants, the more satisfied he/she is. For instance, when we buy a new TV, we expect a good quality picture, good sound, reliable operation, consistency of tuning, etc. This list is pretty basic. You could probably get the same list from a customer survey or a focus group of TV viewers. Our level of satisfaction will be directly related to how well the TV

FIGURE 5.1. Dr. Kano's Three Dimensions of Quality

FIGURE 5.2. Three Dimensions of Quality Contributing to the Whole

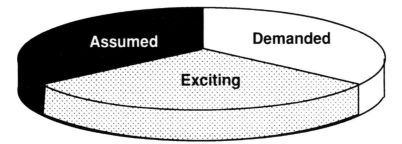

performs with respect to the above features. The better it performs, the higher our satisfaction, and vice versa.

This is the simplest and easiest dimension of customer quality to determine. It is what we get from surveys, specification sheets, market research, and consumer questionnaires. Despite the fact that it is the easiest quality dimension to determine, many organizations do not collect any data to see how well they are meeting demanded customer needs and wants. Many organizations assume they know what their customers want. This is usually the first and, perhaps, the biggest error an organization can make. The second error is to assume that all you have to do to achieve devoted customers is to conduct a customer survey. This is a false assumption. The best you will get is a satisfied customer, and you might not even get that. If you are negligent or behind your competition in either of the other two dimensions, you will still have a dissatisfied customer despite your best efforts.

## ASSUMED QUALITY

Assumed quality is also called "taken for granted quality." This is the most difficult dimension of quality to address. It is difficult because you can't ask customers what they assume. They don't know. So market surveys, questionnaires, and focus groups are a waste of time in terms of this dimension. For instance, airline travelers don't ask that pilots have adequate training. They take this for granted. Studies of restroom facilities found that patrons did not list toilet paper as an expected quality characteristic. It was assumed that all toilets will have toilet paper (at least in North America).

While I was doing some training on the Kano Model with a trucking company, the senior managers tried to think of examples of assumed quality in their business. No one could immediately think of an example. They tried with such ideas as on-time deliveries; good service; clean, friendly drivers; undamaged goods, etc., but all were examples of expected quality. Then someone came up with a perfect example of assumed quality: "Our customers take it for granted that we will not destroy their property when we make a delivery—we won't hit their walls, cars, flower beds, or pets." This was an excellent example; I asked if it ever happened. The employees replied that it happened more often then they cared to think about.

This dimension of assumed quality has properties different from the other two dimensions. If you refer to Figure 5.1, you will notice that it curves and never goes higher than the center line. This means that by meeting all of the customer's assumptions, at best you can only achieve neutral satisfaction. You do not satisfy the customer by providing assumed quality. On the other hand, if you don't provide the elements of assumed quality, customer satisfaction plummets. For instance, a lack of toilet paper when you need it causes your satisfaction with the restaurant or other facility to go way down. It does not matter how many mirrors the restroom has or if it has real cloth towels and the best cologne. When you need the paper and it's not there, you are a most unhappy customer. If the truck driver runs over your dog but has a great uniform and a very polite "Sorry" on his or her lips, you will still probably not give his company a very good rating in terms of quality.

It is hard to determine what customers take for granted. If they don't know, how can you know? You had better make it your business to find out. This is a dimension that can put you out of business in a second. Imagine an airline where the pilots did not have adequate flight training or a hospital that had an absentminded surgeon— big trouble!

So how do you determine what your customers are assuming? Some methods are Unobtrusive Techniques, Participant Observation, Task Analysis, and Critical Incidents. These are all techniques from social science research, anthropology, sociology, and industrial psychology. Each of these methods is a way of looking at the underlying structure of a process or system. They are methods analogous to taking a microscope to a process and determining the essential elements of the process.

Unobtrusive techniques[2] are basically methods for obtaining data that do not involve "intruding" on the customer or participant. For instance, a phone call or survey is intrusive. When Nikon started looking for an idea to improve cameras, the company went to photo developers and asked what their biggest problems in film development were. Nikon found that all too often, customers did not focus their cameras properly, causing their pictures to be out of focus. This led Nikon to the marketing of the autofocus camera. When you put on a customer's shoes and attempt to experience what the customer is experiencing, you are engaged in an unobtrusive technique.

Participant observation simply involves observing customers who are using your product. It might also mean observing potential customers or even customers using one of your competitor's products. For instance, companies such as Procter and Gamble often hire people to participate in projects involving cooking, cleaning, and normal household activities. Their observations of these "customers" help the company find new products that will make life easier for consumers. Motorola is said to have used a version of participant observation in the development of the cellular phone. Motorola researchers observed people using prototypes of the phone, and noticed that people frequently dropped them. It was recognized (to the horror of the engineers) that the phone not only had to be light but also very durable. These are difficult characteristics to achieve simultaneously. A survey of customer preferences probably would not have identified toughness and resiliency as a necessary characteristic. How many customers would plan on repeatedly dropping their phones? Nevertheless, when customers did drop their phones, they would have been most dissatisfied to find their phones in several pieces.

Task Analysis is commonly used to determine criteria for a job description or for job skills training. If you ask someone what he/she does that is essential for a job, often he /she could not tell you. Task Analysis helps to identify the essential elements and steps in a job and ensures that they are addressed. Task Analysis has been used for writing job descriptions and for determining the criteria needed for a new employee. It could be used to look at those elements of a job that people forget or that they take for granted. For instance, what does a delivery person do on the job? By studying the actual work that is done, new and improved products and services could be developed.

The critical incident method is another way to take a snapshot of the various "critical" or essential activities that comprise a job in order to get to get a better idea of the job's requirements and the skills needed to perform the job. Students at the University of Minnesota were hired by the Minneapolis Police Department to ride around with officers and periodically record the various "critical" incidents that comprised the job. By having different students ride with different officers, a much clearer pattern of the job and its activities could be developed than by just studying a few jobs. Furthermore, the "critical" incidents were real time, in that they happened as a part of the normal work that was involved. Often, these kinds of incidents are poorly remembered due to the stress involved when they happen.

The critical incident method has been used by Hewlett Packard, in conjunction with random time sampling, to get a better idea of the work and processes that employees were involved in. It is a very efficient method of studying a process and identifying its main or critical elements. By studying the processes of our customers or would-be customers, it is very easy to identify the problems and gaps that exist in the usability of the product or service. For instance, how many phone systems are truly user friendly? How many times does a customer fail to properly install a new software program? Many people are still unable to program electronic appliances such as clocks, VCRs, etc. There are a whole host of untapped opportunities to observe customers and find those "hidden" or assumed elements which are taken for granted by both the consumer and the product or service provider.

There are many more methods and ideas[3] that can help you to identify the assumed elements of quality. The important thing is that you look for these elements in relationship to a process. You will not find them by studying the product or service independent of how it is used. If you focus all your energy on surveys and questionnaires, you might still be losing customers and never really understand the reasons why they are leaving or buying your competitor's products.

## EXCITING QUALITY

The third dimension of Dr. Kano's model is called Exciting Quality. People often assume that just having exciting quality will create "devoted" customers. This is simply not true because, as we have noted, there are two other dimensions of quality that must be addressed. Exciting quality should be considered as the icing on the cake. If you are doing as well as you can (but always getting better) on the other two dimensions, then exciting quality is the element that will provide the icing on the cake.

You will notice that the exciting quality dimension (Figure 5.1) is also drawn as a curve. This curve shows that exciting quality is often not asked for or wanted by your customers. It may not even be a need that customers have. Thus, if you don't have it, it does not lead to low levels of customer satisfaction. Hence, it never drops below the center line. However, when it is present, it leads to very high levels of customer satisfaction, hence the curve arches way up. Customers are excited about some new feature or gizmo that they have never thought of, and that adds value to their lives.

A recent example of exciting quality for me was when I purchased a minivan: on the way home, I discovered a thermometer display in the overhead panel. At first, I wondered what dingbat thought of this idea. I could not imagine a reason why I would want or need it. It was just another gadget to break and need fixing. My attitude soon changed. Little by little, I found it convenient and helpful to know the outside temperature while traveling. I spend a great deal of time hiking in the woods, and the thermometer has helped me to decide what to take with me on a hike. Now I wouldn't buy another vehicle without this gadget.

There are literally hundreds of examples of exciting quality— products or services that were new or innovative, including Post-It notes, the Apple computer, FedEx overnight delivery, Velcro, Polaroid instant pictures, Gore-Tex rain gear, 24-hour catalog product ordering, mountain bicycles, and so on. The list is literally endless. While there seems to be little in common among the variety of products and services, there is one thing that stands out: in almost all cases, the innovativeness of the product produced a dramatic demand for it, literally changing the nature of an industry overnight and creating a new organization. Those organizations that realized the importance of all three dimensions of quality have remained viable and successful. Organizations that thought innovativeness was all they needed have gone the way of the hula hoop.

So how do you get "exciting" quality? This is perhaps even more problematic than ascertaining assumed quality. Not only do your customers not know what will excite them, but the new feature or service may also add to your costs without significantly increasing customer satisfaction. With exciting quality, you are always taking a gamble. The simple answer is to have creative and innovative people working for you. While creativity and innovation are essential elements in the development of any new ideas that make life easier for people, they are not enough. You also need a systematic effort to accomplish exciting quality. You need to focus your efforts on this objective, not just hope luck or chance will take care of it. Among the many techniques that can be helpful in developing exciting quality are: Value System Analysis, Concept R&D, and Trend Analysis.

Value System Analysis is a way to examine the underlying values which guide people's behaviors. It is a way to explore the differences between needs and wants and also to look at what really matters to people. There are a number of ways that this information can be translated into new products and services that will add value to people's lives. For example, consumers may value leisure, the environment, health, etc. While each of these areas offers opportunities for the creative and innovative organization, it is a mistake to think that values are timeless and unchanging. Values are subject to change, just as are many other elements of social organization. The present concern with the environment has led to many new products and processes that are more in concert with the value of a balanced ecological system. Who knows what tomorrow's values will focus on?

Concept R&D is a way to systematically explore the realm of ideas and thoughts as opposed to looking at needs and wants. Edward de Bono, in his book *Sur Petition*,[4] describes concepts as "the organizers of information and action." De Bono says Concept R&D should "open up possibilities that are then fed into corporate strategy." I created a chart of basic concepts that I sometimes use to find new ideas for services and products. Take, for instance, the following concepts: bigger, smaller, faster, easier, fun, and simpler. These are just a few of the concepts that are on my chart. I can take a product or service and use these to ask myself what would happen if the product was bigger, smaller, faster, etc.

Another useful technique for creating new ideas is associative thinking. Associative thinking involves linking two dissimilar things and then looking for similarities and differences. For instance, how are horticulture and business development related? Thinking about concepts this way can open up many opportunities for developing innovative products and services.

There are many other techniques that one can use for generating new ideas and concepts. Roger Von Oech has published a deck of cards with some of his highly creative and innovative ideas, based on his book, *A Whack on the Side of the Head.*[5] Creativity begins with having the right attitude. After that, it is merely a matter of discipline and allowing the time for creativity to happen.

Trend Analysis is not a new technique. Futurists such as John Naisbitt have made a fortune by studying newspapers, baby boomers, stock market analyses, the elderly, ethnographics, demographics, legal trends, etc. Magazines such as *American Demographics* are full of examples and articles designed to help organizations find new markets and niches for new products. A recent article, titled "Vision in America," was about the declining eyesight of baby boomers who are, of course, getting older. The article noted, "Businesses that ignore older eyes may become invisible to their customers." This eyesight problem will have major impacts on book printers and other publishers of printed material, as well as on manufacturers of products that require customers to read directions or recognize their labels. One night while traveling, I came down with a bug. I went to the lobby of the hotel to purchase some over-the-counter medication. When I returned to my room with it, I found that I could not read the instructions on the label, even with my glasses on!

There are many ways that you can try to predict the future by what is essentially looking at the past and extrapolating from previous events. It is a little like looking down the track to see if a train is coming. If you spot one, there is a good chance it will continue coming, and you should get out of the way. Of course, you always run the risk that the future might change course. It often does. For instance, the growth in e-mail has sometimes been equated with the huge number of people who became CB radio addicts. This has led some to conclude that the Internet may only be a passing fad. However, there are major dissimilarities between e-mail, the Internet, and CB radios. The growth in the Internet and e-mail would seem to be a natural extension of the growth in all mediums of electronic data transfer. From EDI to fax machines to voice mail programs, we are witnessing a fantastic explosion in terms of products, services, and markets. If the Internet and e-mail are a part of this trend, then it seems a very reasonable bet that they will continue to grow. On the other hand, I would predict an eventual demise in the number of new outlets for printed only materials such as books and magazines. Nevertheless, timing plays a great part in the success or failure of any new innovation or idea. But if you are not even out there swinging, you have absolutely no chance of hitting those base hits, much less a home run.

When the bat is in your hand, though, you are risking failure. The dimension of exciting quality involves the possibility of high risk but also high payoff. Why take the risk? There are several good reasons for doing so. External forces are continually changing and shifting the three quality curves. Two major forces, human nature and competition, affect each of the three dimensions of quality. These forces make customer quality a dynamic rather than a static game. Even if you continue to run, you may find you're running in place.

## FORCES AFFECTING THE QUALITY DIMENSIONS

There are two major forces that affect each of the three curves of the Kano model and have the overall effect of keeping the curves shifting. Thus, what is exciting today becomes demanded tomorrow and is assumed the day after. An example is the traditional Thanksgiving turkey given by many organizations to their employees. At first, employees are excited to get it, then they expect it, and finally, they take it for granted. However, if one day the company determines that the turkey has lost its "motivational" power and decides to discontinue giving it, employees may become irate. They have come to believe that they have a right to get a turkey on Thanksgiving, and become angry and resentful when they don't get it. The privilege of getting a free turkey has gone full route and has now become a right. It is like this with many things that involve human nature.

The first force that affects the curves can be directly attributed to human nature. Whatever satisfies us today, we soon become accustomed to, and we now want bigger, better, faster, or something more than we first expected. We fail to be excited by the mundane and familiar. When everybody has one, we lose interest in it. We are thrilled by the unique and exotic, whatever is new is interesting–for a while. We soon lose interest and want something else to intrigue us. Thus, human nature itself ensures that the quality curves are never static.

If human nature was not enough, the second force is competition. No competitor wants to be outdone or lose customers. Thus, competitors keep the curve moving by continually introducing new products and services. Since each curve is relative to customer expectations, competition ensures that our customers' expectations will continually change. Just when customers are satisfied with the new software program or upgrade, the competition comes out with a new program that has even more features. Customers do not gauge quality in a vacuum. Customers are, in a sense, always benchmarking your products and services against your competition's. As long as the competition is not standing still, you cannot afford to.

No organization can afford to only look at one dimension of quality. You may do an excellent job on one dimension, but unless you address the other two dimensions, you will eventually begin to lose customers. Finally, unless you realize that the entire process is dynamic and evolving, you will always be a follower and never a market leader. As long as you are not following too far behind, that may be okay. However, the danger exists that you might just end up so far behind that you have lost sight of the market and your erstwhile customers.

## REFERENCE NOTES

1. Survey conducted by the REL Consultancy Group. Reported in *Quality Progress*, Vol. 28, No. 6. June 1995.

2. Webb, E.J., Campbell, D.T., Schwartz, R.D., and Sechrest, L. *Unobtrusive Measures: Nonreactive Research in the Social Sciences*. Chicago: Rand McNally, 1965.

3. Olson, S.R. "Ideas and Data: The Practice of Social Research." In: *Training and Development Handbook*, edited by R. Craig. New York: McGraw Hill, 1976.

4. de Bono, E. *Sur Petition*. New York: HarperCollins Publishers, Inc., 1992.

5. Von Oech, R. *Creative Whack Pack*. Stamford, CT: U.S. Games Systems, Inc., 1992.

# Chapter 6

# Training That Really Works

Ninety percent of training in American industry is a waste of time and money. Everywhere we turn, we are besieged by courses on Total Quality, Reengineering, Leadership, Communication, Learning Organizations, Team Building, Whole Systems Change, Quality Function Deployment (QFD), Statistical Process Control (SPC), Design of Experiments (DOE), Just In Time (JIT), and so on and on and on. Each course is touted as being essential for organizational success. Many of these courses are very good, but at least an equal number are either impractical or unrealistic in a real organization. Few are truly "indispensable" for organizational success. All too many could be done in half the time at half the cost, but that is the least of the problems with such courses. The biggest problem is that few courses set up the proper conditions to ensure that there will be a transfer of learning to the work environment.

There are four major elements that a successful continuous improvement training effort must address to ensure that what is learned in class will make a difference in the workplace. Most training efforts address some but not all of these elements.

It should be noted that much of what is said in this chapter will apply to all training efforts, but this chapter is primarily concerned with efforts to construct a continuous improvement effort or total quality improvement system. The area of job skills is another issue and, while fundamental to the success of any organization, is not the focus of this chapter.

The four elements needed for successful training and for the transfer of training to the workplace are (1) A clear focus, goal, or purpose for the training; (2) Motivated and willing employees; (3) Management support; and (4) Adequate training preparation. Each of the elements is necessary, but each alone is not sufficient for a successful, continuous improvement effort. All four must be present at the right time. When they are put together in this way, you go beyond Just-In-Time (JIT) training to JIT quality improvement. This is as it should be, since quality improvement, not training, must be the goal of the training department. Most problems with training classes stem from the planner's failure to adequately address each of these elements before the training takes place. All too often, it is only after the training (when real-world problems arise) that these elements are addressed. A little bit of planning can save a great deal of effort later on.

## *A CLEAR FOCUS AND GOAL FOR THE TRAINING*

This can be called the "What comes next?" issue. "What comes next?" is the first question that should be answered before any training takes place. Unfortunately, it is seldom answered either before or after training. If training is being done in support of a major goal such as Total Quality or Continuous Improvement, there should be a plan, prepared before any training begins, that provides a goal and rationale for all training. The goal should be specific, and there should be accountability in the system to determine to what extent the goals were reached. Some organizations think that becoming a "learning" organization is an adequate goal. Obviously, they value learning, but to what end? Why are they learning? How will their learning help add value for the customers and stakeholders of the organization? To become a learning organization sounds like a lofty goal, but it is pure pedantry if divorced from any real-world value.

Imagine giving someone a course in welding or word processing without also giving him/her a word processor or welding equipment. What would happen? He/she would probably soon forget the skills he/she learned in the training class. What about skills such as law, medicine, or quality improvement? The old adage, "Use it or lose it," applies to word processing, welding, law, medicine, etc. Providing training without a plan for utilizing the skills or tools after the training is a waste of time, energy, and money. Anyone responsible for training in an organization should answer three key questions: (1) What will trainees do after the training?; (2) How can we ensure that the training is used in the organization?; and (3) How do we help others benefit from the training? These questions imply that there is some purpose or focus for the training. It is expected that trainees will be able to use what they have learned to help add more value to the organization or to further the goals of continuous improvement. These questions also help to leverage the time and money spent on training to benefit the rest of the organization. For instance, 3M corporation videotapes all speakers and training classes in its Technical Services Division. The company retains the right to use these tapes internally and to distribute them to its other divisions. This helps 3M to "leverage" both the time and money that it spends on speakers and trainers.

If the organization has a very specific problem or process in mind (some organizations train employees in teams who are assigned specific problems/processes to study), it should also be sure that such problems/processes meet the criteria of Meaningful, Measurable, and Manageable. Meaningful problems/processes make a crucial difference to customers or to stakeholders. Solving such problems or improving such processes will likely improve customer satisfaction, increase profits, reduce costs, make a job easier, or simply keep you ahead of the competition. Measurable problems/processes can be flowcharted, and critical variables identified that can be measured and analyzed to determine the impact on desired process outcomes. Manageable problems/processes can be tackled, given the finite resources of the organization and the ability to allocate these resources to the problem.

When issues are identified that will be addressed through quality training, they should meet the criteria of Meaningful, Measurable, and Manageable. Problems/processes that don't meet these criteria may be great for pure research, but they are unlikely to have much impact on your bottom line, quality, or customer satisfaction. Furthermore, the best training in the world will be ineffective if no one cares about the problems/processes, the resources do not exist to tackle the problem, or the problem is so esoteric that there is no way to measure its impact. When problems/processes are not tied to training, the training is purposeless. When problems/processes are not meaningful, measurable, and manageable, the best training in the world will be useless.

## MOTIVATED AND WILLING EMPLOYEES

Training is useless if employees lack the desire or interest in solving problems. Since most employees want to do a good job, we know that motivation is a natural state of being human. If motivation is a problem, then it exists because of "demotivators" in the organization. As Dr. Deming repeatedly told us, the problem is with management, not with the workers. Taking demotivators out of the system is the job of management. Deming's eighth principle is "Drive out fear." Most employees are afraid of management, since management typically provides rewards and punishments. There is no such thing as "unconditional love" in organizations. Employees are constantly told that if they do not perform, they will be gone.

Several years ago, a client who had been a quality assurance (QA) inspector for over twenty years told me that all the statistical training in the world is useless if employees fear for their jobs. He said that employees had kept control charts for years in his organization (a food company). Whenever he came around to look at them, the charts were absolutely perfect. They showed no defects, special causes, or out-of-control points. The charts were too good to be true, and my client knew that the data had been "doctored." Data is critical to the quality effort, but it must be reliable data. Anything that leads to "unreliable" data is a major barrier to continuous quality improvement.

In Business Process Reengineering (BPR) efforts, the issue of fear is just as critical. In any task, the more creativity that is required, the higher the element of risk. BPR asks for high levels of creativity, ergo high risk taking. Employees who fear for their jobs or fear even making a mistake will not be willing to take the kinds of risks required in BPR. It is amazing how many people think that you can have creativity without risk taking. Without creativity, there can be no improvement or innovation of any kind in an organization. Anything that decreases creativity can only have a negative impact on long-term organizational survival. Fear is the single most devastating and pervasive destroyer of creativity known to humans.

Employees who have fear for any reason will seek safety in the comfort of conformity and routine.

Fear, one of the prime employee "demotivators," is not the only one that makes training ineffective. Barriers, because of language, role modeling, and status also play a part. I remember visiting a client company with a colleague, a female statistician, and having a woman manager enthusiastically tell me how great it was to have a woman statistician to help them. She then somewhat apologetically explained that she meant no offense to me, but that there were not enough women role models in our business, and it was something that was important to the women in her organization.

Status quo can be a built-in inhibitor to new ways of doing things. In some organizations, it is called the "not invented here" syndrome. A manager once told me that when he was first hired, he went to his new boss to explain a procedure that he thought would improve things. He had learned this procedure while at this former company. His boss told him to keep his ideas to himself for at least five years, because his organization would not entertain ideas from anyone who had not been with the company for at least five years. The new manager's method of doing things would have improved operations, but it was not until five years later that the company was able to benefit from his previous experience. He was not alone. Many managers reject new ideas brought in by trainers or employees who have attended outside training sessions.

Training programs often bring in consultants and trainers with great presentation skills and entertaining stories. But even as employees are listening to the consultants and trainers, they are thinking, "This will never work here," "The organization's not ready for this," or "Management will never change." While it is important to have someone who knows the subject and has good teaching skills, training programs often overlook the need to have managers and employees involved in the training, both as teachers and role models. The involvement of managers will show commitment to the ideas and theories being taught. Furthermore, the involvement of managers and employees can help ground the theories in the real-world experiences of the organization. Employees who are trained by their co-workers will more easily believe that the new training is something that works, and something that they, too, can learn and use. The more diverse the workforce, the more need to have a variety of role models and, of course, they should not all come from any one level of the organization.

Another "demotivator" is to be told that you must attend such and such training–tomorrow. The participant has no choice, no chance to change prior plans, and no input into when and where he or she will take the training. The trainee naturally resents such an imposition, and the trainer, upon asking why someone is taking the course, hates to hear, "My boss told me yesterday that I had to be here today." Employees should be asked if they want to attend the training, when it would be convenient for them to attend, and what they need to know to help prepare them for the training. This sounds like common sense, but it is seldom done.

A problem directly opposite to "mandatory" training attendance is "catch as catch can" training. This typically occurs in large bureaucratic organizations. Here, the quality training sessions are often offered as a form of "smorgasbord." People can sign up for whatever they want, whenever they want it. This can create many problems for the instructor as well as the trainee. For instance, the specific course might require a prerequisite class or it might be a class that assumes the trainee's manager will be supportive of the course content and that the trainee will have the time to practice the skills or contents back on the job. At the very least, trainees should have some idea as to how the course fits in with the goals of the organization and how it is expected to impact their work. It should be required that whoever approves the attendance of anyone at a training session have some way of ensuring that trainees know what the course is about, why the organization is offering the course, and what he or she will be expected to do with the ideas and skills learned in the class.

Addressing each of the points noted above will help to ensure that everyone comes to the training session in a prepared state of mind. Trainees will be more open to the ideas in the training, have a better sense of the organizational context in which the training fits, and a much better idea of how they can use the training in their daily work. The content and context of the course will have more validity, and trainees will have less resistance to new ideas offered in the course.

## MANAGEMENT SUPPORT

The term "management support" has been used so often that most of us automatically assume that we know what it means. In fact, most people do not really know what it means. Within the context of organizational behavior, management support must address three areas: prioritization, accountability, and resource allocation.

In most organizations, that which is not a priority does not get done. When something is a priority, it gets built into the daily work flow of the organization. For instance, if an organization planned to build a new plant or start a new product line, a manager would use some type of project management tool such as a PERT (Program Evaluation and Review Technique) chart or a Gantt Chart to help in the process. Such tools would help to define a plan of action, budget, roles, time frames, and expected milestones. Planning would ensure that needed actions are prioritized and placed in the daily work flow. But how often do a manager's supportive efforts make it to his or her daily calendar? Very few managers demonstrate that continuous improvement is a priority by making it a part of their calendars or by subjecting actions in support of continuous improvement to project management guidelines. Actions to support continuous improvement are seldom built into the financial plan or the annual business plan. Furthermore, one seldom sees good measurement of continuous improvement or reviews of quality as a monthly or weekly item in operations meetings. How many organizational meetings discuss the level of organizational learning, the degree of risk taking, or review specific measures of continuous quality improvement? Continuous improvement requires prioritization and systemization. Without prioritization, continuous improvement is an ad hoc activity, not an organizational priority.

The second part of management support concerns accountability. There is a big difference between accountability and responsibility. Responsibility is to accountability as people are to process. People are only one element of a process. However, people are traditionally the only element we focus on when something goes wrong. When we focus on the process, we also look at equipment, materials, methods, and the environment. We must take into consideration all of these elements if we want to understand the process. Similarly, responsibility is only one element of accountability. Responsibility is the "who" of accountability. Responsibility rests with one or more people, but accountability rests in the system.

Accountability includes what must happen, when it is expected to happen, and how success will be measured. When only responsibility is assigned, the system has no way to monitor what must be done, when it will be done, or even if it is done. This means accountability for the support activities themselves, not just for the quality improvement effort. Thus, management support gets defined as a set of specific actions where responsibility is assigned along with a time schedule and a process to review success and failure of the management support activities themselves. Accountability can take many forms. It can be a presidential audit, an annual quality survey, or just a quick review of last month's minutes or last week's scheduled action items. This sounds so simple, yet I've seen many meetings where there is little or no accountability for the issues and actions discussed. It is as though they are just expected to happen.

The third element of management support concerns the allocation of necessary resources, both tangible and intangible. Equipment, space, tools, capital, training, and time are resources that must be provided. These resources seldom present much of a problem, despite the fact that most organizations say that they don't have the time or the money to obtain such resources. The most problematic area is concerned with employee empowerment. This is a nebulous concept that has to do with power and management rights and prerogatives. Power is, of course, a function of budget and authority. While empowerment sometimes seems nebulous, the more you think about how it takes place in some organizations, the less nebulous it becomes. For instance, organizations can talk about empowerment all day long but, in reality, it often comes down to the question of how much money and authority will employees be trusted with? Will employees be allowed to stop the assembly line as they did at Ford Motor Company? Will all employees be given $500 discretionary authorization to solve customer complaints as Embassy Suites in Coronado, California has done? Employees are often entrusted with a million dollar piece of equipment but not with a ten dollar discretionary cash fund. Management support must include authorization of budgetary allocations to teams and individuals. Until employees are trusted to make financial decisions affecting their jobs, management support will only be a token concept.

## *ADEQUATE TRAINING PREPARATION*

I have yet to see a training course in the area of continuous quality improvement where the course is rated as to its level of usability. Don Campbell and Stu Tait from INCO (Ontario division) and I jointly devised the following scale of usability that could be universally applied to training courses. The scale has five levels of course usability.

- Level I: Awareness
- Level II: Recognition
- Level III: User
- Level IV: Teacher
- Level V: Innovator

A Level I (Awareness) course is designed to make you aware that something exists. For example, a one-day course on trucks might show certain types of trucks and introduce the trainee to the world of trucking. I have seen five-day courses on continuous quality improvement which do not do much more than make you aware of the different quality concepts and philosophies. Such training is important for providing the individual with the "big picture" of the issue that will be further explored and for orienting him/her to the concepts, ideas, language, and problems that are part of the discipline or subject. Each subject or discipline seems to have its own jargon and language. Anthropologists have one language and managers have another language. A good Level I course can introduce the fundamental ideas required for further progress by the trainee.

A Level II (Recognition) course on trucking would be designed to help the trainee recognize the different parts of a truck, the differences between types of trucks, and the reasons for these differences. The course would go beyond simple awareness to a more concrete recognition level. Such a course might involve a field trip to a trucking site or operation. In the area of quality improvement, such a course might be an intensive four-day session on the Crosby or Deming philosophy.

A Level III (User) course would be designed to help the trainee learn how to operate the many functions of a truck. To become a certified or licensed truck driver would also require experience gained from hours behind the wheel or with a driving simulator. In continuous quality improvement, this might be a three- or four-day course in statistical process control tools or in team effectiveness training.

A Level IV (Teacher) course would be designed to help someone with the talent and skills to become a trainer or instructor of other individuals who wanted to learn how to operate a truck. If this person was studying SPC, it might mean several weeks of training on SPC, interspersed with experiential opportunities, or even getting a master's degree in statistics.

A Level V (Innovator) course would help someone go beyond the teacher level to the innovator level. Individuals at this level are able to find truly innovative uses for trucks, and are capable of devising innovative trucking methods and procedures. Not all people have the ability or aptitude to reach this level. Training is probably not nearly as useful as experience in reaching Level V.

It is important to realize that training alone cannot advance you up through the levels. If you view each level as a step, then the lift between the steps is provided by experience as well as training. Some type of practical experience is necessary to advance from Level I to Level V. It is also apparent that not everyone has the ability, desire, or aptitude to reach the higher levels.

The ultimate goal of training is to help as many people as practical in the organization to reach Level V. In the short term, this is a very impractical goal. Massive amounts of money could be spent on this effort with few immediate benefits. A more practical goal is to set up a training plan that identifies the quality training needed by the organization and who needs to receive it, at what level and when. The concept of levels is important because all too often, managers are seduced into thinking that a two-day course in SPC will make the attendees into users or, even worse, into teachers.

The concept of levels of training can be applied to all the training in your quality effort. You will probably not want all people trained to the innovator level in terms of quality concepts, but you will probably want most of the organization trained to at least the awareness level. In terms of problem-solving tools, you might want a large chunk of employees trained to the user level, and a smaller group trained to the teacher level. These "teachers" can then be in-house trainers and coaches for the rest of the organization. Not much time should be spent worrying about the innovator level, as this is a level we probably do not know how to train people for. Nevertheless, innovators are critical to the success of the organization; they should be identified and nurtured so the organization does everything it can to ensure innovators' loyalty and commitment to the organization. It's not good to lose your most creative people to other organizations.

Previously, it was mentioned that there were specific kinds of training needed in a continuous improvement effort. There are basically three areas in which training is needed for continuous quality improvement. As has been noted already, this assumes that the organization has adequate levels of basic skills in terms of its core competencies and production requirements. Quality training is not designed to provide these basic job skills. Quality training helps the organization and its employees learn the tools needed for continuously improving products, processes, and customer satisfaction.

The first quality training area concerns basic quality concepts and philosophies. For example, what is a process? Who is an internal customer? What does Deming mean by "profound knowledge"? The study of quality philosophies could be a three-day or life-long study. Do not think that a three-day course is going to take you to the innovator level in terms of quality concepts and philosophies. Many people are still mystified by the Deming philosophy even after attending his seminar and reading his books.

The second basic area for quality training is in problem solving. There are many different problem-solving methodologies and hundreds of problem-solving tools. Dr. Kaoru Ishikawa, the noted Japanese quality expert, said that as many as 95 percent of all problems in organizations could be solved by using the seven basic QC tools. These seven tools are the Pareto diagram, histogram, run chart, control chart, Ishikawa diagram, checklist, and flowchart. In terms of the Pareto principle (better known as the 80/20 rule), this is a good place to focus your training money. Nevertheless, advanced tools in problem solving, such as design of experiments, Taguchi methods, and multivariate analysis, may be essential for some organizations. In these cases, the organization will want to spend the time and money to develop key employees who can use such specialized training and help others. Remember, few employees will be able to get to the teacher level or even the user level with only a two- or three-day course in problem-solving tools. It takes at least five years of academic preparation to produce a good statistician and several years of organizational experience for such an individual to become truly effective working in a specific organization.

The third area for quality training is in the so-called "New Leadership Skills." Beware! This can easily be a bottomless pit in terms of time and money. No one knows for sure how to develop leaders or, in fact, whether or not it is more a case of the right person at the right time or of leaders simply being born. Nevertheless, good courses in team effectiveness, team leadership, and facilitator skills are an indispensable part of a quality improvement effort. It is essential for key managers to take part in some form of ongoing leadership development and coaching. Few individuals can accurately assess how they impact other people and what actions they need to take to improve their organizational skills. A good coach or mentor can provide the type of objective feedback that all individuals need to improve their leadership skills. This should be an ongoing effort, not a one-shot deal. Furthermore, when it comes to the area of human relations skills, it takes many years to see change and to be able to assess the impact of training. This is an area that almost has to be taken on faith, where no one should be expecting to link bottom line results to specific training courses. Efforts to do such measurement will generally cost more than they are worth.

# Chapter 7

# Building a Sustainable Organization

Only a few years ago, if you had mentioned "business" and "environment" in the same breath, you would have been labeled a "tree hugger." In the world of free enterprise, everyone knew that an "environmentalist" was really a pseudonym for anyone who was anticapitalist, pro government regulations, and on the side of spotted owls and snails, as opposed to the side of economic and social progress. We also knew that there had to be a trade-off between free enterprise and the environment. You could only achieve the goals of one by sacrificing the goals of the other. To attain economic growth, some snails would have to be squashed, and some owls made homeless. If you wanted to save the owls and snails, then forget about your condominium with the great view.

The stereotypes described above, and the shortsighted thinking that perpetuated them, appear to be changing. Farsighted organizations are now picking up the banner of "environmentalism" and "sustainable economic development." Progressive organizations have embraced the concept of environmentalism as a new corporate ethic and value. Everywhere you look, organizations are including it in their mission statements, values, and organizational policies.

In 1993, twenty-one of the most progressive companies in the total quality movement (most of them *Fortune 500* organizations) developed an *Environmental Self-Assessment Program* to provide a system and methodology for integrating total quality and sustainable development into the business arena. The group of companies is calling its effort the "Global Environmental Management Initiative" (GEMI). To their considerable credit, they are permitting and encouraging reproduction and dissemination of their program as long as full credit is given to the authors and the report is not altered or changed in any way.

Before looking at how the *Environmental Self-Assessment Program* (ESAP) can be used in your business to support total quality or continuous improvement, we need to discuss just what "sustainable development" means and why it is essential for any organization that is focused on improving itself through continuous improvement, total quality management, business process reengineering, or other programs.

Businesses are hearing the word "sustainable" with increasing frequency, and many of us have wondered what this term means. We hear it used in conjunction with a number of other words which render its meaning even more confusing. We hear of sustainable growth, sustainable economic development, sustainable society, environmentally sustainable economies, sustainable industrial growth, and sustainable agriculture, but we seldom are given a definition of what these words mean or what they will entail in practice.

The UN Conference on the Environment (AKA, "Earth Summit") was held in Rio de Janeiro in June of 1992 to discuss the issue of how to protect the world's ecosphere. It was attended by over 35,000 people and more than 100 heads of state. It was the biggest gathering of world leaders ever held. At the conference, a debate over the definition of the term "sustainable economic development" produced 50 or so definitions of the term. It was finally decided that it was useless to try to promote one definition of sustainable economic development as the "right" one. The inability of the "experts" to agree on a definition creates a problem for those who want to be able to understand the concept or use it in a meaningful way. If we look up the word "sustainable" in the dictionary, we find the following definitions: "(1) To support, hold, or bear up from below. (2) To bear a burden. (3) To undergo loss without yielding." Thus, something that can "sustain" something else can support something. Brown, Flavin, and Postel in their book, *Saving the Planet*, define a "sustainable society" as "one that satisfies its needs without jeopardizing the prospects of future generations."

Donella Meadows, professor of Environmental Studies at Dartmouth, has said, "The systematic social pursuit of quality will almost inevitably lead to productivity, literacy, health, and freedom. On the other hand, the pursuit of GNP or literacy or any other quality indices for their own sake, without underlying quality, will be a counterproductive exercise."[1] There is a remarkable parallel between Dr. Meadow's statement and Dr. Deming's famous statement, "If you pursue lower costs, you will get lower quality and lower productivity. If you pursue quality, you will get lower costs and higher productivity." Dr. Deming made this comment in one of his seminars titled, "Quality, Productivity, and Competitive Position." Clearly, there appears to be some confluence and common bridge between the thinking of those in the quality improvement movement and those who are considered to be in the "environmentalist" camp.

I propose the following definition of the term "sustainable economic development" for those who are in the total quality field or other business endeavors aimed at continuous improvement of products, processes, and services. This is not meant to be a definitive definition, but rather is suggested simply to provide a starting point for discussion and common understanding.

> Sustainable economic development is the production of goods and services that optimize total value* to society by meeting the needs of today's customers and stakeholders, while also meeting the needs of future customers and stakeholders.

If, as the experts at the Earth Summit felt, the dialogue and process of discussion is more important than the words, then we need to create a vision for sustainable economic development that is unique to each organization. A mere definition or statement of the environment will not suffice. It is similar to creating a vision for your organization's products, services, and culture—there is no way you can copy others. Each organization must struggle to understand the purpose of sustainable economic development and then create its own vision which is consistent with the organization's goals and beliefs as well as the needs and desires of its customers and stakeholders.

It is important for organizations to identify and discuss the important questions that will impact their understanding and implementation of sustainable economic development. Organizations need to start asking a variety of questions: How do our products and ser-

---

*I would define "total value" as "providing products and services that will create a world in which people would like to live 20 to 200 years from now."

vices fit with our vision of the future? Are we creating products and services that will produce a future society we would want our children to live in? What are the trade-offs between short-term value and long-term value, and how can we ensure that trade-offs do not jeopardize the future of our world?

Many organizations still do not believe that sustainable economic development is compatible with long-term business success or even with a continuous improvement effort. The following three reasons for developing a value around sustainable economic development should convince even the most die-hard pessimists.

- Your customers want it, and many demand it.
- It will provide long-term profitability.
- Your competitors will be offering it.

### CUSTOMERS WANT IT

Consumers are more educated, informed, and concerned then they were twenty years ago. Consumers' awareness of and respect for the environment is being demonstrated by their spending in the marketplace. Consumers are asking for biodegradable products, recycled paper products, reusable and nondisposable containers, clean air regulations, waste disposal facilities to handle recycled plastics and other materials, clean water standards, and many other requirements designed to protect the environment. Many businesses are waking up to the demands of consumers, realizing that they can meet such demands as well as make a profit. There is a win/win situation for consumers and astute business owners.

Anita Roddick founded a chain of cosmetic shops, The Body Shop, based on the idea that a businessperson can make money and still support the needs of the environment.* Roddick sells products that use all natural ingredients, have not been tested on animals, and

---

*There has been some controversy about the ethics that The Body Shop espouses and the company's real adherence to these in practice. Some see Ms. Roddick as just a shrewd, manipulative businessperson who is capitalizing on a good thing. Others, including the authors, believe she is sincere and that the criticisms come from those who do not believe that business and the environment can coexist.

"wonder of wonders," tells customers the truth about what her products can and cannot do for them. There has been an explosive growth in the number of new businesses started which attempt to follow such principles. The recycling industry is being created because of the demand by consumers to do something about the waste that is glutting our environment. The green revolution is infusing businesses with new ideas for products and services. Progressive consumers and the new knowledge workers are beginning to understand that quality and sustainable development are not luxuries but are rights as valuable as truth, justice, and equality. Businesses will need to address these issues or risk obsolescence.

The issue of health is also fundamental to sustainable economic development. Much of the evidence on cancer shows that its continued growth is caused by carcinogens that are created by economic growth and development. There are some who believe the war on cancer would be better won by spending money on preventive measures and regulations to address pollutants and carcinogens rather than on basic cancer research.

The question of health is connected to sustainability because the health of the environment affects the health of the consumer. The two cannot be separated. As people become more concerned about health and preventing health problems (continuous quality improvement programs are now mandatory in most health care organizations and have become part of the Joint Commission for the Accreditation of Health Care Organization's certification requirements), they will quite naturally address both personal health needs and health needs generated by environmental problems.

Consumers are increasingly challenging the use of materials that impact the environment. We have already witnessed challenges to such industrial practices as fluorocarbons in spray cans, asbestos in materials, lead in gasoline, and saccharine in soft drinks. Those businesses that adversely impact the health of society will find themselves ostracized and denigrated by consumers. The cigarette industry continues to decline in the United States, but is growing worldwide by exporting its products to third world and developing countries and marketing to the young, who believe that they will live forever. The practices of the cigarette industry have come under increasing criticism and appear to be short-term thinking that will do little to provide long-term value to consumers and society. Industries that find themselves on the wrong side of health and sustainable development must use their profits to cast off their old products and find new products with which to make a profit and also add long-term value to society.

## *IT WILL PROVIDE LONG-TERM PROFITABILITY*

Profitability is essential for organizational survival. If you are not profitable, you will not survive. The benefits of sustainable economic development create conditions that are conducive to both increased survival and increased profitability. For example, there are direct benefits to an organization in terms of reduced costs due to the reduction of waste and rework. An optical lens manufacturer in Minnesota was stuck with 500 tons of waste by-product per year and no place to dispose of it. The company found another organization that would take all of the waste away for a fee. It was not exactly the type of customer most of us have in mind, but the optical lens manufacturer was exuberant to find a solution to its problem. However, its goal is to ultimately reduce the amount of waste in the first place.

This example points out some of the problems with waste production. First, there is the cost of the wasted material and labor. The material and labor could have been used to create products that made money. Second, there is the cost of the wasted energy involved in the process. In many organizations, the cost of energy is the biggest single factor in production. Disposal is the third problem. There is often no place to put it or no one who wants it. So the handling and storage of waste are high-cost, nonvalue-added activities associated with its production. An extreme example of these problems can be seen in the nuclear power industry, where the problem of waste disposal is unparalleled. Not only does no one want it, but many do not even want to let it be transported across their property. The problem is further complicated by the difficulty in containing the waste and, of course, the length of time it takes for the nuclear waste to degrade. The hazardous lifetime for low-level waste is estimated at between 100-500 years and approximately 10,000 years for high-level waste.*

So we have multiple costs associated with the problem of environmental sustainability. If one adds the cost of inspection of hazardous waste to these other costs, the overall costs to our society are clearly prohibitive. Dr. Deming said repeatedly (Point #2) that we are in a new economic era and we can no longer afford or tolerate commonly accepted levels of mistakes, defects, waste, poor or inadequate material, or handling damage. The costs of quality are, in effect, one and the same as the costs of economic sustainability. A quality organization is an organization that is also economically sustainable.

One reason that many in industry and business have not understood the linkage between quality and sustainable development lies in our traditional accounting system. The traditional economic accounting system does not identify the hidden costs associated with waste, rework, poor quality, and lack of sustainable development. In many respects, our economic accounting system parallels our organizational accounting systems. In both of these, the emphasis has been on short-term costs calculated in such a way that the figures tell us little or nothing about costs associated with the processes that produce the products and services. Lester Brown states, "Our existing economic accounting system makes it difficult to assess the effect on the economy of both environmental degradation and the inherent constraints imposed by the carrying capacity of natural systems" (*State of the World,* 1993).

There are many who believe that these "hidden" costs may be slowly destroying our long-term economic viability as well as our physical health. However, even as these words are being written, associations such as the Canadian Association of Chartered Accountants have formed special task forces to rectify the situation in respect to environmental accounting. Part of the reason for this is

---

*These figures were provided by the Nuclear Energy Institute in Washington DC. We tried to find out this information from our local energy provider, Northern States Power Company, and were told by the company's information services spokesperson that no such information was available from their organization. This struck us as peculiar since Northern States Power Company runs at least one nuclear reactor in the state of Minnesota.

quite pragmatic. With the increasing potential of liability over environmental issues, it is imperative for organizations to be able to accurately assess the impact of environmental issues on the financial planning of the organization. Part of the reason (we'd like to think) is due to sincere concerns about methods and strategies to better protect the environment. Many other organizations are also developing and testing new models for environmental accounting.[2] These studies demonstrate that there are costs associated with all decisions that an organization makes, and that by capturing these costs we are in a better position to judge the wisdom of decisions that might jeopardize our future.

## YOUR COMPETITORS ARE DOING IT

While it is not true in all industries, there are many organizations which are beginning to see the competitive advantage in "sustainable economic development." Christopher Flavin and John Young of the Worldwatch Institute staff maintain:

> The need to achieve an environmentally sustainable world is now shaping the evolution of the world economy. During the 1990s, ecological pressures will increasingly influence economic decisions, making some industries obsolete while opening up a host of new investment opportunities. Companies and nations that fail to invest strategically in the new technologies, products, and processes will fall behind economically–and will miss out on the jobs that these new industries provide. (*State of the World*, 1993)

Surprisingly, these two scientists are not at all in favor of imposing more government regulations on business in order to protect the business. In fact, they point out that such laws often make the situation worse by exchanging one problem for another. Increasingly, informed scientists, politicians, and environmentalists are not against free enterprise or economic development. Clearly, free enterprise is essential for a free society. It is also clear that there must not be any conflict between "sustainability" and "economic development." But it is also clear that these issues are too important to be left just to scientists, politicians, and environmentalists. Business leaders and all consumers need the knowledge and information to participate in the process of purchasing and allocating resources in a way that will contribute to long-term growth and development. We are all responsible; we all must participate in the process. For those who have not started the journey, or even for those who have begun, the *Environmental Self-Assessment Program* can be an invaluable tool to help your organization complete the journey.

## *THE GLOBAL ENVIRONMENTAL MANAGEMENT INITIATIVE (GEMI)*

GEMI[3] is a group of leading companies (initially, twenty-one) dedicated to fostering environmental excellence in businesses worldwide. It includes such companies as AT&T, Eastman Kodak, Procter & Gamble, Boeing, Dow Chemical, and Occidental Petroleum. The *Environmental Self-Assessment Program* (ESAP) was prepared by Deloitte & Touche as an offshoot of the work sponsored by GEMI. The ESAP is similar to the Malcolm Baldrige process in terms of the way it is structured and organized. It is designed to be used as a form of internal self-assessment and is based on sixteen key principles for environmental management that were identified by the International Chamber of Commerce Business Charter for Sustainable Development. The sixteen key principles are the following:

1. Corporate Priority
2. Integrated Management
3. Process Improvement
4. Employee Education
5. Prior Assessment
6. Products and Services
7. Customer Advice
8. Facilities and Operations
9. Research
10. Precautionary Approach
11. Contractors and Suppliers
12. Emergency Preparedness
13. Transfer of Technology

14. Contributing to the Common Effort
15. Openness to Concerns
16. Compliance and Reporting

Each principle is divided into a number of elements which describe the activities needed to implement the principles in more detail. Each element can be scored on one of four progressively more advanced performance levels. For example, under Principle 1: Corporate Priority, the first element (1.1) is Scope of Corporate Policy. On this element, you can score from 0 to 4. Level 1 is compliance, Level 2 is Systems Development and Implementation, Level 3 is Integration into General Business Functions, and Level 4 is Total Quality Approach. There is also a "Not Applicable" rating that indicates the element is not relevant to an organization's operations. If you reach level 4, it means that your integrated environmental management systems are applied to operations globally and are continually evaluated for improvement opportunities. There is also a rating scale that allows you to assign an importance rating to each element; this is then factored into the final scoring.

When your organization has completed its environmental self-assessment, you will have a profile that identifies your organization's overall strengths and weaknesses in terms of its environmental management effort. You will be able to see where your organization stands in terms of integrating environmental issues into its business practices.

For any organization that is serious about continuous improvement, the ESAP should be an essential component of its ongoing effort. The time will come when such criteria will be part of the criteria for a quality organization and, no doubt, will be incorporated into the criteria for ISO Certification and such quality award processes as the Canadian Awards for Business Excellence, the Malcolm Baldrige National Quality Award, the European Award for Quality, and the Japanese Prize for Quality. Even more important, these criteria will determine whether your organization remains viable and competitive for the long term in the global economy. It is certainly going to be essential if your organization wants a "sustainable" competitive advantage.

## REFERENCE NOTES

1. National Geographic Society. *Changing Geographic Perspectives.* Proceedings of the Centennial Symposium, 1988.

2. For a collection of articles and case studies in this area, see *Green Ledgers: Case Studies in Corporate Environmental Accounting,* edited by Ditz, Ranganathan, and Banks, published by the World Resources Institute, Baltimore, Maryland. Call 1-800-822-0504 or 1-410-516-6963.

3. *Environmental Self-Assessment Program.* Washington, DC: Global Environmental Management Initiative, September, 1992. Call 202-296-7449 or fax 202-296-7442 for a free copy of Environmental Self-Assessment Program.

# PART III:
# INNOVATION

Innovation has always been an important factor in the success of any business. Throughout the history of business, the innovative organizations have been the ones to jump the market and grab the lion's share of new technology, products, and services. Many would challenge the assumption that innovation has not been a value in the past. This assumption could be defended, but that is not the point of this book. Even if innovation has always been a core business value (and we don't think it has been in many organizations), it is not only more important than it has ever been, it is also different than it has been in the past.

A strong emphasis on creating new products and services, not just improving the old products and services, is being enhanced by such new tools and information technology as Quality Function Deployment (QFD), concurrent engineering, Business Process Reengineering, Mass Customization, Point of Purchase Information, the Internet, Groupware, and Electronic Data Interchange (EDI) between customers and suppliers. Never before in history has the world seen the linkage of so many different tools and methodologies for the purpose of generating innovation in business products and services.

Innovation is regarded by many as the single best way to get ahead and stay ahead of the pack as well as the most important strategy for leapfrogging the competition. This has led to a relentless drive to dramatically reduce the time it takes to develop new products. Software development, for example, has increased so dramatically that the customer barely has time to learn how to use the product before a newer version is out. The pressure to be the first to market with a product puts pressure on every area of an organization. Marketing, engineering, customer service, production, and delivery must all be able to accelerate their operations as the length of time for new product or service development fails. No one in the organization is immune to the pressure of producing new products and services faster and faster.

In the past, innovation was considered the brainchild of a few gifted people in the organization. The marketing department, the CEO, or the research and development (R&D) department were generally looked to as the source of new ideas. It was generally assumed that only a few people in the organization were creative, and those people could be put together in one area to provide all the creativity that the organization needed. Hypercompetition has rendered such assumptions obsolete. Increasingly, any organization that does not enlist every brain it has in the search for new products, services, and ideas is running at less than full capacity. Today, no organization can be innovative merely by relying on the wisdom of a few of its members, no matter how gifted they are. People throughout the organization must be tapped into for their creativity and new ideas. As more organizations realize this, it becomes a basic business necessity rather than a competitive advantage.

In the past, organizations were content to do basic research in line with producing new products and services. Today, astute organizations realize that they must be innovative in terms of creating new concepts. Concepts are the basic foundations for all innovation. Organizations that are able to create fundamentally new concepts will have a head start on the competition. For instance, the concept of groupware gave rise to the highly successful product called "Lotus Notes" which links people in an organization together. Use of Lotus Notes creates the corporate equivalent of the beehive. In a beehive, when one bee finds honey, it returns to report this to the entire hive. In a short period of time, this new knowledge becomes common throughout the hive. This greatly facilitates the speed and organization required to bring the honey back to the hive in an efficient and effective manner. Lotus Notes essentially does the same thing for organizations. The product is so powerful that IBM acquired the Lotus Corporation principally on the power of this one product. Lotus has done an excellent job of jumping the market and gaining significant market share. Imitators are only now starting to come out, but Lotus is already working on version five of its product.

These facts point to a significant new role (or at least a significantly heightened one) for innovation in organizations. The chapters in this section will explore some basic strategies, concepts, and tactics that you can use in your organization to become more innovative. We have chosen several different processes that are highly dependent on the role of innovation for their success. For instance, strategy development has become a bureaucratic procedure in many organizations. We will demonstrate how, with the infusion of innovative thinking, you can restore strategy formation to its rightful role as a means of developing plans for outpositioning and outmaneuvering your competition.

# Chapter 8

# Innovation and Creativity: Cornerstones for Prosperity

Some time ago, I was listening to a radio talk show while driving to work. The topic was the issue of innovation. One of the participants, a management professor at a local university, was relating a story about an evening MBA class that she was teaching. Many of her students were older adults coming back to school for career advancement. Most already held lower or middle management positions at various Twin Cities organizations. During the discussion on innovation and creativity, all of her students agreed that in the coming millennium, organizations need to be much more innovative and creative. In a world of "hypercompetition," the ability to compete is based on being able to continually find new and innovative ways to satisfy the customer. Those organizations that cannot manage intellectual capital will not be able to manage innovation.

While talking about innovation, the professor casually asked members of her class if they knew of Prince, the Twin Cities' rock star and entrepreneur. The entire class did. She then asked her students if any of them would hire Prince if he/she had a job opening. Surprised by the question, the class' general response was, "Well no, we are not in the music business. What would we do with a rock musician?" Not one student in the class said that he/she would hire Prince, mainly because Prince would not fit into his/her organization. There is a message of great importance to American business in this story which we shall come back to later.

First, let's talk about Business Process Reengineering (BPR). Since BPR was introduced to the world by Dr. Hammer and Dr. Champy,[1] it has become the subject of seminars, courses, conferences, and several other books. For many, it has replaced Total Quality Management as the new business phenomenon. Nevertheless, there are those who would argue that it is nothing new. Proponents of this position maintain that innovation was always a part of Total Quality Management (TQM). Many leading quality gurus have said that in TQM, organizations need innovation as well as improvement of products, services, and processes. W. Edwards Deming, in his book, *Out of the Crisis,*[2] stated the following:

> Innovate. Allocate resources for long-term planning. . . . One requirement for innovation is faith that there will be a future. Innovation, the foundation of the future, cannot thrive unless the top management have declared unshakable commitment to quality and productivity. (p. 25)

Indeed, one could argue that Deming's first point of his famous 14 Points for Management is all about innovation. Point number one is "Create constancy of purpose for improvement of product and service." Many other experts in TQM have also pointed out the role of innovation in continuous quality improvement. Ishikawa noted, "Ours is the age of rapid technological innovation and worldwide competition. If the top management cannot assume leadership in breaking through the existing barriers, their company is going to be left behind"[3] J. M. Juran has said, "The most decisive factor in the competition for quality leadership is the rate of continuous improvement. . . . Companies must continually evolve new product features and new processes to produce those features."[4]   And Imai, in his book *Kaizen,* states emphatically that "both innovation and Kaizen are needed if a company is to survive and grow."[5] So it is difficult to see how Hammer, Champy, and other advocates of BPR can maintain that total quality is only concerned with small incremental improvements and not with major breakthroughs.

On the other hand, to be fair to the BPR advocates, there are at least three good reasons why BPR is an important concept* for the

---

*A brief literature review into the field of management or quality literature would demonstrate that BPR does not deserve the status of a new theory or even a new body of knowledge. Robert Coles noted in his review of Hammer and Champy's book the following: "As shorthand, scholars are turned off because they see little value-added content in the reengineering concept, and much sloppy, if not deceptive thinking. It appears to be a classic case of product differentiation driven by the consultant industry" (Cole, R. "Reengineering the Corporation: A Review Essay." *The Quality Management Journal,* July 1994). When asked what he thought of reengineering, Dr. Joseph Juran replied, "Well, there are only so many hills around, so you either have to knock someone off their hill or create your own hill."

quality field. The first reason is that the concept of innovation is usually thought of only as it relates to the introduction of new products and, in some instances, services. All too often, the subject of process innovation is missed or downplayed. Thus, the distinction Hammer and Champy make concerning how a typical quality improvement team looks at a process versus how a BPR team looks at a process is often a valid one.

Hammer and Champy note that the quality team would generally start by flowcharting the process. After a series of steps, the team might end up eliminating parts of the process or streamlining others. Team members probably would not radically redesign the process. (Sometimes, given the available resources, it is nearly impossible to do this anyway.) Nevertheless, it is useful to contemplate the idea of radical redesign from the start. Many processes have evolved out of tradition, custom, habit, and the "We have always done it this way" mentality. The BPR team would start with a blank sheet, not with a flowchart of the way it is usually done. Instead, the team members would start from scratch and see how they could design the process with what they now know about it. They would attempt to design the ideal process from the start. Such an approach has the advantage of allowing for truly innovative departures from the "way we have always done things around here."

The second area in which BPR offers some new insights concerns where most of its applications have been applied. Despite those who maintain that manufacturing processes have been slow to apply BPR, its greatest strength lies in helping the staff and service areas in an organization. Areas such as management information systems, human resource development, accounting, purchasing, payroll, legal, engineering, and customer service typically do not feel that they are part of the total quality effort. Sometimes this is a result of an overemphasis on quality in the production areas. It is here management typically starts to look for the big bucks and quick fixes. After all, if its products are not up to the competition, the organization will not stay in business long.

Another reason for the neglect in staff areas is that professionals in these areas often do not believe that the quality methodology and tools used by people in the production and manufacturing areas will be useful for their problems. Indeed, employees in staff functions such as customer service, purchasing, and marketing do face problems different from those in manufacturing and production. Many staffers argue that such tools as Statistical Process Control, Design of Experiments, Quality Function Deployment, and the Seven-Step Problem-Solving Methodology are useless when dealing with nonquantifiable or nonnumerical processes. There is, in fact, some validity to these arguments. Many abstract problems are not handled as readily as production or machine-type problems, which more easily succumb to such linear problem-solving methods as the Seven-Step Process or Statistical Process Control. Indeed, our experience has given us some sympathy to these complaints.*

The BPR methodology gives employees in many staff areas a new and potentially very powerful concept for dealing with their problems and processes. Rather than putting a bandage on problems, BPR allows a critical reexamination of the fundamental premises and assumptions underlying the processes. As was noted, staff processes were often developed with a set of contingencies in mind which may no longer be valid. Only through a radical redesign of process can many such processes and problems be eliminated. Thus, we must not only ask, "Even if it ain't broke, how can we continually improve it?" We must also ask, "How can we continually innovate it?" Herein lies the strongest case for the overzealous claims made for BPR. When an entire process is eliminated that no one needed in the first place, it is truly a fantastic breakthrough in innovation and thinking. Such breakthroughs can save an organization thousands or even millions of dollars. Nevertheless, such breakthrough thinking must be coupled with a process for continuous improvement if further gains are going to be made. No organization should merely rely on breakthroughs for product and service improvements and innovation.

The third reason for viewing BPR as a new concept is that it is the first methodology to recognize the inherent and critical interdepen-

---

*However, I still remain an advocate of the position that everyone in an organization should be able to use SPC and the Seven-Step Problem-Solving method and that they can be of substantial help to any area of the organization. There are indeed more abstract problems in staff areas, but there are still many problems that staffers face which can be resolved by a linear analytical approach.

dencies between organizational processes and the computer. Many years ago, Armand Feigenbaum said that if you automated an inefficient process, you would only produce faster inefficiencies. BPR has truly pointed out that the automation of inefficiency is what has been done in staff areas since the introduction of the personal computer. Thus, in many organizations, billing clerks still handle the billing process the way it was done as Frederick Taylor recommended in the early days of industrialization. Under the Taylor system of management, every process in the organization was divided into the smallest possible task that could be done routinely. Each employee only completed one task. Riveters would rivet, welders would do the same weld repeatedly, and office clerks would routinely complete the same form, again and again. For office people, personal computers did not change the nature or routine of the task. The only difference was that employees were completing the same form using a computer rather than a typewriter.

BPR challenges organizations to use computer technology as a way to empower employees, not to just speed up their work. When employees are empowered to use the knowledge provided by computers, they are often able to radically redesign processes and cut process times by incredible amounts. For instance, electronic data interchange (EDI) is now creating invoiceless offices where the information needed for payment or billing is placed right into the computers of the supplier or customer. EDI not only creates less paperwork but also significantly eliminates many time-consuming, routine, tedious tasks that were formerly part of purchasing and warehousing. There are many other areas in organizations undergoing similar transitions. No doubt, we have only just begun to see really radical workplace designs based on the interaction of people and new technologies. We can thank BPR for many of these insights.

Returning to the issue of innovation, it should be clear by now that for BPR to be successful, you need innovative people. For instance, what would happen if you put your people together to work on a process and gave each of them a blank sheet of paper–but none of them could think of any way that the process could be different? In real life, this seldom happens because people are basically creative. Furthermore, those with knowledge of the process will have pent-up lists of ideas. In many organizations, there is a backlog of good employee ideas stemming from years of believing that managers think and employees do. Nevertheless, there are constraints on the innovative abilities of employees. For instance, Deming noted that customers often cannot tell you what they want in the future. "How would they know?" asked Deming. It takes someone with foresight and imagination to identify new products and services that will make people's lives easier. The same holds true with the innovation of new processes. Organizations will not have process innovation unless they have employees with foresight, imagination, and lack of fear. Employees who fear repercussions from taking chances or sticking their necks out can never be innovative and creative.

A critical issue for organizations (at least those that want to stay in business) concerns developing a workforce that can contribute to organizational innovation and creativity. How can an organization accomplish this? One answer is to go out and hire people gifted with foresight and imagination. Find people like Prince and hire them. While this might seem like an easy solution, it is not easy for several reasons. First, many managers would not recognize an innovative person if they saw one; second, innovative people do not fit well in most American corporations; third, an innovative person probably would not want to work for you and, finally, if you are like the managers in the story, you would not hire a truly innovative person anyway. We are being somewhat facetious here. However, numerous pragmatic constraints are going to mediate against any wholesale hiring of innovative and creative people. Nevertheless, perhaps these characteristics should be part of an organization's hiring requirements in the coming decade.

The most realistic option for becoming an innovative organization is to create truly creative people from those employees already in your organization. But this approach is not without problems. If so many managers can't recognize innovation, are afraid of it, and expect blind conformance to their demands and requirements, will it really be worth creating innovation? You might be creating your own Frankenstein monster. If you are a command-and-control manager, you will not want people who can think for themselves and challenge you. On the other hand, if you are really committed to creating a "learning organization," you will have no choice. Many now view the ability to continually learn and incorporate new ideas and knowledge to be fundamental to the long-term success of organizations in a hypercompetitive global economy. Creativity and innovation are as much a part of learning as is the simpleminded assimilation of facts and figures that are associated with traditional learning. One could argue that simply learning new theories and ideas are not enough if those ideas are not translated into new products and services to thrill and delight customers. Indeed, we believe that many organizations should try to become thinking organizations as well as learning organizations. Your customers don't really care if you are philosophers or sages if the product does not meet specification or if your competitor has better quality and customer service. Creativity is to thinking as intuition is to analysis. One is predominantly a right-brain exercise and the other is a left-brain exercise. A true thinking and learning organization must ensure a holistic integration of the human skills which are available. Either set of skills is valuable but, in a knowledge-based society, both are essential.

Fortunately, it is possible to create the conditions necessary for creativity and innovation to thrive in an organization. Your task begins by recognizing the fundamental elements of innovation and creating these in your organization. The following elements are the key components of innovation: fertilization, recreation, hybridization, cross-pollination, incubation, and maturation. Each is a necessary condition for innovation, but each alone is not sufficient. You need all conditions for innovation to take place. Let's look at each of these elements and their roles in promoting innovation in products, services, and processes.

## *FERTILIZATION*

Just as seeds cannot grow on barren ground, ideas will not grow when certain conditions do not exist. Principal among these conditions is the absence of fear. If people are afraid for their jobs, their positions, their self-esteem, or their respect from others, they will not have a soil conducive to the growth and development of their new ideas. There are many sources of fear in an organization. There are still some managers who argue that "a little fear is good." Such managers use fear as a motivator and, since they find that it often works, they believe it is useful. This is short-term thinking. What those types of managers never notice is the loss of risk taking by their employees, the unwillingness to challenge the system, or the apathy that their management methods create in the workplace. At the very least, fear creates an "everyone for himself/herself" attitude which is hardly conducive to teamwork and risk taking. You cannot have innovation without risk taking; and you will have less risk taking where there is fear. No fear is good if you want creative, innovative employees.

### *RECREATION*

The word "create" comes from the word recreation. Play and recreation are essential for innovation. Play can take many forms: brainstorming, daydreaming, working with people you like, working on a challenging product, or taking a vacation. When we play, we momentarily suspend judgment about what we are doing. We are able to relax and allow new insights to come into our minds. When we "recreate," we simply accept what is, without judgment. There is no such thing as a stupid or bad idea. A key rule in brainstorming is that there are no bad ideas. By suspending judgment, we acknowledge the concept of equifinality. Equifinality means that there are multiple paths to the same goal or, in plain English, "There is more than one way to skin a cat."

Another essential attribute of recreation is the suspension of a goal orientation. In recreating, one doesn't worry about the right answers or if the effort will lead to the correct solution. When we recreate, we are simply trying to explore new ideas and possibilities. Many managers have a hard time with this. They go to a training session, each asking, "Will I get anything out of this?" or "Will I learn anything?" They attend a retreat for strategic planning, but only with the caveat, "We'd better have a strategic plan by the time we leave." Each manager feels quite satisfied if he/she comes back with a long "to do" list, even if most of the items lack any coherence or relationship to the true needs of the organization or its customers.

Very few organizations think of free time or idle time as a contributor to creativity and innovation. In most organizations, people know that they will be penalized if they are not busy or at least look busy. So they spend large amounts of energy in wasted efforts to look busy or in make-work activities. How much more productive would they be if they were allowed to read a book or just take a walk outside and spend an hour or two daydreaming? Imagine an organization with a "Department of Daydreaming." In such a place, perhaps today's dreams could become tomorrow's innovative products, processes, and services.

## *HYBRIDIZATION*

One definition of hybridization is this: "Formed from heterogeneous elements, produced by the interaction or crossbreeding of two unlike cultures or traditions." In biology, something that is a hybrid has genes from two or more distinct elements. Hybrids might be considered a form of diversity in action since anything that is hybrid exhibits characteristics from multiple elements. In the *Star Trek* series, the character Spock came from a species, the Vulcans, whose primary value was called the IDIC principle. This stands for "Infinite Diversity through Infinite Combination." Thus, Vulcans exhibited a true value for diversity. Generally, this is not a trait that we human beings seem to really exhibit. We are much better at creating hybrid plants and goldfish than we are at creating diversity of ideas and thoughts.

Some people are exceptions to the above rules. I once met a psychologist at a Deming conference and asked him how he became interested in Deming and TQM. He replied that, until he came to the conference, he had never heard of either Deming or Total Quality. Curious, I persisted by asking him why he came to the conference. He certainly did not fit in with the management or quality executives who frequented Deming's conferences. He told me that every year he picked a conference to go to, the subject of which he knew nothing about. This kept his thinking fresh and gave him new perspectives on his own field of clinical psychology. This is truly radical behavior. If it does not seem radical, imagine one of your employees applying to attend the next annual horticulture conference or the next annual conference on "Theories of Dinosaur Extinction." Would your training department or management pay for his/her time off and the cost of the conference? In most organizations, the answer would be a resounding NO! All too often, the question is answered by the manager asking, "Does it relate to his/her job?" Such questions will not produce hybridization nor create a culture that values new ideas. A learning organization is one where curiosity and inquiry are fostered. This is done by helping employees find new ideas and theories outside the narrow disciplines that most of them are boxed into at work and school.

## CROSS-POLLINATION

The word "cross-pollinate" is defined as "the transfer of pollen from the flower of one plant to the flower of another plant having a different genetic constitution." This is not as radical a step as hybridization. We use this metaphor in organizations to imply creating innovation by taking a good idea and putting it in a new place. Hybridization is creating an entirely new idea from two different ideas. Cross-pollination is simply introducing an old idea into a new place. For instance, espresso coffeehouses have been standard in Europe for decades. Recently, they have been popping up all over the United States as the idea of upscale gourmet coffeehouses gets transplanted, first from Europe, then from one U.S. city to another. Another good example of cross-pollination concerns the quality movement. TQM started in manufacturing industries in Japan, spread to manufacturing industries in North America and Europe, and has gradually been introduced into service industries, hospitals, and even police departments. Good ideas need both exposure and receptivity to ensure their ability to find fertile ground and take root.

It is not easy to create an organization open to such novel changes. Deming described sixteen barriers to quality.[6] Most consultants are familiar with the "not invented here" syndrome. In other words, "it is only a good idea if it is created by our organization, our group, our department, or our team." Ideas emanating elsewhere are automatically rejected. A second idea killer noted by Deming is the "search for examples." The argument is, "Yes, but our industry is different. Could you show us how it would apply here? Could you give us examples of other industries such as ours where this has been done successfully?" Of course, even if you can provide such examples, it is still futile because you will inevitably be told that those other cases are different, so your examples are meaningless. Deming believed such organizations are not ready for quality and, indeed, may never be ready. After all, as he said, "Survival is not compulsory."

If you want an innovative organization, you will have to create processes that foster cross-pollination. This means that you will have to look across disciplines, departments, industries, and even nations to find ideas that work. You will need to give people the tools to search out such ideas and the time to "recreate" with them. Employees must be encouraged to play with such ideas and to explore the relevance of those ideas to their industry. Many excellent ideas and breakthroughs in history have come about by the cross-pollination of ideas and concepts. For instance, the industrial age was actually born in England, but reached its zenith in the United States. The ability to innovate was critical to its development. It took the fertile ground that the United States offered, plus the abilities of the Carnegies, Mellons, Fords, Rockefellers, and many others to produce the systems that have led the United States to be the dominant economic power in the world. The sociotechnical movement was also born in England as an experiment to raise productivity in the coal mines. Even though it was very successful, it was not until Einar Thorsrud took its concepts to Sweden that the movement really caught on. The Saab and Volvo plants in Sweden demonstrated to the world that plants organized around the needs of the workers could be at least as efficient as those organized around the principles of F.W. Taylor.

The Japanese have often been criticized for being "copy cats" due to their propensity to adopt patents and inventions created by other nations. The VCR was patented in the United States, but the Japanese developed it and made it into a household staple. Robert Cole noted in 1985 that every major U.S. trade, technical, and scientific journal in the United States was translated by the Japanese so their managers and scientists could benefit from American ideas. Conversely, in 1986, not a single Japanese journal was translated into English in the United States. This fact has now been somewhat rectified, but it demonstrates that arrogance and egotism are perhaps the biggest single barriers to innovation. As long as an organization or a country feels that it is "Number One" or the "Best in the Business," it has a tendency to feel that there is nothing to learn from anyone else. Such attitudes usually precede an inevitable decline in innovation.

## *INCUBATION*

Throughout history, many ideas have been ahead of their time. Mendel's theories of genetics took over fifty years to be recognized by mainstream science. Walter Shewhart introduced statistics to the U.S. industrial world in 1931 with his book, *Economic Control of Quality of Manufactured Product.*[7] It wasn't until the 1950s that statistics really caught on as a major industrial tool, and it was in Japan rather than in the United States. It took another thirty-five years for its use to be "rediscovered" by U.S. industries. Many other great innovations came about because someone "slept" on the problem. The classic story of the discovery of the benzene molecule by the father of organic chemistry, Frederick Kekule, illustrates this point. Kekule had been working on this problem for months when, all of a sudden, he pictured the molecule in a dream he was having. He immediately woke up and drew a picture of the molecule as he had seen it in his dream. His interpretation was correct. Many people have such visions and solve problems in their sleep, but most of them roll over and go back to sleep.

Organizations cannot expect to see all their problems resolved just because they buy a new piece of equipment, spend millions on training, or have hundreds of process improvement and reengineering teams. Management's attitudes play a major role in the successful incubation of organizational ideas. For example, one team in an optical lens company worked on a problem for nearly a year, only to be told by top management that, "Never have so many people worked on a problem for so long with so few results." Nothing could have been more demoralizing to this team and nothing could have been further from the truth. In terms of new knowledge and greater understanding of the process, this team accomplished a great deal. Not one of the people on the team felt that it was a waste of time. Each one felt that he/she had learned a great deal about the process and that this learning would be of major benefit to the company. The team had identified the major barriers to streamlining the process, had identified the actual amount of time that was spent on non-value-added activities, and identified the true capability of the process that produced the lens. Previously, there was no actual data as to the capability of the process. While it is true that there were no major breakthroughs, there was a greater understanding of the process and system. Such knowledge often lays the groundwork for subsequent breakthroughs and innovations. Nevertheless, management felt that such "process" understanding was a waste of time. Apparently, anything that did not convert to greater sales or lower costs was not deemed of value in this organization.

"Instant pudding" was often noted by Deming as management's unrelenting search for results without efforts, increased sales without increased knowledge of the customer, lower costs without an understanding of the processes that produce waste and rework, and a more harmonious work environment with a management that creates "fear" in the workplace as a normal standard for doing business. It is naive and unrealistic to expect "instant pudding." Assigning a team to work on a problem will not necessarily produce earthshaking results. The production of knowledge and new ideas are often only the first step in generating theories and hypotheses that can be tested. Only by testing ideas, assumptions, and theories will employees be able to find answers to many of the problems that trouble their organizations. Creating a learning organization requires the realization that solutions take time and that knowledge and theories must be developed before solutions can be found. The learning process cannot be quantified in dollars and cents. If this is true, then the more you pay for a book, the better the ideas should be. Personally, we have found some of our best ideas in books that were on the bargain table.

## *MATURATION*

Let us assume that the ground is fertile, the seed is in the ground, and we have a robust hybrid planted. We should be expecting good results come harvest time, right? Not necessarily. The plant still must be tended to. There must be adequate water, sunlight, nutrients, and protection from the ravages of nature. So, too, with good ideas and innovation. There must be an infrastructure in the organization that provides the necessary ongoing conditions that will allow good ideas to reach their full potential. Many good ideas die on the vine because they do not receive enough support from the organization. If you just allow or expect natural selection to weed out the best ideas, you may miss a lot of worthwhile ideas.

This takes us back to some of the issues brought up by the story about Prince, related at the beginning of this chapter. For example, how do you keep innovative people who may seem like misfits in a traditional organization? How do you create an infrastructure that fosters and nourishes new ideas and innovation? These are not easy questions to answer. There are some answers to these questions and some things that we know for sure will impede innovation and creativity. We will never have a creative, innovative organization if we are saddled with bureaucracy, hierarchy, and traditional stereo-typical managers and employees. We will need to rethink the systems and policies that support such structures. They were not created to foster innovation but instead to support top-down direction and control. In traditional organizations, employees were expected to do what they were told and not to think for themselves. We cannot have an innovative learning organization when structures and systems limit access to information and where information is based on a "need to know" military-style paradigm or travels only top down in the organization.

An innovative learning organization cannot exist when the needs of the employee are discounted or ignored. When some people get perks and others don't, teamwork is destroyed. Instead, conditions are created for "rugged" individualism and competition. When employees are expected to not have feelings and to leave their family lives at home, organizations are creating an arbitrary distinction between work and family which only superficially exists. The needs of employees for integration of work and family life are a reality in the modern corporation. Many of the best employees are leaving corporate America to work for themselves because businesses will not provide the quality of life conducive to doing a good job and having a good family life. Many businesses think nothing of uprooting and transplanting employees for the good of the organization, regardless of the familial needs of the employees. Women also find it difficult to advance in organizations because of the "glass ceiling" and the lack of support systems which are needed for women to advance. There can be no fertile ground for innovation and creativity if the natural needs of the employee for family, social life, and spiritual development are either discounted or not taken into consideration. People want to work in a democratic culture based on trust and mutual respect. They also want to be recognized as "holistic" beings who need to develop professionally, socially, and physically. Organizations that want to be industry leaders will recognize these natural needs and, within limits, take them into consideration when conducting business.

We cannot have an innovative learning organization where there is fear; fear is generated by the very way we choose to structure our organizations and by the organization's policies and procedures. Positive discipline programs, performance evaluation systems, piecework systems, pay for performance, distinctions between hourly and salaried people, union work rules, the collective bargaining agreement, and management's commitment to providing employment security all impact efforts to create an innovative workplace. One can talk to employees in any number of organizations and find numerous such practices that instill fear and stifle innovation. Management will need to find new policies and new procedures if it wants to foster learning and innovation instead of fear and control.

Finally, a truly innovative and creative workplace will make a total and unequivocal commitment to the lifelong training, education, and development of all employees. This will not be a random effort. It will be a systematic effort that is continually improved and innovated. Many organizations adopt a tuition reimbursement program, start training courses for employees, or send a few employees off to seminars once in a while, and think that they have become a learning organization. Such serendipitous educational activities may have value for the organization, but they fall woefully short of creating the conditions for ongoing learning and development.

One study found that while most major organizations had a tuition reimbursement program, on the average, only 2 percent of employees used it. There were three major reasons for the lack of use. First, the release time policies of the organizations prohibited employees from taking time off when most local colleges or trade schools offered courses. Second, there was a lack of courses available during the hours when employees were off and could attend courses. The third reason was the reimbursement policies. Many required a grade of B or better to get reimbursed. Many employees never received higher than a C during the entire time they were in grade school and high school, and were too intimidated by the need to get a B to want to take the risk of taking an outside course. If employees did not pass, they would not be reimbursed or, worse, they would have to pay back the cost of the course (if the company had already paid). This study demonstrated that tuition reimbursement policies are often a mere token effort to provide for ongoing training and development of employees. Furthermore, we have yet to find an organization that actually tracks the number of employees who use tuition assistance and actively tries to find ways to continually improve this number. Organizations that want to create the conditions for innovation must go beyond such serendipitous approaches to education and learning.

A learning organization will make a sustained and systematic effort to foster the fundamental elements of innovation that have been identified in this chapter. When any employee in an organization, whether he or she is at the management level or not, can take some time to "think about things," or perhaps to just read a book, that organization will have begun its journey toward becoming a learning organization.

## REFERENCE NOTES

1. Hammer, M. and Champy, J. *Reengineering the Corporation.* New York: Harper Business, 1993.

2. Deming, W.E. *Out of the Crisis.* Cambridge, MA: Massachusetts Institute of Technology, 1982.

3. Ishikawa, K. *What Is Total Quality Control?* Translated by David J. Lu. Englewood Cliffs, NJ: Prentice-Hall, Inc., 1985.

4. Juran, J.M. *Juran on Leadership for Quality.* New York: The Free Press, 1989.

5. Imai, M. *Kaizen.* New York: Random House Business Division, 1986.

6. Deming, 1982.

7. Shewhart, W.A. *Economic Control of Quality of Manufactured Product.* New York: Van Nostrand Co., 1931.

# Chapter 9

# Developing Strategies
# for Long-Term Success

Despite what many think, it is not essential to have a strategic thinking/planning process in an organization. There is much evidence that such processes are, at best, a waste of time and, at worst, can have a negative impact on corporate performance. Much of the traditional strategic planning that has dominated American industry has amounted to little more than developing copious lists of action items and budgets that were then delegated to lower-level managers or staff planners to implement. About every five years, those responsible for planning would dust off and revise the old strategic plan. Plans lacked creativity and intuitive thinking, the very factors that built most organizations in the first place.

The term "strategic thinking/planning" will be used in this chapter to distinguish between the "traditional" system of strategic planning that is found in most organizations, and the concept of strategic thinking/planning that is the subject of this chapter. Many people (particularly planners) have confused or misunderstood what strategic thinking/planning is all about and its role in organizations. They have lost sight of the forest because of the trees. This is probably not surprising given the number of books and experts describing how strategic thinking/planning should be done.[1] Most such books promote a reductionistic method of strategic thinking which tends to ignore or exclude entire sets of factors critical to the success of an organization. For instance, there are several new books that tout a Vision-Mission-Objectives model for strategic planning. These books tell you how to create a vision, how to create a shared vision, the difference between a mission and a vision, how to set objectives, etc. Unfortunately, your competitors are probably reading the same books. In the world of strategy, the phenomenon of shared information has the tendency to put everybody at the same point. As long as the focus of these books is on copying a strategy, not on understanding the implications of strategic thinking, you will never be any better or further ahead than your competitors, assuming they can also read.

Strategic thinking/planning is a means to an end. In the business world, the end is to add value. Value helps make a customer's life easier, better, or more pleasant. Strategy is all about the best means to accomplish these goals. Strategy involves being open to many dimensions and influences that impact an organization. It is not about coming up with the "best possible plan" or the one right way. It is about probabilities as much as it is about certainties, and opportunities as much as about action items. To try to separate any of these factors is to diminish the role that strategic thinking can play in an organization.

As an example of how a strategy gets confused with "strategic thinking," let's look at the widespread adoption of total quality programs. For the past ten years, Total Quality Management (TQM) has been the most popular strategy for helping organizations to add value and to achieve increased organizational competitiveness. However, many managers believe that Total Quality Management is an end in itself. They do not understand that TQM is only one of a number of strategies that can add value. Since 1900, there have been at least twelve major strategies that organizations have pursued; some of these have been pursued simultaneously. In an approximate sequence, these included the following:

1. Monopolization (dominate the market)
2. Financial Strategies (find the tax loopholes)
3. Empirical Modeling (study and imitate successful traits of successful organizations)
4. Vertical Integration (purchases and acquisitions to find economies of scale)
5. Horizontal Integration (takeovers and mergers to buffer the company from market downturns)
6. Strategic Forecasting (predict where the market will be going and be there first)

7. Deconglomeration (sell off to achieve strategic focus)
8. Total Quality (be the lowest cost and highest quality producer)
9. Create the Future (forget prediction; get a vision and make it happen)
10. Strategic Alliances (get a partner or get close to the customer)
11. Core Competencies (know thyself)
12. Reengineering (quality is too slow; abolish the entire processes)

There are probably even more, but the point is that since 1900, there have been a variety of "means" pursued by organizations to enhance competitive position. Each of these means has its particular strengths and weaknesses. However, by merely copying a strategy without understanding its strengths and weaknesses, organizations limit their options and are more likely to be overwhelmed by their competitors. One of the key rules of strategic thinking/planning is to have as many available options as possible.

To discover options for planning, we have identified eight continuums of strategy. A continuum is a dimension that exists between two linked points. For instance, between light and dark or good and evil. A continuum recognizes the possibility that an infinite number of points can be possible between the two extreme points that anchor the continuum. There is no right or wrong place to be on any continuum, however, a flexible dynamic organization will try to pursue a balanced posture in respect to each of the possibilities represented by a continuum. By examining where your organization is and where your competitors are on each of these continuums, you will be able to achieve a more dynamic and viable strategic thinking/planning process. These continuums will highlight options and opportunities that you will then need to convert into tangible action items. The implementation of the "opportunities" is not the subject of this chapter since this process is very well described in most of the recent literature on strategic thinking/planning.[2] The eight continuums are listed here:

1. Continuous–Discrete
2. Emergent–Predictive

3. Internal–External
4. Competitive–Cooperative
5. Growth–Development
6. Historical–Ahistorical
7. Tangible–Intangible
8. Innovate–Improve

It is important to understand that every organization has a strategy, either by default or design. Design is not always better than default; however, an organization that is unaware of its key strategies is surely operating with many potential blind spots. For instance, one organization was pursuing a somewhat informal strategy of buying every competitor it could. It soon achieved what some might think was an enviable state of market dominance. Within a very short time of achieving this state, however, it found that government officials had been notified by customers who were concerned that they had little or no market choice. This organization is now facing the possibility of having to break up what it spent considerable time, energy, and dollars to develop, as well as possible legal fees to defend its position and market.

A key function of strategic thinking/planning should be to eliminate as many blind spots as possible. Strategic thinking/planning cannot eliminate all of the uncertainties of the future, but it can help organizations to be better prepared to meet these uncertainties. Any organization that takes the time to continually examine its strategic posture in respect to the eight continuums (while not eliminating all uncertainties or blind spots) will eliminate at least some of its blind spots and be in a much stronger position to anticipate, and perhaps even control, some of its future, rather than just reacting to what the future brings.


## CONTINUOUS–DISCRETE

Strategic thinking/planning should be a continuous ongoing process; management's key function is strategic thinking. Those who think that it is a joke that Komatsu, the Japanese construction equipment manufacturer, has a 200-year plan fail to see the real point. The point is that organizations should always be looking at the options and possibilities that the future might bring. The future will present many discrete possibilities. A military battle or skirmish is a discrete event in what may or may not be a long-term war that is part of a larger political issue. For instance, the military intervention by the United States in Honduras was a discrete event compared to the ongoing military activities and problems in the Middle East or to the problems faced by the British in Northern Ireland.

Organizations face many discrete events which call for focused short-term planning. Such events do not wait until the next planning retreat to present themselves. Organizations must balance continuous with discrete planning. Once-a-year planning sessions for the next fiscal year should be discarded in favor of a more continuous planning process. It is absolutely absurd to think that the forces affecting an organization can be planned for or thought about on a once-a-year time schedule. Strategic thinking should be so ingrained in the daily activities of the organization that it becomes like eating or drinking. Organizations must have a process to make this a reality and to ensure that strategic thoughts become strategic actions. As your strategy group looks at this continuum, it should be asking the following questions:

- How do we do our strategic planning?
- Is strategic planning an event or is it part of a continuous process?
- Do we create conditions for everyone in the organization to think strategically?
- Do we confuse planning with strategic thinking?
- How good is our current planning process? How do we know?

## *EMERGENT–PREDICTIVE*

Many people suppose that all planning is predictive, that planning is always about anticipating what is going to happen. In actuality, most strategies deal with emergent events. For instance, in a chess game, one is continually faced with unexpected moves. Your opposition is always trying to predict what you will do. Each competitor is, in effect, trying to cancel out the advantages that the other side has obtained. (In business, this is perhaps through a prior study of the market or some strategic or technological breakthrough.) So, one must be equally prepared to deal with events that happen today, not just in the future. Because a chess player is thinking five moves ahead does not mean that he/she can or will be able to make each of those moves.

You have to plan to take advantage of the unpredictable. The irony or paradox of planning is that only by trying to predict the unpredictable will an organization be able to eliminate many of the uncertainties that the future will surely bring. People who cannot understand such paradoxes will generally not make good strategic planners. Strategic thinking is all about handling paradoxes that arise because of the tensions that life presents us. We must balance work and family, long-range planning with short-term planning, concern for things with concern for people, and the needs of stakeholders versus the needs of customers. One sign of success is when you begin to understand that life is both infinitely complex and infinitely simple. Such issues are not ideal philosophical speculations, they are the core of strategic thinking. As your strategy group looks at this continuum, it should be asking the following questions:

- Do we try to anticipate the future or do we just respond to events?
- What data do we collect to anticipate the future?
- How do we use the data in our planning process?
- How do we use intuition and creativity in our thinking/planning?
- What kinds of predicting do our competitors do?
- How do we deal with paradox and conceptual thinking?
- Do we encourage challenges to our thinking and the organization?

## INTERNAL–EXTERNAL

Strategies can deal with the organization itself (internal strategies) or the environment (external strategies) within which the organization operates. For instance, in terms of internal strategies, the concept of core competencies[3] lays the foundation for a strategy to better understand your own organization's knowledge, skills, and abilities, indicating what could be more profitably outsourced. TQM, as practiced by many organizations, is basically an internally focused method for removing waste and non-value-added activities from within an organization. Contrast these strategies with such externally focused strategies as empirical modeling or strategic alliances. Empirical modeling is a strategy for looking at what has worked in an organization or industry and adapting it to your own organization. Strategic alliances attempt to meld the strengths of one organization with those of another. The goal of a strategic alliance is to help the organization either fend off encroachments on its market or to be in a more competitive position. Organizations that think they can be successful merely by pursuing strategic alliances or the core competency strategy should think about Sun Tzu's dictum: "If you know only yourself you will win as many battles as you lose. If you know only your enemy you will also win as many battles as you lose. But if you know both yourself and your enemy, you will never lose any battles."[4] Sun Tzu's point is that no business or endeavor can only look inward or only look outward and think it will find success. At best, it will be wrong as often as it is right. It is imperative to understand the reality within your organization as well as the reality outside your organization. To ignore one or the other is to act as though they do not exist. As your strategy group looks at this continuum, it should be asking the following questions:

- How well do we understand our own strengths and weaknesses?
- What do we do best? What do our competitors do best?
- Do we focus all our energy internally or externally?
- What kinds of a balance do we have in respect to these two positions? What are the forces in the environment that could affect us? Would a traditional SWOT (strengths, weaknesses, opportunities, threats) analysis help us?
- How do we measure ourselves? How good is our data?

## COMPETITIVE–COOPERATIVE

Organizations that see the world only in terms of competition are severely limiting their possible options. It has long been part of political and military strategy to create advantageous alliances. Beginning with supplier partnerships and moving into customer partnerships and alliances with competitors, more and more organizations are beginning to recognize that there needs to be a balance between competition and cooperation. Overemphasizing either one leads to an imbalance that is, in the long run, counterproductive.

There is a major trend in business today to form partnerships with suppliers, and strategic alliances with customers and potential competitors. There are pros and cons to such strategies. Supplier partnerships and customer partnerships take a considerable amount of time and energy to develop. Furthermore, as James Brian Quinn notes in his book, *Intelligent Enterprise*, suppliers and competitors who acquire your capabilities may decide that they don't need you, that they can deal directly with your customers. Why should suppliers and distributors split the profits with you if they can provide what the customer wants without you?

To treat any competitive or cooperative strategy as though it were without any disadvantages is to be extremely naive. Furthermore, such thinking underlies a more profound limitation that seems inherent in many organizations–the tendency to jump on a bandwagon, believing that it has some sort of magical or omnipotent powers that will guarantee success and longevity. Each new program is seen as unblemished and perfect. Thus, in many businesses, competition is out and cooperation is in. Organizations would be well advised to think about the pros and cons of any strategy they adopt. If they cannot find pros and cons to each strategy, they are suffering from terminal myopia or equally terminal "group think." These organizations would be well advised to bring in some fresh perspectives. As your strategy group looks at this continuum, it should be asking the following questions:

- Are we only focused on competitive strategies?
- Do we form strategic alliances? What are the pros and cons of doing so?
- How do we identify possible beneficial alliances?

- Do we examine and protect ourselves from the possible downsides of a cooperative strategy?
- Are we focused only on cooperative strategies?
- What are some competitive strategies that might help our organization?
- What are the downsides to the competitive strategies?

### GROWTH–DEVELOPMENT

Organizations pursue growth through many different strategies. One common strategy is diversification. Through such tactics as mergers, acquisitions, takeovers, and leveraged buyouts, an organization can double in size almost overnight. Furthermore, when the right skills and abilities are put together, a synergy can be created that can lead to competitive advantage. However, when the organization ignores its own development and focuses only on growth strategies, it risks losing the long-term ability needed to capitalize on any gains from growth. If this happened, growth can leave the organization in a worse competitive position.

There are many examples from the 1970s (sort of the apex of times for acquisitions and mergers) of organizations that later found they were in a worse position after the merger or takeover than before. Organizations that were chasing acquisitions and mergers sometimes found they had acquired a hornet's nest. In some cases, these problem acquisitions were difficult to manage because they simply didn't fit with the skills and abilities of the dominant organization. In other cases, it was just that the difference between the two organizational cultures was too great. Many times, the relationship between the organizations was so poor that it was detrimental to the survival of one company or the other. Harley-Davidson was a good example of this. Acquired by the AMF Corporation in 1969, by the late 1970s its sales and performance were so poor that AMF tried to sell it off but could not find a buyer. An in-house group of Harley-Davidson and AMF employees bought the company in 1981. Under their leadership, and with the adoption of the Total Quality strategy in 1985, the company started an uphill battle against Japanese motorcycles.

Harley-Davidson's turnaround and subsequent success made it one of the success stories in the Total Quality field. However, this change in operational strategy would probably not have been possible if Harley-Davidson had not divested itself from the AMF Corporation. There were so many situations similar to this that the end of the 1980s saw a wholesale selling off of many companies that had once been acquired. Diversification led to divestiture. Although managers still fantasize about unbridled growth, in reality, the theme of growth seems to have been replaced by the theme of "downsizing" in American industry.

Russell Ackoff, in his book *Creating the Corporate Future*, says, "Most managers see growth as an objective that is second only to survival. To be sure, they speak of corporate development, but they normally think of it as equivalent to corporate growth. Growth and development are not the same thing. Growth can take place with or without development, and development can take place with or without growth."[5] Ackoff defined growth as an increase in size. Development is a process by which an organization increases its ability to satisfy its needs and those of its customers. Development cannot be achieved by merely buying or selling other organizations. Many managers believe the dictum, "Grow or die." They should remember that "Grow and die" may be equally true. As your strategy group looks at this continuum, it should be asking the following questions:

- Are we managing growth or being driven by growth?
- What are our development needs? How well are we meeting them?
- How do our competitors balance growth and development?
- How will growth help us and what will we accomplish by more growth?
- How much growth is healthy for us?
- Will we better serve our customers by our growth?
- How do our growth strategies fit with our vision and mission?
- How do we determine the development needed to support our planned growth?
- How will we handle unplanned growth?

## *HISTORICAL–AHISTORICAL*

The historical point on this continuum refers to the knowledge and information that is tied up with the past or with what others have done before. It is the practices and principles that history and experience have to offer. The ahistorical point on the continuum refers to uniqueness and novelty. It is the potential for discontinuities that have no historical precedents. Ahistorical strategies are new, innovative, and involve creating goals and plans that have never before existed. Tendencies exist to ignore or overemphasize one or the other of these points.

Many managers believe that there is little value in studying the past. It is "ancient history" they say. They fail to recognize that adopting "best practices" is, in a sense, studying the past. When you copy the "best practices" identified by market studies such as PIMS or by benchmarking the "best in class," you are borrowing from the past and what has been already shown to work in one context. On the other hand, adopting best practices can be a form of mindless incorporation of practices ("copying" as Deming labeled it) without the necessary understanding of why and how the practice worked for the other party. Dr. Kevin Dooley of the University of Minnesota noted,

> If one tends to view the organization as a single entity–which tends to obscure context–then little can be learned from a historical perspective. If, however, one studies the dynamics of the organization, namely how it adapted and coevolved with the environment, then I think valuable lessons can be learned. Adaptive responses and coevolutionary tendencies are what may be repeated, not absolute principles devoid of context.[6]

Copying is harmful when the organization fails to truly understand the context that the practice or historical episode was rooted in. Indeed, the organizational propensity to jump on bandwagons and blindly follow the latest fads and fashions reported in the business journals has led to the term "Program of the Month." Yesterday, it was the "One Minute Manager," today, it is Total Quality Management; tomorrow, it might be Business Process Reengineering. Deming repeatedly warned managers of the dangers of copying.

He used the terms "analytic" and "enumerative" to distinguish the concepts managers must understand in order to avoid copying. He was simply saying that you can't predict the future from the past. No amount of counting how many times something happened will prove either that it will continue to happen or ever happen again. The gambler's fallacy illustrates this erroneous thinking very well. The gambler's fallacy refers to the well-known tendency for people to believe that, in a toss of a coin, if heads comes up two or three times in a row, tails now has a better chance of coming up. The fact is (if the coin is fair) that the odds are still fifty-fifty on any toss of the coin. Regardless of how many times heads or tails has come up in the past, it still does not change the probability of how many times it will come up in the future.

We need innovative or ahistorical thinking that breaks with past precedents and with what others in the industry are doing. Lou Schultz, an author and CEO of Process Management International, said in a personal discussion that "You will never stand out by following where everybody else is going."

You will also be better able to deal with the future by understanding what worked and what did not work in the past or, as history professors are fond of saying, "The past can't predict the future, but the past is pregnant with the future." Studying the past can often show us trends that have a nasty habit of recurring. While there is no guarantee that they will, many events do repeat themselves. Periodically, the Mississippi River overflows its banks. No one can predict with absolute certainty which years it will happen or if it will ever happen again. However, there is a strong probability that it will overflow at least several more times in each of our lifetimes. If we assume that this is true, we can take steps to plan remedial actions. The whole concept of strategic thinking is based upon the belief that if we cannot predict the future, at least we can anticipate it.

The solution for strategic thinkers is to create a balance between studying the past and thinking about the future. You must strike a balance between understanding the theory behind what you are doing and spending time on innovation and creating new strategies that will separate your organization from the pack. You cannot ignore the past, but you cannot mindlessly copy it either. As your strategy group looks at this continuum, it should be asking the following questions:

- Do we examine our failures as well as our successes?
- Do we really understand what works and what doesn't work in our organization?
- Do we examine the successes and failures of our competitors?
- How much time do we spend studying the past?
- How much time do we spend creating new concepts and ideas?
- Do we really understand why and how our organization was/is successful?

### INTANGIBLES–TANGIBLES

This continuum is concerned with the products and services that an organization has to offer. However, simply listing all of the products and services that an organization provides to its customers could hide much of the value that it provides. So, while products are generally tangible and services are generally intangible, thinking about tangibles and intangibles is one way of determining all of the value provided to customers, whether associated with a product or service, sold for a price, or given away free. Some of the intangibles that you provide for your customers may be the real reason that they do business with you. For instance, Nordstrom's is known for providing excellent customer service and McDonald's for its quality, low-cost food. Nevertheless, both of these organizations are also providing intangibles that are at least as important as their primary products and services. When customers patronize McDonald's, they know it will be clean and its product quality consistent. When consumers go to Nordstrom's, they know its product quality is high and that someone will really want to help them find what they need. No one at Nordstrom's will say, "It's not my department." The McDonald's and Nordstrom's customer is really paying for convenience, even though it is not listed on the receipt or at the checkout register.

Organizations need to be clear about the tangibles that they provide their customers and what value these add for the customers. These organizations also need to understand what intangibles they are providing their customers and how these impact their customer relationships. Strategic thinking must balance thinking about the intangibles and tangibles. The mission of the organization will be directly impacted by the value that the customer places on what the organization can and cannot do for him or her. The value from the intangibles can be a subtle signal that the marketplace is changing. Such signals could provide the early warning signals that your organization needs in order to reposition itself for the future. As your strategy group looks at this continuum, it should be asking the following questions:

- What are the primary tangibles and intangibles that we provide for our customers?
- How do our customers rate our tangibles and intangibles? What value do they receive from them?
- How do we compare against our competitors in these areas?
- How do we find new needs to provide value for our customers?
- Do we change customer responsibilities into opportunities for our organization?
- Do we really understand our customers, their needs, hopes, desires, and what they want for the future, even if the customers themselves are not aware of them?

### INNOVATION–IMPROVEMENT

Many people believe that the difference between an improvement and an innovation is simply a matter of degree. We believe there is a greater difference, but there is indeed an area of overlap where what is an innovation and what is an improvement cannot be distinguished. To conceptualize the difference, we define improvement as taking something which already exists and making it better. Innovation is defined simply as creating something new. The gray area is when what is old becomes changed into something that is new. Again, herein lies another paradox which may be more of a problem with semantics than with reality.

In the business world, to only continually improve the old can lead to obsolescence. Organizations must work on improvements to products and services and also work on new products and services. Furthermore, organizations can only create new products and services if they are working on creating new knowledge. Organizations must balance technical R&D with concept R&D.

Concept R&D means creating new ideas which can add value to the organization, its stakeholders, or its customers. Concept R&D adds value by helping organizations to rethink existing assumptions and paradigms about how business is conducted and why certain practices are accepted. New concepts are the foundation for new thinking and for new products and services. Only concepts can be changed into new services and products. Concept R&D can help organizations find new ideas that can lead to new products and services. The organization that enlists all of its employees as conceptual thinkers and as producers of new ideas and strategies will surpass the traditional organization where these responsibilities are trusted only to managers. As your strategy group looks at this continuum, it should be asking the following questions:

- What is our mix of innovation and improvement?
- How much time do we spend on concept R&D?
- How do we involve all of our people in producing innovations as well as improvements?
- What are our competitors doing in this area?
- What forces represent our "hidden competition" (new concepts, products or services that might replace our core competencies and value-added activities)?
- What impact could this "hidden competition" have on our organization?

Some general rules and guidelines that will be helpful for you and your planning team to keep in mind are the following:

1. Seek to balance the eight continuum of strategy.
2. Do not confuse means with ends, but recognize that means and ends are interdependent; there is no such thing as the ends justifies the means or vice versa.
3. Strategic planning should be a process, not an event. It is not a once-a-year, three-day planning session.

4. All strategies have pros and cons. Try to understand the limitations and strengths of any strategy you use.
5. Beware of making strategy an end in itself. Always be clear of the end and keep it in mind.
6. Strategy must be a creative process. There is no room for fear or a "My way or the highway" approach. Also, it is not a straight line effort; you must be able to work with a great deal of ambiguity and paradox.
7. Strategies are never independent of the prevailing economic milieu or what the Germans call "Zeitgeist." There is sort of a "Law of Efficient Strategic Planning," something like the "Law of Efficient Market Theory." According to this law, once something is known about the market, everybody gets the same information and it nullifies any real competitive advantage. The same is true with strategic thinking/ planning. Strategies and plans have a definite phase (maybe a curve) where they give maximum competitive advantage. Once an advantage begins to be recognized, everyone jumps on the bandwagon, thus negating the advantage. Always understand what your competitors are doing, but don't mistake the bandwagon for the road to success.

## REFERENCE NOTES

1. For an outstanding critique of strategic planning, including its pitfalls, fallacies, and poor record of performance, see H. Mintzberg's *The Rise and Fall of Strategic Planning* (The Free Press, 1994). Mintzberg describes the confusion among the leading proponents of strategic planning concerning its use and even a definition of the process. He shows that most research supports his premise that strategic planning has become a bureaucratic process and that "planning" and "plans" have taken precedence over thinking, creativity, and intuition. Planning in organizations has tended to institutionalize the status quo and drive out change and innovation.

2. For perhaps the best overall planning system yet to be devised, see Yoji Akao's book, *Hoshin Kanri: Policy Deployment for Successful TQM* (Productivity Press, 1991). The Japanese have been using an integrated system of planning and implementation since the early 1970s. Their system has been tested and refined. Nevertheless, it is very complex and should not represent the starting point for an organization that has never had an effective strategic thinking/planning process. Furthermore, the Japanese system is weak on the intuition, innova-

tion, and creativity that is essential to strategic thinking. The eight continuums address this weakness.

3. See G. Hamel and C.K. Prahalad's book, *Competing for the Future* (Harvard Business Press, 1994), for a more thorough understanding of core competencies as well as a number of breakthrough strategies for "seizing control of your industry and creating the markets of tomorrow." Core competencies is a great concept, but like many others in the marketplace, it has been oversold as a panacea and a recipe for success.

4. Tzu, S. *The Art of War*, translated by S. B. Griffith (Oxford University Press, 1963). Writing in 500 BC, Sun Tzu is perhaps the most interesting and persuasive advocate of strategic thinking. He has been rediscovered by legions of business planners and business writers.

5. Ackoff, R.L. *Creating the Corporate Future* (John Wiley and Sons, 1981).

6. Remarks from personal correspondence with the author.

# Chapter 10

# Deeper Organizations

For many years, it was common to find corporate mission statements proclaiming an organization's desire to be the "best in the industry." With the advent of Total Quality Management (TQM), many organizations began to understand that a more important focus was to concentrate on being "better and better" and not necessarily to worry about being the "best." Many quality experts felt that a focus on being better and better (continually improving) constituted the heart of TQM. Today, many organizations have dropped the term TQM in favor of the term "Continuous Quality Improvement" (CQI) or just "Continuous Improvement."

To go from trying to be the "best" to trying to be "better and better" necessitates a basic fundamental change in attitudes, values, and concepts. It takes years for organizations to understand and implement this major paradigm shift. Organizations that can make these changes will add decades to their organizational life spans. Organizations that cannot become more responsive and adaptive will not survive in the twenty-first-century marketplace.

There is an even more significant and profound challenge facing American corporations, a challenge so radical that success could translate into the survival of an organization for centuries, not just decades. That challenge to corporations is to become deeper and deeper. This is a challenge of depth rather than breadth.

Organizations may make many changes in structure. They can become more fluid, more flexible, more adaptable, or more dynamic. They can align themselves by becoming more decentralized, more organic, more holistic, or more Holonic. They can change from hierarchical structures to starburst, spider web, cluster, team-based, or networked structures, but these are all superficial changes. All of these changes are merely methods that help an organization to accommodate and adapt to a new business environment. The deep organization fundamentally controls its environment, shaping and modifying its environment at will.

In the history of the human race, the most successful organizations of all time have been religious and educational institutions. They have the longest records of survival and have touched more lives than any other organizations. They are still considered by many to be the most important institutions in any society. Fundamentally, these are deep organizations. It is not just their religious or educational orientations that make them deep organizations. Any organization can be a deep organization. A deep organization is one that adds long-term value to its stakeholders, employees, customers, and society. A deep organization is not merely profitable or successful. Many organizations are profitable but do not provide long-term value to anyone. We have all heard of wealthy people who live twisted, sad lives. Some organizations conduct their business in the same way. They seem to lack scruples or any type of humanistic considerations for either their customers or society.

Even organizations that are scrupulous and ethical often are only able to achieve temporary success. Having achieved success, they soon see it slip away. Such companies may be labeled as having the "Best Buy" stocks or being the "Fastest Growing." They may even make the *Fortune 500* list. Companies highlighted in Peters and Waterman's book, *In Search of Excellence*, demonstrate this point. Less than ten years after Peters and Waterman wrote their book, many of these "excellent" companies were having financial difficulties.

Research shows that the average life span of a *Fortune 500* Company is about fifty years. There is a reason for the early death of most businesses: many organizations are shallow. A "shallow" organization is one that measures survival in terms of years rather than centuries. A shallow organization may achieve temporary success by selling pet rocks or hula hoops, but it soon finds it difficult, if not impossible, to repeat such success. It may achieve success by selling products that have little or no long-term benefits to humanity or society. Indeed, such products may even be harmful to people or the environment. The "shallow" organization feels no need to connect to the deeper needs of humanity. It is like a noxious weed rather than an edible plant. In time, people will find a way to exterminate it. Deep organizations sink strong roots into the soil. Like the giant redwood trees, the deep organization can exist for centuries. Deep organizations achieve success not by merely selling a product or service, they also achieve success by meeting moral and ethical obligations to shareholders, customers, employees, and society.

Anyone thinking that this all sounds very "spiritual" or "moralistic" is experiencing one of the boundaries of the "old" business paradigm. Business schools have taught for many years that profits and "deepness" do not go together. Harvard MBA programs do not teach managers how to build "deep" organizations. Managers are not challenged by Executive Management Programs to worry about how they can make organizations "deeper." MBA students may have to take a course in ethics, but ethical thinking is not "deepness." In fact, ethical thinking is only one aspect of the deep organization. Even morality is only one aspect of "deepness." Ethics and morality constitute part of being a deep organization, but the deep organization succeeds by balancing many different dimensions. Few organizations worry about the need to achieve such balance. Furthermore, the deep organization challenges itself not just to be better and better, but also to be deeper and deeper. It is much more difficult to become deeper and deeper than it is to become better and better.

If we told you that we knew a person who was very successful, you might ask how that person became successful. If we replied, "He/she made a great deal of money in a very short period of time," you would probably ask, "How?" again. If we answered that he/she had robbed a bank, your opinion of this person would probably plummet. However, even if we replied that he/she made the money quite honestly, this wouldn't necessarily cause you to strongly admire this person or to feel that he or she was a great person. But suppose we described a person who was honest, caring, thoughtful, open, consistent, flexible, tolerant, ethical, focused, and wise. You would no doubt have more admiration for such an individual than for anyone who had robbed a bank or even made a fortune on the stock market. Your admiration for this person would far surpass the level of admiration you felt for the "very successful" person.

What if we combined the two people that we have described? In other words, what if we added very successful and wealthy to the list of noted virtues, creating someone who is wealthy, wise, caring, and tolerant? Sadly, it is hard for us to conceive of such people. Even the terms sound contradictory. We don't usually think that the two sets of qualities can go together. This is an important point. As long as we think that the qualities of success and virtue are mutually exclusive in people, we will continue to believe that such characteristics are mutually exclusive in organizations. If, however, we can unite them in organizations, we can create organizations that are successful, profitable, honest, caring, thoughtful, open, consistent, flexible, tolerant, ethical, focused, and wise. Such organizations will measure success in centuries rather than mere years or even decades.

Deep organizations are essential for our economic future, as well as for the economic future of the world. Deep organizations are sustainable and contribute to long-term economic growth and development that is socially and environmentally compatible. They create sustainable economic development rather than short-term economic prosperity. As the issue of sustainable economic development becomes ever more important, we must ask if it is possible to achieve such development with disposable organizations. If even the best organizations only survive some fifty-odd years, how can we develop a long-term, sustainable economic system that is capable of adding value to the world for centuries to come?

There are hundreds of examples of organizations that meet the standard for being labeled "shallow." These organizations have given us thalidomide, DDT, fluorocarbons, the Dalkon Shield, silicone breast implants, asbestos insulation, "sugar-enhanced" foods, and lead-based petrochemicals. We are all familiar with many of these products and their harmful side effects. However, such products only mask the underlying business practices that lead to "shallowness." Dr. Deming labeled some of these practices as the "Seven Deadly Diseases of Management." He repeatedly warned that such practices would "kill" an organization. If practices and policies that lead to "shallowness" can kill organizations, then those practices which lead to "deepness" must become fundamental for organizations that want to achieve long-term survival and success.

There are ten key dimensions that leaders can use to help create a deep organization. Some organizations are outstanding on a few of these dimensions, some are outstanding on several, but few are outstanding on all of the dimensions. By enhancing organizational performance on each of these ten key dimensions, organizations that are already successful in the marketplace will ensure long-term success, respect, and prosperity.

Figure 10.1 shows a starplot diagram with the ten dimensions that contribute to making a deep organization. The starplot has also been called a radar diagram, a spider diagram, and a glyph. It is one of the seven Japanese management and planning tools. This plot can be used in conjunction with the following descriptions and questions to

FIGURE 10.1. Deeper Organizations

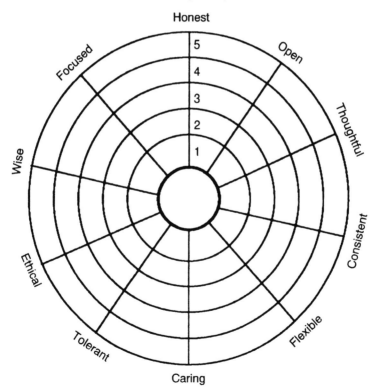

help your organization start thinking about this issue. You may plot your progress on the starplot, utilizing the questions asked at the end of each section in this chapter.

You could do a random sample of customers, employees, and managers, asking them to rate your organization on each of the ten dimensions. The farther from the center that you are, the better you are doing. The starplot can be used to plot the responses from the different stakeholders and also to plot changes over time. Stakeholder responses could be plotted in different colors. A new starplot could be made each year and compared from one year to the next to see improvements.

## *DIMENSION ONE: HONESTY*

The characteristic of honesty tops the list of almost every survey of key management traits. If honesty is so important to us as human beings, should not our organizations also be measured on the trait of honesty? Should we not ask ourselves how deep our organization's honesty is? Superficially, honesty means giving people their money's worth. If we go deeper into the dimension of honesty, we find that there is a whole set of issues that we often neglect in our dealings with employees and customers. We may avoid research that shows our product in a bad light, we may ignore complaints from certain customers because they might cost us money, or we might not tell employees the whole truth about financial events. A deeply honest organization will act and look much different from a superficially honest organization. Key questions to ask as you explore this dimension are listed here:

- Is your organization honest with employees, customers, and suppliers?
- Do people know where they stand in the organization or must they play a guessing game to find out?
- Does your organization admit when it is wrong to customers, suppliers, and employees?
- Are you always as honest as you could or should be?

## DIMENSION TWO: OPENNESS

Recently, President Clinton and Secretary of Labor Robert Reich facilitated a joint business, government, and labor conference called "The Future of the American Workplace." One participant (formerly a so-called "blue-collar worker") spoke about the open management at his organization. He noted that in the old system, most information was secret, which kept workers uninformed and out of touch with the realities of the business world. Under new leadership, his organization had decided that there would be no secrets, that everything would be open. It was interesting to note that both President Clinton and Secretary Reich kept referring to this new and important concept of "openness." Openness itself is a new key concept that in its own way is every bit as important and profound as the concept of Quality or Continuous Improvement.

If you apply the concept of Quality in a shallow, traditional way, it will probably not change much in your business. However, organizations that have spent time defining and trying to understand the implications of Quality have reaped huge rewards. The same rewards can accrue from the time and attention spent trying to understand and define the concept of openness, as well as for each of the ten dimensions. If you merely pass over them or say your organization is already "open," you will be like the hundreds of organizations that maintain, "We don't need a quality effort because we already have quality." The following are key questions to ask as you explore this dimension:

- Do all employees have access to the information they need to do their jobs?
- Are major decisions made secretly behind closed doors, or are decisions made openly?
- Do employees get to see the big picture or are they kept in the dark?
- Are we as open as we could be with all of our stakeholders? If no, why not?
- Do we keep secrets in our organization?

## *DIMENSION THREE: THOUGHTFULNESS*

The thoughtful organization is just that–full of thoughts and ideas. It is an organization that values thinking ahead as well as thinking for the sake of thinking. It measures success by what it has learned and is learning. There are no "mistakes" in the thoughtful organization, only lessons to be learned. As we go deeper into thoughtfulness, we think about our stakeholders and our employees. We ask how we can make things better for them and we involve them in these discussions. The thoughtful organization plans ahead and regards continual firefighting as a failure of thought. The thoughtful organization thinks about its purpose, mission, and vision often, not just once in a while. They are made meaningful by the time, attention, and effort that go into thinking about them. The thoughtful organization is a contemplative one that is as interested in thinking about itself as it is in thinking about the world. However, it realizes that it must balance inward-looking strategies with outward-looking strategies; it must balance thinking with feeling and doing. Key questions to ask as you explore this dimension are the following:

- Does your organization plan ahead or is it always reacting to crises?
- Does your organization try to see the big picture?
- Are decisions made in a systematic manner using all available data?
- Does the organization value learning?
- Does the organization foster a continuous learning environment?

## *DIMENSION FOUR: CONSISTENCY*

Consistency relates to the concept of reliability. Do you do what you say you are going to do and do you do it reliably and faithfully? Consistency is also related to the concept of fairness. A consistent organization is one that applies rules and privileges to all. It is one where the concept of variation is understood. Consistency and the concept of variation are closely related. Unless you understand the concept of "normal distribution" and "statistical variation," you cannot avoid the variation and inconsistencies caused by bonus systems, pay-for-performance plans, and piecework systems. Organizations spend a great deal of time and effort on policies and procedures, but seldom evaluate how consistently and reliably they are administered. In many organizations, the inconsistent application of these policies is a major cause of poor morale and grievances. The concept of consistency is related to the issue of equity.

In an equitable organization, people are treated the same regardless of sex, age, race, or religious beliefs. It is a sad commentary on American organizations that one repeatedly reads about companies that transgress in these areas. We should all be ashamed of this occurrence in a country founded on democratic values.

The concept of consistency is also related to the goals and objectives of the organization. Do the various departments share and align themselves around these goals or are individual chimneys and fiefdoms rampant in the organization? Many organizations create departments that are so narrowly focused (hence the name chimneys or smokestacks) that they act as though they have little or nothing in common with the rest of the organization. Some areas grab as much power as they can and create "fiefdoms" where power and influence reign supreme. Other fiefdoms and their members are treated as potential competitors or allies, often with little regard for customers. There is room for a multiplicity of values in an organization. In fact, if you create an organization that respects diversity, you will create an organization with diverse values. The key is to ensure that personal values are expressed in such a way that benefits both customers and stakeholders. Key questions to ask as you explore this dimension are listed here:

- Are policies and procedures applied uniformly to all employees?
- Do policies change to fit the whim or convenience of a few?
- Are department goals in sync with each other and with overall organizational goals?

## *DIMENSION FIVE: FLEXIBILITY*

Flexibility entails the ability to adapt rapidly when needed, to adjust and deal with the unpredictable and the chaotic, not taking rigid positions that will lead to stagnation or paralysis. France's Maginot Line in World War I provides a good example of organizational rigidity and stagnation. The French army set up a line of "impenetrable" defenses that it assumed the German army would never be able to get through. The French were right; the German army could not get through, so it went around the Maginot Line.

Flexibility is a state pertaining to both mind and body, process and structure. An organization can be flexible in structure but rigid in process. It may be creative in developing new products, but seldom looks at new ways to organize work or production. Flexibility is related to creativity and innovation. A flexible organization is open to new ideas and new concepts. It is willing to take the risk of trying new adventures and new ways of doing things. It is not an organization where people advance or are listened to only on the basis of seniority or status in the organization.

Flexibility is also related to training and knowledge. A flexible organization has people who can do a wide variety of tasks and are imbued with knowledge and talents from a wide array of disciplines. Flexibility is related to diversity. In an ecological system, the richer the genetic diversity, the better the chance a species has to adapt to change and, thus, survive. A diverse workforce, with people who have widely differing views and ways of looking at the world, is much more likely to help the organization survive than one where everybody thinks alike. The WASP Club and "Old Boys' Club" are prescriptions for early organizational death.

Ralph Waldo Emerson once said, "A foolish consistency is the hobgoblin of little minds." Flexibility means balancing the concept of consistency with the need for inconsistency. This is no contradiction, merely a fact of life. Long-term success is a question of dynamic and strategic balance between a number of issues necessary for survival. Quality must be balanced with quantity, value must be balanced with cost, and so on. In the same manner, each of the ten dimensions must be creatively and strategically balanced with each other. This entails an ongoing process, not an event. You will never "get it right." There is no "better and better." In this game, it is simply a question of deeper and deeper. As you go deeper into each concept, the question of balance resolves itself. Issues that seem contradictory at one level will appear completely compatible at another level. The following key questions to ask as you explore this dimension:

- How does your organization adapt to the changing times?
- How does your organization accept and nourish diversity?
- Does your organization value flexibility and new ways of doing things?
- Is risk taking rewarded or punished in your organization?
- How do you distinguish between special causes and common causes in terms of understanding whether something is a unique problem or a system problem?

## *DIMENSION SIX: CARING*

There is a part in Dicken's *A Christmas Carol* where Ebenezer Scrooge says to Marley, "You were always a good man of business." Marley thunders back, "Mankind was my business!" Dr. Deming exemplified this aspect of "caring." Several of Dr. Deming's 14 principles had to do with how we treat people in our organizations: Drive out Fear; Institute Pride of Work; and Eliminate Slogans and Exhortations. Dr. Deming repeatedly said that if you hire someone, you have made a commitment to that person. Thus, you have a responsibility to help the person succeed. If you have a responsibility to a person, you must care about that person. How can you discharge a responsibility to people if you don't care about them as people? In the shallow organization, people are merely a commodity to be bought and sold when it is convenient. Since the organization is not going to be around for long, why worry about people? People are merely another disposable resource. This is shallow thinking, not deep thinking.

In some "new style" organizations, managers are beginning to understand that people are more than mere resources. People are creative and can think, which are things that machines, robots, and even computers can't do. Only people can find ways to add new and more value for customers. Nevertheless, if the only reason we care about our employees is because they add "value" to the production process, we are still viewing people from a strictly utilitarian approach. "We will keep people because they add value" can easily be changed to "We will keep people as long as they add value." This might be a little better than the old way of treating employees as "disposable," but it is still not "caring" about them. At best, it is caring in the most shallow sense imaginable. It is an eye for an eye approach. You do for me and I'll do for you. Granted, there is a mutual responsibility on the part of employee and employer, but can we not discharge our responsibilities while still caring about each other?

Sadly, many people and organizations do not really know how to care. "Caring" is a term we talk about often, but seldom associate with the working world. Dr. Deming associated it when he said that people are entitled to experience joy in work. He noted that in America, we do not believe that meaningful activity, fun, and learning can take place in the same environment. Thus, we go to school to learn and must be serious—no fooling around please! We go to work to do meaningful activity, but are not expected to learn much; we are expected to know it all when we are hired and, please, no fooling around here either. When we are home on a Saturday, that is the time for fooling around, but please don't learn anything or do any meaningful useful activity because it's Saturday and we are supposed to take it easy.

Dr. Deming wondered why we could not unite all three activities in the workplace, school, and home. Why couldn't schools be places where meaningful work, play, and learning were all united? Why can't the workplace and home also unite these three important activities? When we begin to explore the deeper implications of caring about people, we will begin to see the necessity of accomplishing this unity. Can you imagine the life of a person who, no matter where he/she is, can say that he/she is accomplishing a meaningful, useful activity while having fun and learning something? Wouldn't you like to be that person? Key questions to ask as you explore this dimension are the following:

- Does your organization care about the well-being of employees?
- Does the organization care about its customers?
- Do your employees feel that their work is meaningful and useful?
- Are your employees learning and having fun while they work?
- Does your organization demonstrate with actions that it really cares about its long-term contribution to society?

## DIMENSION SEVEN: TOLERANCE

I will always remember a quote I once read that said, "The test of courage comes when we are in the minority; the test of tolerance comes when we are in the majority."[1] Tolerance is a willingness to accept variation. It is focusing on the process, not blaming the people. Tolerance accepts errors and weaknesses and, instead of assigning blame, looks for ways to strengthen and educate. It relates to flexibility because tolerant people are able to deal with people who are different and who have different needs. Tolerance relates to diversity because it understands that differences are not necessarily deficits. To be physically challenged may mean that other abilities and skills are heightened. To be young confers some advantages and to be old confers other advantages. Tolerance accepts differences and inconsistencies in terms of work habits, work patterns, and learning styles. Tolerance recognizes that a bell-shaped curve exists for most phenomena and does not try to force people or events into the same mold. Key questions to ask as you explore this dimension are listed here:

- Does your organization blame people for mistakes or does it study the process and system?
- Is your organization tolerant and fair to those who make mistakes?
- Does the organization allow some slack to people when special problems arise?
- Does management accept coresponsibility for helping people overcome difficulties and problems?

## *DIMENSION EIGHT: ETHICS*

Ethics is described in the dictionary as "The discipline dealing with what is good and bad and with moral duty and obligation." An ethical organization is concerned with what is good and bad as well as with moral duty and obligation. We know that we can make money without being concerned with ethics, at least in the short run. We have countless examples of businesses that have proved this point. The major question for many business people is, "Can we be both profitable and ethical?" Some organizations have proved that you can do both. Those organizations will outlast those that do not balance the two concerns. Furthermore, it is a tragic waste of time, effort, and resources to separate the two. There is a common saying that what goes around comes around. If we create products and goods that ignore fundamental issues of good and bad and right and wrong, we will only be asking for trouble in the future. A concern with ethics is not and should not be thought of as a "luxury." Ethics is critical to the long-term survival of an organization and of our society as a whole. Key questions to ask as you explore this dimension are the following:

- Does your organization consider the long-term value of its products and services?
- Are customers and consumer groups really listened to?
- Is the sole goal of your organization to make as much money as possible in as short a period of time as possible?
- How does your organization deal with the negative impacts of its products and services?
- How does your organization deal with the question of social good and ethics?

## *DIMENSION NINE: WISDOM*

In Webster's dictionary, it is noted that the term "wise" suggests "great understanding of people and of situations and unusual discernment and judgment in dealing with them." We all know that you don't become wise just by reading the encyclopedia or getting a college degree. Unfortunately, age alone does not seem to make one wiser either. Wisdom seems to come from a combination of both knowledge and experience, perhaps tempered by caring, tolerance, thoughtfulness, honesty, and openness. It has been said that "knowledge helps you to make a living, but wisdom helps you to make a life." When it comes to wisdom, we seldom, if ever, associate it with an organization. How many wise organizations come to mind? Is this only because we associate wisdom with people? Even if wisdom is usually associated with people, could we not create wise organizations?

At one time in history, an educational institution would probably have been considered to be a "wise" organization. People who came out of schools and academies in the past were generally considered as knowledgeable, if not "wise" individuals. "Doctor" was a title that meant "learned person." Today, many schools give graduates credentials and diplomas for doing little more than showing up for four years or parroting back the answers that the instructors want to hear. You certainly don't get a degree by thinking for yourself or expressing original thoughts. This is because our educational institutions have failed to adapt to the newly emerging era. They have lost flexibility; today, few would consider them as repositories for wisdom. Nevertheless, all organizations have the potential to become wise or, at least, wiser. As with quality, wisdom is more a state of mind than it is an absolute measurable quantity. In most cases, wisdom is perhaps best defined by the customer. Thus, a survey on "wise" organizations would ask customers what values they think constitute a "wise" organization. Answers to what constitutes a wise organization would suggest many of the topics and issues that we have been talking about. A "wise" business organization is able to balance all of these dimensions, make a profit, and satisfy its customers. Key questions to ask as you explore this dimension are the following:

- Would your customers describe your organization as "wise"? Why or why not?
- What would wisdom mean in your business?

- Do you provide conditions to encourage the integration of knowledge, experience, and values in your organization? How?
- What else could your organization do to become "wiser?"

## DIMENSION TEN: FOCUS

Focus relates to having a sense of purpose and being able to stick to it. Vision and focus are flip sides of the coin. Many organizations seek a grand vision with which to rally employees to the cause. By concentrating so much on finding a vision, organizations often neglect or forget the important aspect of focus. Focus is the discipline to stick to your vision through the many trials and tribulations that litter the pathway. It is not enough to have a great vision if you are continually letting obstacles divert you from the path. Abraham Zaleznik, in his book, *Learning Leadership,*[2] said,

> While much is made of vision in leadership, too little may be made of focus. The ability to remain grounded in reality, and to focus attention on the elements of advantage in any economic situation, and to remain committed to allowing the elements of advantage to work in one's favor, probably accounts for as much success in business as vision. To foresee a future is vision. To understand and apply focus is clarity of thinking and perseverance.

Exploring the concept of focus in depth, going deeper and deeper in thinking about this concept, can lead to some unique insights for all businesses. Key questions to ask as you explore this dimension are listed here:

- Does your organization have a clear purpose?
- Is the organization able to stay on target?
- Does everyone in the organization share the purpose?
- How deep is your focus and how do you create a deeper and deeper focus?

These thoughts and ideas should help you examine your organization and think about your business in a different light. If form follows function, then it makes sense to think about these issues before you deal with the issues of how your organization should be structured. Many organizations are more concerned with form than with substance. They endlessly redo the organizational chart and change managers from one department to another. Such practices ignore more important underlying problems. It has been said that the character of people can be told by the visions they have and by the values that they stand for. The same will one day be used to measure our social and economic organizations. History, society, and the global marketplace will judge economic organizations by the visions those organizations had and by the values they stood for. Those organizations that stand for nothing or that are shallow and trivial will be easily forgotten.

## REFERENCE NOTES

1. I remember reading this in the *Reader's Digest* Famous Quotes section several years ago, but have since been unable to remember or find the origin of this quote.

2. Zaleznik, A. *Learning Leadership*. Chicago: Bonus Books, Inc., 1993.

# Chapter 11

# Crime and Quality

What do continuous quality improvement and crime have to do with each other? You have probably never seen these two topics together at any conferences and you probably have seen few lawyers, judges, or police sporting total quality banners. In 1989, I published an article in *Judicature* that described this connection and called for the adoption of a quality approach to the problem of criminal justice in America. This was well before the O.J. Simpson trial or the Menendez brothers' trials. The article received a great deal of interest, but little or no action on its premises. It has taken the Simpson trial to make Americans realize how ludicrous the criminal justice system has become. The arguments in this chapter can help point the way to a new judicial system, one that provides equal justice to all regardless of race or economic background.

Crime seems to be a national epidemic, drug use is greater than ever, the "just say no" campaign is just another slogan effort, trials have become judicial farces and mockeries of criminal justice and, while some reports say that violent crime is declining, no one in his/her right mind would walk in any American inner city at night alone and feel comfortable. Surveys consistently show us that more people are afraid to walk the streets, juvenile crime is more violent, the number of people in prisons is still increasing faster then we can build prisons, and the visible cost of crime is about 300 billion dollars per year and continues rising. If Dr. Deming was still alive, I am sure that he would add crime to his list of seven deadly diseases of industry. Crime is, in fact, the eighth and deadliest of all deadly diseases. The cost of crime is born not just by every man, woman, and child in society, but by every organization and business in America.

## THE "MODERN" CRIMINAL JUSTICE PARADIGM

In America, we have people who break laws (criminals), people who catch criminals (police officers), people who defend and prosecute criminals (lawyers), people who decide on sentences for criminals (judges and juries), and people who oversee the care and feeding of criminals and keep them off the streets (wardens and correctional people). People who break certain laws are tried according to laws and guidelines that prescribe certain punishments and retribution. The victims are a relative nonentity in the system, since the only thing that matters is whether justice was prescribed in accordance with the law. In this system, every crime is investigated and every accused person is accorded a trial with respect to being able to prove or disprove the charges against him/her. If convicted, the guilty party is assigned a sentence to "correct" his/her deviant behavior, which may or may not involve being sent to a correctional institution for a specified period of time. Admittedly, this is a fairly simplistic picture of the system, since there are, of course, many other players in the process. However, it is sufficient for our purposes, and does in fact reflect the core functions and purpose of the American criminal justice system. Keep in mind that we have addressed the system as it is supposed to work, not as it often does. All too often, the police and lawyers make mistakes, the judges and juries appear to be swayed by subjective biases, the social service and correctional institutions are unable to help "correct" deviance, and the public is apathetic about crime—until it comes to their neighborhoods. Even then, the public soon learns to effect a "barricades" mentality, protecting themselves behind locks, neighborhood watches, or gated communities.

## THE CONTINUOUS QUALITY IMPROVEMENT MODEL OF CRIME

Using continuous quality improvement as a model or metaphor for crime helps us to see the system in a different light. Instead of criminals, the people who commit crimes would be viewed as system "defects." The police officers are actually inspectors in the system and as with all inspection, add little or no "value" to the process. Lawyers and judges are the system managers and, in this respect, are analogous to the old-time supervisors whose job was to take names and "kick butt." Lawyers and judges help decide the penalties for violating "workplace" rules. The "defects" are then shipped to warehouses (prisons) for either storage or rework (rework is called rehabilitation and is less than 20 percent effective). Thus, the warden and his staff are really warehouse people who must continually find space for the inventory and keep it in good condition. Of course, inventory depreciates with the passage of time. Even more problematic is the fact that some "defects" are deemed unworkable and must be destroyed. This costs even more money and lowers the overall productivity of the system, not that it is very productive to begin with.

One of the worst parts about the warehouse system is that we are running out of space. As more prisoners receive longer sentences, we can no longer find a place to keep them all. John Philips, the District Attorney in Stockton, California, has told police chiefs that he cannot afford to prosecute certain crimes and will have to let the offenders go free (stated in *Time* magazine, May 17, 1993). This type of story is repeating itself all over the country.

## SENTENCING

The purpose of sentencing is to deter crime. This has been the purpose throughout recorded history. For the last twenty or so years, the emphasis has been on both stricter sentences and mandatory sentencing guidelines. Politicians on both sides hurl epithets at their opposition, accusing them of being "soft" on crime. Afraid of begin labeled as "soft on crime," politicians outdo each other in calls for longer and "tougher" sentences. To be "soft" on crime is the equivalent of the kiss of death to any aspiring politician. It does not matter that he/she knows stricter sentences and longer sentences do not deter crime; no politician in his/her right mind would dare bring up such a fact.

Sentencing guidelines are somewhat analogous to specifications in industry. However, consider what happens when a system's capabilities (the control limits) are outside of the system's specifications.

The system is not capable and will produce lots of defects and higher rework costs, no matter what you think should happen. Furthermore, tightening the specifications will only make matters worse. Of course, if the system is out of control then it does not matter where we put the specifications (sentences) because we have no way of knowing where they should be put anyway. In a completely random arbitrary system, there is no way of telling what the tendency of the system is and, hence, no way to set control limits or any other types of specifications. Many people feel that this is the case with crime in America, that it is totally out of control. In the usual sense of the word, they are right, but from the perspective of continuous quality improvement they are dead wrong.

## CONTROL SYSTEMS AND CRIME

It might surprise you to know that most, if not all, crime in America is not "out of control," if we mean "control" in the sense that the system is stable, measurable, and fairly predictable. For instance, consider murders or homicides. Give or take a few percentage points, the data suggests that for any given month, in most large American cities, we can predict the murder rate with a high degree of accuracy. This is similar to knowing the defect rate on an assembly line. We can't know for sure which items will be defective, but if the system is in control, we can predict the defect rate with a high degree of accuracy. This is a very important point because, if it is true, then we do not need to do 100 percent sampling. In fact, such sampling will tell us less about how to improve the system than random sampling will.

Imagine the implications. If the murder system in America is in control (predictable), then inspecting and investigating every murder is not needed to improve the system. Furthermore, it would only be tampering (and drive up costs) since it is treating each common cause factor as though it is a special cause. In quality improvement, we learn that investigating each defect in a system that is in control is a waste of time, money, effort, and will not improve the system anyway. Why should this not be true in the case of murders, robberies, rapes, or any other crimes? Have the last fifty years of murder investigations in the United States or anywhere else improved the murder rate? Has increased incarceration and longer sentences slowed the growth in crime? All the available crime data and FBI statistics say it has not. In fact, over the last twenty years or so, it has become decidedly worse throughout America. One hundred percent inspection does not work in industry and it does not work in crime. As unbelievable as it might seem, we cannot improve the criminal justice system by catching every crook, murderer, and rapist in America and putting them away for the rest of their lives. We can no more improve the criminal justice system by such tactics than we can create higher quality or lower defect rates in a manufacturing process by the use of 100 percent inspection. And this assumes that it is possible to catch every "defect" and keep him/her out of the system forever.

## *REDESIGNING THE CRIMINAL JUSTICE SYSTEM*

It makes many of us feel better to know that some "lowlife" has received severe and immediate punishment. However, the data shows that this does not improve the system. It also does not decrease the recidivism rate, or make adequate restitution to most victims. What the present system does do very well is keep us in a situation where we now have over one million people in jail at an average cost of $35,000 per year per convict. This means that over $35 billion dollars a year is spent just for incarceration alone. This does not count the losses to society and victims or the costs of police, lawyers, probation offices, hearing boards, juries, and judges. We cannot afford this system anymore. It is the same system that was bankrupting American industry and forcing us to be less competitive than Japan. We need a realization that the criminal justice system in America is broke. If we can accept this fact, then we can start a movement to redesign and continually improve the criminal justice system in this country so that it provides justice, not just laws, for the good of all Americans. If we don't do it soon, none of us will be safe in our homes.

I was asked to speak at a conference on correctional procedures shortly after my first article on crime was published. It was a conference attended primarily by corrections people and people with relatives in jail. Some had read the article; most were unsure what I was advocating. I spoke on the same concepts I have described above. No one really understood the article or the talk because the quality concepts were foreign to them. The corrections people assumed that I was simply another critic of the prisons and "soft" on crime—anyone criticizing the "enforcers" of the system must be "soft" on crime. The relatives of prisoners were also disappointed because I was not advocating early release, better rehabilitation programs, or some other sort of offender benefits. It appeared that I was against both sides. In truth, I was not taking sides. So neither side was particularly interested in what I had to say or what continuous quality improvement concepts had to offer the criminal justice system.

I have since been challenged many times to state how I would improve the criminal justice system. I can offer the tools and concepts to redesign the system and institute continuous quality improvement. But without the help of the people in the system, no amount of outside "expertise" will be enough to make the major changes needed in the criminal justice system or any other system.

The ultimate goal is to reduce crime rates and decrease the cost of running the criminal justice system in this country. The first thing I would do is start a "redesign" group in each city in America. Each group would be composed of legislators, judges, lawyers, police officers, and correctional officers. Each group would be trained in the concepts of Total Quality and would be charged with collecting or developing the data to help it understand its individual processes and to see the justice system as an integrated whole. The "redesign" group would be responsible for identifying recommendations that would optimize the system, rather then just deal with each part separately.

Second, the group would need to reach consensus that the primary goal of a justice system was not retribution but continual improvement. What does it matter to the "next" victim that last week's murderer is now in jail? The focus of the system must be on prevention, not detection, inspection, and rehabilitation. There are, of course, emotional issues that have to be taken into consideration, but continuous improvement must be based on the needs of present and future customers. This means trying to eliminate defects for the future by improving the process as far upstream as possible. In manufacturing, we have tried to stop placing blame on people for defects and, instead, have empowered people to take responsibility for their work. Responsibility must be substituted for blame in the criminal justice system.

Finally, we must focus on the whole system by using systematic data to identify the major factors that contribute to crime. Massive citywide projects in every state in the country should be started to identify cause and effect relationships between proposed solutions and outcomes. Can this be done? Is it possible to understand crime as a system? Many experts already have some of the answers. For instance, the data clearly says that the "system" is part of the problem.

One way the system is to blame is by manufacturing and distributing guns and weapons on a scale that is unprecedented in the civilized world. We have more murders per capita than any other developed country in the world. We also have the most handguns per capita in the world. The correlation to any intelligent person would suggest some sort of a relationship. Can anyone show that an increase in handguns has led to a decrease in crime or murders? Guns are necessary in a society that does not feel safe and where no one trusts the system. I am not suggesting that guns cause the high crime rate. I am suggesting that handgun possession escalates the murder rate. However, citizens feel the need to possess handguns when they don't trust the legal system to protect them from potentially violent situations. Thus, the increase in handgun possession is both a cause of violent crime (murders) and an effect of increasing crime rates. I would not try to restrict the distribution of handguns until people felt that they could trust the system to protect them. If we can get a safe, dependable criminal justice system, most people will willingly give up their handguns.

We also know that there is a relationship between crime and unemployment, between poverty and crime, between pornography and crime, between TV and crime, between alcoholism and crime, and between drugs and crime. Again, these are all system problems. It is naive to view the problem of crime as monocausal and to think that any one solution will fix the problem. Such simplistic theorizing leads to fruitless arguments about why some people who are poor don't become criminals, or why some people who have guns don't kill other people. This is a lot like asking why some items on an assembly line are not defects. No doubt, the system works some of the time, but does it work often enough and consistently enough that we trust it?

To reduce the crime rate, we must focus on the overall criminal justice system. We must collect data and analyze the data in a valid statistical manner. We must be willing to spend the time and effort to identify cause and effect relationships and to test theories in the Shewhart manner of Plan-Do-Check-Act. When legislators, lawyers, judges, prison officials, and police officers are working side by side to accomplish these tasks, we will see the beginning of the end of crime in America.

The following paraphrases Deming's 14 points for the criminal justice system in America.

1. Create constancy of purpose toward improvement of society and service, with the aim to reduce crime, to stay productive, and to provide a safe environment.
2. Adopt the new philosophy. We are in a new economic era. Leaders in the criminal justice system must awaken to the challenge, must learn their responsibilities, and must take on the leadership for changing the entire system from retribution to prevention.
3. Eliminate the need for police and prisons to catch and remove defects from society. Fix the process by creating a society which balances rights and responsibilities and equity and equality.
4. Minimize total cost through the sharing of resources by all customers and suppliers in the system and working together in long-term relationships of loyalty and trust.
5. Improve constantly and forever the criminal justice system and thus constantly decrease costs to victims and societies.
6. Institute training that will help make criminals a productive part of society.
7. Institute leadership that helps those in the system to do a better job. Eliminate the old-style hierarchical management practices in all crime agencies. Develop a sense of customer between crime agencies and society.
8. Drive out fear so that everyone in the system may work together for the good of society. The court system must be

changed so that victims do not get treated as though they are the guilty parties. Minorities and women are second-class citizens in the criminal justice system.

9. Break down barriers between all parts of the criminal justice system. The courts, police, and prisons must all work together for the good of society.

10. Eliminate slogans and exhortations such as "Get tough on crime," "Just say no," and the "War on Drugs." Such exhortations do nothing to reduce crime.

11. Eliminate quotas and numerical goals for all workers in the criminal justice system. The only goal should be the systematic and continuous improvement of all processes in the criminal justice system.

12. Remove barriers that rob those in the criminal justice system of their pride of work. The system abounds with negative stereotypes of law enforcement officials. Changing the role of the job from detection to prevention would help to erase some of these barriers.

13. Institute a vigorous program of education and self-improvement for all those in the system, criminals as well as employees.

14. Put everybody in the system to work to accomplish the transformation of the American criminal justice system.

# PART IV:
# INCLUSION

Inclusion is the act of including. It means to make something a part of some whole or to contain something. It is teamwork, shared resources, open communication, cooperation, respect for diversity, shared vision, common values, broad-band job descriptions, dialogue, win-win, and all one world rolled into one tidy value. It is a fundamentally new business value.

For the past 100 years or so, most large businesses valued hierarchy, status, strict job classifications, information on a "need to know" basis, independent fiefdoms throughout the organization, and pitting one unit, one department, or one division against another. Each unit would be measured not on how it cooperated with other units, but on how well it measured up against other units in terms of financial performance. Such systems fostered a value on "exclusion." Incentives in the organization were designed to ensure that "exclusion" was the norm. Pay-for-performance systems, manager bonus systems, and merit systems pitted one employee and one manager against another in a win-lose situation. "Why should I help you, when it will cost me my bonus and maybe my job?" In hindsight, it is very difficult to see how businesses could have become as successful as they did with such a value system. Dr. W. Edwards Deming credited the success of American management not to a superior system, but to the lack of global competition from 1945 until about 1975. This does not explain its success from 1900 to 1945. Clearly, even during the earlier time frame, American businesses were very successful.

A more fundamental reason for a shift in values can be found in the emergence of a democratic ethos in organizations. Throughout the world, there has been a constant but inexorable spread of democratic values. The workplace has, perhaps, been the last bastion of resistance. In the workplace, one can still find rulers and ruled. In the past, owners and managers were kings with the power to hire, discipline, and fire at will. This may be true in some industries but, for the most part, it is a relic of bygone days. It is the rare manager today who can fire or discipline or even hire at will. Increasingly, policies and committees are in place to ensure that employees are subject to democratic principles in respect to how they are treated. Employees no longer regard themselves as "corporate chattel." Today, employees ask for respect and the right (a democratic right) to be part of the organization and to be treated in an open and trusting manner.

The spread of democratic values to the workplace, the highly educated worker, increased global competition, and the need to use the brainpower of all employees have reached a convergence out of which has emerged the new value of inclusion. Books such as Block's *Stewardship: Choosing Service Over Self-Interest* and Greenleaf's *Servant Leadership* are enormously popular because they describe the new roles for leaders and followers in organizations that adopt the value of inclusion. In the inclusive organization, the distinction between followers and leaders becomes blurred. Anyone can be a leader and everyone must be a follower. Time, knowledge, experience, motivation, and desire have more to do with determining leadership and follower roles than corporate status or position on the organizational chart. In the inclusive organization, roles are dynamic and variable.

# Chapter 12

# The Inclusive Organization

Inclusion is one of the five most important value drivers for the twenty-first-century organization. The other four key value drivers for the twenty-first-century organization are Information, Incentives, Improvement, and Innovation. Each is essential for organizational success in the next century, but no single one of them will suffice to make your organization successful. However, inclusion is the key linkage between all five. Unless you are creating an inclusive organization, no amount of innovation or improvement will be enough to provide long-term success. Inclusion is the ingredient that helps meld the people, machines, methods, materials, and information in your organization into a harmonious unit. Organizations that lack the value of inclusion are usually nonharmonious blends of people, customers, stakeholders, suppliers, unions, and managers, all working at cross purposes with each other.

To really understand what inclusion means, it is helpful to look at its opposite: exclusion. Until recently, most organizations were exclusive rather than inclusive. To be exclusive means to leave out or not to work together with. Webster's defines exclusive as "Excluding others from participating; snobbish; aloof; having power to control; limiting or limited to possession." This description is an accurate characterization of the way that many people were treated by organizations in the past and, in some cases, are treated in the present. Suppliers were traditionally kept at an arm's length relationship at best and, at worst, in an adversarial relationship. In many organizations, suppliers were pitted against each other in bidding contests designed to ensure that the lowest cost was obtained. Often, the end result was that long-term value to the organization was eroded. Business was usually dangled in front of suppliers from year to year. Seldom was any supplier trusted enough to be offered a long-term contract. Only the odd-ball company would subscribe to Dr. Deming's idea of working with one supplier in a long-term relationship of trust. Information was not routinely shared with suppliers, and suppliers were not involved in helping customers innovate and improve. The only incentive for suppliers was the hope that they would not lose the contract that they already had. Suppliers were seldom rewarded for doing things well.

Customers were also excluded from participation in most organizations. They were not considered important enough to provide input into the way that the organization conducted its business. Customer partnerships were unheard of and customers were often told the single most common business advice: *caveat emptor*, "Let the buyer beware." Only recently have organizations started to actively solicit customer input into the quality of services and products. Many companies still only passively solicit such input by leaving customer service surveys on the check-out register, the table top, or underneath the windshield wiper. One wonders what companies do with the data from such worthless efforts. As for the government, it is still unusual to find any city, state, or federal agency that truly seems to care about what its customers think or how they feel.

Boards of directors and external stakeholders were not usually included in providing active input into how most businesses were run. This was also true for state boards that oversee cities, universities, and other government agencies. In general, the role of such external stakeholders usually is to provide capital or to meet federal requirements for some oversight direction. Any actual decision making would generally be deemed as meddling. Most stakeholders would not have the slightest clue about what the organization was doing, how it was doing, or what it needed to do. There are some exceptions to this situation in the nonprofit area. Often, the boards overseeing nonprofit organizations are much more active in the actual running and decision making than is the case in government and for-profit organizations. Indeed, some people have called for the more active inclusion of stakeholders and boards of directors in the running of public (e.g., utilities), for-profit, and government organizations.

In terms of employees and even many managers, most organizations practice the most blatant exclusionary practices. How often have you heard the following?

- "I just work around here."
- "No one tells me anything."
- "They treat us like mushrooms, keep us in the dark and feed us manure."
- "They don't have a need to know."

Numerous employees and managers have complained about not having any idea where their organizations are going, their organizations' long-term goals, or their organizations' visions for the future. I have worked in several organizations where I did not have the necessary information to do my job. I had restricted access to computer databases because I was told that I didn't need this information to complete my work.

I have seen many employees who had not the slightest clue who their internal customers were, what their internal customers needed from them, or how well they were satisfying the needs of their internal customers. In many organizations, the supervisors and foremen are the "information" carriers. It is their job to dole out the information that the production people need to do their work. Is it any wonder that so many middle managers are finding themselves out of work? Peter Drucker noted years ago that computers would replace middle managers as information providers. It only remains for senior managers to take off the conceptual blinders that allow them to restrict information access based on an outdated idea of "need to know" or corporate secrecy. To try to keep secrets from competitors is probably futile anyway. To keep secrets from employees is worse than futile, it is a means for ensuring their nonparticipation in the organization.

We could also talk about the concept of exclusion as it applies to competitors. Indeed, I think that even today, many managers would find it peculiar to think about "including" competitors in the business of their organization, not merely because there are antitrust laws that prohibit some forms of "inclusion" between competitors, but primarily because we have a tradition of excluding competitors. The tradition stems from the commonly accepted premise that if competitors knew what we were planning, they would contrive to "steal our lunch" or "thwart our plans." No doubt, there is some basis for truth in this logic. However, this is the logic of adversarialism. The logic of adversarialism is also the logic of exclusion. The logic of win-win is the logic of inclusion. Many organizations are beginning to understand that the logic of inclusion, or win-win, can lead to gains for both parties. Under the logic of adversarialism, the best that can be hoped for is a win-lose, while other possibilities include a stalemate and a lose-lose. Many organizations have fought their competitors to the death only to find that some other organization arrives to take over the whole game.

This brings us to the final group that is usually excluded from active input in the running of the organization: the union. Unions legally represent the workers and look out for the best interests of the workers. For the most part, unions try to ensure that in the business of making a profit, a fair share of the rewards are set aside for the workers. While this might sound fair and reasonable, for the most part unions are viewed by managers as a big pain. Few managers would willingly invite a union into their organizations to talk to employees. Management organizations have consistently fought any efforts by unions that would extend union influence or do anything to disrupt the "balance of power" that is perceived to exist between management and unions today. This is particularly true when the power that unions want is to have more influence or input into decision making, planning, quality improvement, or any other decisions affecting how the business is run. In the majority of organizations, unions are effectively excluded from direct input into strategic decisions that will affect how the organizations are run.

From management's perspective, excluding the union seems to make sense. Why should the union have a say in how the business is run, in how capital is spent, or how work is assigned? These are the traditional prerogatives of management. On the other hand, one could argue that the union, a key stakeholder and legal representative, has a vested interest in how the business is run. It is conceivable that by including employees and their legal representatives in key decisions, the organization might be more successful and avoid making some disastrous mistakes. From a democratic perspective, it makes sense to secure the greatest amount of informed input into any decision that is going to have a major impact on either the organization or society. Are not organizations part of society? What defense can there be for the twenty-first-century organization to systematically exclude the legally elected representative of the majority of the workforce? Such exclusion has led to many costly and protracted labor battles that have created lose-lose situations for both sides. It is time to move beyond such short-range thinking and set up inclusive partnerships with unions and labor for the good of all.

By now, we should have sufficiently explained what "exclusion" is and how it works to harm an organization. However, merely understanding the negative side of something is not the same as understanding the positive side of something. Inclusion is not merely the reverse of exclusion. You will not create an "inclusive" organization just by stopping the negative practices associated with "exclusion." There is much more to creating an inclusive organization than that. To create an inclusive organization, you must understand the key elements of an inclusive relationship.

Many of us are able to create inclusive relationships in our lives and organizations, but have not really thought about the key elements that make up an inclusive relationship. Recently, we came across a study by Paul W. Mettessich and Barbara R. Monsey for the Amheart H. Wilder Foundation of St. Paul, Minnesota. This is a nonprofit organization that is involved in many social service and community help projects throughout the greater St. Paul/Minneapolis metropolitan area. The stated goals of this study were to "Review and summarize the existing research literature on factors which influence the success of collaboration." In other words, what factors were necessary and essential for a successful win-win relationship or partnership between two independent entities? These factors were culled from over 133 studies. From these studies, the researchers identified nineteen factors that were reported as most influential to the success of a collaborative effort, and grouped these factors into six categories. Keep in mind that these factors were looked at from the perspective of a social service agency. So, while the terminology is different from private business, the concepts and basic ideas are still valid. We have used these concepts and ideas with organizations that were interested in both supplier and customer partnerships and also in forming a win-win relationship with their respective unions. We believe this list has even more applications to foster inclusiveness than the ones we have found so far.

What is required to use this list is some imagination and work. The six categories and factors are listed here:

I. Factors Relating to the Environment:
   1. A history of collaboration exists
   2. The collaborative groups are seen as leaders in the community (could be industry)
   3. Political/social climate is favorable

II. Factors Relating to Membership Characteristics:
   4. Mutual respect, understanding, and trust
   5. Appropriate membership
   6. Members see collaboration in their self-interest
   7. Ability to compromise

III. Factors Relating to Process/Structure:
   8. Members share a stake in both process and outcome
   9. Multiple layers of decision making
   10. Flexibility
   11. Development of clear roles and policy guidelines
   12. Adaptability

IV. Factors Relating to Communication:
   13. Open and frequent communication
   14. Established formal and informal communication links

V. Factors Relating to Purpose:
   15. Concrete, attainable goals and directives
   16. Shared vision
   17. Unique purpose

VI. Factors Related to Resources:
   18. Sufficient funds
   19. Skilled organizers and initiators

We have found that the Wilder study provides extremely useful guidelines in helping to set up relationships that are collaborative, win-win, and inclusive. There are five essential elements that provide the foundation for all of the other factors. This is not to say that all of the nineteen factors are not important. They all must be considered. However, some may be less important than others. For instance, number one, a history of collaboration exists, cannot be true if you are pioneering a new type of relationship with your union, suppliers, or board of directors. Likewise, while number three (political/social climate) is also important and needs to be considered, it cannot stand in the way if you are pioneering a new effort. When this is the case, you will be leading the industry and society, not the other way around.

Of the concepts and factors which are discussed in this study, as well as drawing on our experience, we have distilled the five factors which are the most important. Without them, we cannot see any collaborative or inclusive effort standing a chance. We will briefly explain the role of each of these factors in establishing an inclusive or win-win relationship. The five key factors are trust, respect, choice, caring, and vulnerability.

## *TRUST*

Trust is a word that gets used a great deal in social science literature. It seems as though everyone is continually told that they must trust. Trust others, trust your employees, trust your suppliers, trust your managers, trust your customers, trust your union. Despite such admonitions, many people find it difficult to trust. I am one of those people. I have thought about this a great deal, and believe that there are two divergent views on how and when you should trust. I have found that on the issue of trust, people can be divided along these views.

When I spoke at one of the annual Labor Management conferences in Washington, DC, I was asked to facilitate a discussion group in the evening for attendees. About fifty people showed up at my session. I chose the topic of trust to start the discussion. It was soon clear that there were, indeed, two seemingly divergent viewpoints.

One position was that you did not have to have trust at the beginning of a relationship. Trust was earned as each side demonstrated that it could be trusted and its members were willing to accept responsibility for the effort and the relationship. The other position that emerged (about equal numbers of attendees subscribed to each position) was that you needed trust from the start or the effort would never get off the ground. The attendees believed that trust was not something that was earned, but was something in one's nature that was brought to the relationship—an almost innate belief that people wanted to do a good job and could be trusted to do a good job. Dr. Deming always voiced this type of belief in workers.

It became apparent to me that there is really no conflict between the two positions. It's really a matter of the chicken and the egg. I believe that the false dichotomy stems from our treatment of trust as though it were black and white or a finite element such as electricity. We treat trust as though it is something that can be turned completely on or off. This is never the case. Trust is essential at the start of any relationship. However, trust can also be built up over time as both sides demonstrate their commitment to the relationship. Trust can be eroded, but even if it is completely destroyed by hostile actions of the other side, it can eventually be built up again. Witness our government's current relationships with Germany and Japan.

Trust, like hope, seems to be a quality or value that we need in our lives. No one can go through life without trusting someone or something and no one can go through life without being disappointed. If we are going to establish "inclusive" organizations, it is essential that we learn to trust others. It is also essential that we do not become so naive that we think our trust will never be damaged. People make mistakes and do things which conflict with our judgment. Until we become perfect ourselves, we must learn to accept such differences and errors.

## *RESPECT*

Every time I hear the word "respect," I think of the song by Aretha Franklin of the same name. I can hear her words repeating in my mind, "All I want is a little respect." I once worked at a company where the employees identified communication as the biggest problem in the organization. The management asked that a team of employees and managers look at the problem from a continuous improvement viewpoint. We decided to apply the TQM tools that we had been taught and use them in the framework of the seven-step problem-solving method also known as the "Quality Story."

After extensive interviews with employees and some focus groups, the team met to put our data together. We had a great deal of quantitative and qualitative data. We used pareto charts, affinity diagrams, interrelationship diagrams, and fish bone diagrams to try to make sense out of the data, and finally narrowed the problem down. What employees really meant when they said, "Communication is poor," was that they did not feel respected. We were somewhat surprised by this interpretation of the traditional problem of "poor communication." We found that older people, younger people, office people, women, minorities, managers, and professional people all felt, at one time or another, personally disrespected. We had a pervasive, if not systematic, culture of "disrespect." People did not feel personally or professionally valued. The only thing that mattered was how much money the organization was making. If profits were up, then all was well. When profits were down, then people were excluded from decision making and from participation in key events and meetings. People were solely valued on the basis of the money that they were perceived to be making for the organization. There was little, if any, real value placed on diversity or on the different ideas and opinions of employees in the organization. The only ideas that really mattered came from senior management.

Respect is defined in Webster's dictionary as "Paying particular attention to something; a high or special regard; to refrain from interfering with; the state of being esteemed." In other words, respect is listening to people, allowing them to make mistakes, and not interfering with the way they are doing something or the way that they would like to do something. However, it is more than just listening to people and not tampering with their decisions. You must "esteem" or have a high regard for the opinions and ideas of others. You cannot just do a perfunctory "MBWA" (Management By Wandering Around) and politely ask people how their day is going or what is new on the job. You must earnestly seek out new and different ideas from people and you must really want to know what employees are thinking. It cannot just be an exercise or a prescription given in a communications skills training course. You must fundamentally respect each individual, and the organization must create a culture of respect.

## *CHOICE*

I have generally argued that continuous improvement teams must be entered into voluntarily and that a TQM effort should be started with those employees and managers who believe in it and are committed to it. However, the issue of choice is really much broader than the subject of voluntarism. Without choice, it is difficult to have a culture of respect. People must have a choice in the work they do, the way they do the work, and even the conditions under which they do the work. Many choices are implicit or de facto in organizations. Thus, by joining a company, we make a choice about certain things which include the type of work we will do and the conditions under which we will work. There is nothing wrong with such contracts since, of course, they are entered into voluntarily. Though it still exists in some places, slavery and enforced work is now a thing of the past in most of the world.

Nevertheless, there is a great deal more that we can do to ensure that our organizations really provide for continually higher levels of choice for employees. The real issue is how we can continually increase the choices that we give our employees. Some organizations have started to find ways to include employees in making choices concerning equipment that they will be using and in setting goals and objectives that address their workload. Other organizations are trying to find ways (e.g., search conferences, visioning workshops) to include employees in more strategic choices that will affect the long-term viability of the organization. These efforts represent a start toward providing for continually higher levels of choice in the workplace.

We also need to think about the subject of choice with respect to suppliers, customers, and other stakeholders. Perhaps it is ludicrous to think about choice in respect to competitors, but perhaps not. Maybe it is only our old paradigm of win-lose that makes it seem ridiculous to apply the concept of choice to relationships with competitors. Certainly, we would agree that networks and strategic alliances must be entered into willingly. The same would also apply to partnerships with suppliers and unions. Beyond the initial entry requirement, all relationships with all collaborators must be characterized by choices that are made with full understanding and a full willingness to share the rewards and risks.

## CARING

To care for someone is to have a sense of responsibility for someone. It is to have an interest in and a liking for the person. When an organization (whether Japanese, European, or American) takes great care to ensure the long-term job security of its employees, it is demonstrating the quality of caring. Establishing a plan or a system to ensure employment security is one way employers show they care for their employees.

When Johnson & Johnson immediately took Excedrin off the market after the death scares in Chicago several years ago, the company demonstrated to customers that it really cared about them. This demonstration of caring is perhaps the underlying reason that Johnson & Johnson was able to regain its market share. Do you think if Johnson & Johnson had demonstrated "caveat emptor," that all the advertising in the world would have helped it regain market share? Contrast Johnson & Johnson's behavior with the behavior of Nestle. (At one time, Nestle was being boycotted for its claim to Third World women that Nestle infant formula was better than breast milk. The boycott lasted until Nestle finally compromised on a settlement.) or with that of the A.H. Robbins Co., the makers of the Dalkon Shield. Who would you rather do business with or work for?

The above examples demonstrate that caring is not just another "touchy-feely" concept from the soft sciences. It is a real, tangible commodity that is worth something and can be traded. It can be gained and it can be lost. It definitely affects the bottom line, customer satisfaction, and probably the long-term viability of the organization. Organizations that care more about their customers and stakeholders probably live longer and are more prosperous than organizations that don't give a whit. There is no way to create an inclusive organization if you don't really care about the other people with whom you work. If you believe as we do, then maybe you should look for ways to find out how to measure caring and see how caring your organization is. Perhaps this question should be part of the metrics that you use to assess how well your organization is doing. As your financial reports demonstrate the short-term viability of your organization, your "Caring Report" will demonstrate the long-term viability of your organization.

## *VULNERABILITY*

To care for someone is not an easy task. It requires a certain amount of vulnerability to care. To be vulnerable means to be open to damage or harm, to be susceptible to being hurt. When we are open, we risk being hurt. Only someone who is completely closed is invulnerable and beyond hurt. However, if we are completely closed, we cannot hear others and are not open to understanding the ideas and opinions of others. Paradoxically, the invulnerable person or manager has put himself or herself in the most dangerous and vulnerable position of all. By becoming closed off from the ideas, opinions, and feelings of others around them, he/she risks losing all. Like the dinosaurs, he/she faces extinction by failing to be open and adaptive to his/her surroundings. Such people cannot see or hear the warning signs that will tell them they are making a mistake or heading in the wrong direction.

When we try to really understand others, it is often very scary. In the first place, if we empathize with others, we risk feeling what they feel. (Empathy is a key skill needed for openness and caring.) The downside is that when we empathize with others, we become open to understanding how they feel and what they think. We might understand why they worry about job security, their ability to do the job with improper training, about what our customers are saying about the company, or about how the organization deals with suppliers and the union. Such understanding can be very risky because we might just gain a different opinion of our employees or, heaven forbid, we might just change our minds about some of the ideas and practices that we take for granted in the organization.

Unless risk can be minimized or eliminated (something most managers assume is an intelligent thing to do, while forgetting that the most risky things in life provide the highest potential for new growth and development), vulnerability is a condition that must be accepted and even applauded. It is only by being somewhat vulnerable that we allow ourselves to be open to risk, to new ideas, and to understanding the feelings of others around us. We need to better understand the advantages that vulnerability gives us in helping us to set up relationships with our customers, suppliers, employees, unions, and even competitors. The invulnerable organization is essentially a closed, nonlearning organization. A twenty-first-century organization must be vulnerable if it is going to be flexible and adaptive.

# Chapter 13

# Quality as a Lifestyle

Dr. W. Edwards Deming used to tell people that they don't really understand quality until it becomes personal. This thought was intriguing to me, but I did not really understand it until I came home from work one day and found a jar of jam on the counter with the lid off and jelly spilled on the counter. Raised in an Italian family that struggled to put food on the table every day, I was brought up with the rule that you did not waste one drop of food. Even in school, the nuns would chastise us about cleaning our plates, with the reminder that there were thousands of peasants starving in India. So I was incensed to see food treated with such disregard and started yelling, "Who left the food out? Who left the food out? Who left the food out?" Karen (my spouse), who was also in the kitchen, turned to me and said, "I thought you were supposed to ask 'Why?' five times, not 'Who?' five times."* At this point, quality became personal for me. I suddenly understood what Deming meant when he used the technique of asking "why" in order to get to the true crux of the matter.

Once quality became personal, it was no longer an abstract theory of management. I could see that I had to practice what I had been preaching for seven years as a consultant. Furthermore, I began to realize that I had a long way to go to apply it to my own life. However, this was essential, because if I could not do it, I could not

---

*The question of "who" made the mistake, rather than "why" the mistake was made, has often been associated with Amercian-style management. It refers to the tendency to be more concerned with assigning blame than with fixing or improving the process. It also treats the system as though it is entirely controlled by human factors and ignores the role that methods, materials, equipment, and the environment all have in the process.

ask others to do it. I have come to truly believe that unless each of us starts applying quality personally, as well as professionally, we will never achieve a true quality organization, never mind a true quality society. Organizations and societies are made by people, not machines and equipment. If we as individuals are unhappy, abusive, discriminatory, or unethical, we will not be able to create joyful, dynamic, and creative workplaces or societies. I think this issue is so important that I would like to explore some of the problems that I have faced and that I think every individual will face if he/she accepts the commitment and effort it takes to become a "Total Quality Person."

Most workplaces in the world (including in the United States) have tolerated and condoned abusive behavior. Historically, physical abuse was legal. It was once permissible to beat slaves. It was not uncommon in the military for recruits to get the stuffing beaten out of them almost on a regular basis as part of their basic training. In some workplaces, the foremen were picked because they were the biggest, toughest dudes on the crew. No one would dare give them any lip because it was assumed, and sometimes demonstrated, that a "kick in the pants" would be forthcoming. It was literally true that a foreman's job was to "kick ass and take names." Today, legally and morally, our organizations no longer tolerate such overt forms of abuse. However, abuse (including physical abuse) still exists at unacceptable levels in our workplaces and society.

Psychologists and sociologists generally identify three different categories of abuse: physical, verbal, and emotional. Physical abuse includes assaults, battering, sexual, and any other form of unwanted, undesired, or unsolicited touching. Verbal abuse includes insults, name calling, yelling, and sarcasm directed at people, as well as discriminatory remarks made toward minorities, women, disabled, or other protected or disadvantaged groups. Emotional abuse is much more benign and difficult to define. Certainly, discrimination is a major form of emotional abuse in the workplace. However, I would label emotional abuse as practices that put "fear" in the workplace or any practices that lead to employees feeling humiliated, denigrated, demeaned, or disrespected.

Some of you may be saying, "Yes, abuse is bad, but what does this have to do with quality or with me personally?" Several years ago, I felt the same way. Abusers were creepy, low-life people who were dirty, illiterate, and unemployable. They skulked around back alleys waiting to pounce on defenseless women and children. They did not hold respectable positions in major corporations and they certainly did not have PhD degrees. You can imagine my surprise when the divorce counselor my former spouse and I were seeing said that I had an "anger" problem and suggested I get "help" for it. For several sessions, I admitted that I had a temper, but I certainly did not have a problem. Besides, if anyone was on the receiving end of my temper, he or she deserved it; it was his/her fault. I did not start arguments, but I sure could end them. When I was younger, I prided myself on always championing the underdog and never starting any fights.

At some point in our counseling sessions (my spouse and I had already separated and I continued to see the counselor on my own), I finally agreed to call a couple of numbers that the counselor recommended where I could get "help" dealing with my anger. These places were called "Domestic Abuse Centers."

It took several months for me to make contact with a center. I made my first calls somewhat reluctantly. I felt like I was doing the centers a favor since I considered myself potential business. The few in my area appeared to have more "business" than they could handle. I talked to a staff member at one of the the centers; after some discussion, we set up an interview. During the first interview, the intake counselor asked a number of questions that I felt were demeaning and degrading. I could feel my temper beginning to rise and I was on the verge of walking out. My typical response to most questions was that it was not my fault and "they" only got what they deserved. I said that I never started fights, but I would protect myself if physically or verbally attacked. I would make damn sure that I did not get the worse end of the battle. Suddenly, the intake counselor said to me, "You have an abuse problem. You can start in with our next group if you desire." The "group" (I presumed a bunch of derelicts and lowlifes) would meet for four hours, twice a week, for sixteen weeks. You didn't miss a session without a good reason. Otherwise, you would not be permitted to continue with the group.

I still don't know why I decided to attend, but I did. I did not think that I had any problem whatsoever. I did not particularly like the attitude of the people with whom I had talked so far, either. They seemed arrogant and condescending. I went to the first meeting expecting it to be my last. I felt superior because I was not a lowlife who couldn't hold a job or support himself. I certainly would not be like the rest of the people in the group. I would soon be finishing my PhD program, I had a very respectable position, and I had a work history that would be the envy of many. I expected to attend the first session, prove to myself and the ignorant counselors that I was different, and leave feeling vindicated. This would be my first, last, and only "domestic abuse" session.

I completed thirty-two sessions over the next sixteen weeks and continued with a Monday evening support group for another two and one-half years. My "low-life" group turned out to be a cross section of American society. It was an all-male group that included a doctor, a lawyer, a school principal, several managers, a few small business owners, mechanics, welders, bus drivers, construction workers, and one PhD candidate. Twelve years later, several of these "low-lifes" have remained good friends of mine. I found out very quickly that I had more in common with all of them than I could ever have admitted. Most of us had grown up in tough neighborhoods with abusive fathers. We had quickly learned that the best defense is a good offense, and that it was better to get the last hit than the first hit. We all learned that not one of us liked the way we felt after we had been in a fight and that we all went through the same cycle of escalation, explosion, and contrition. Together we learned how to break this cycle and stop blaming our problems and anger on others. It took many sessions of confrontation and painful honesty to make progress, but everyone who stayed for the full sixteen weeks eventually saw the light.

I finally admitted that I had an abuse problem and that I was responsible for the problem. I began to see that my problem did, in fact, affect my work life and that employees and co-workers were afraid of my temper. I realized that I had been treating people as tools and objects that could either help or inhibit me from accomplishing certain goals. Employees to me were not people who had home lives, personal problems, stresses, and demons of their own to battle. The only problems that mattered were mine and they generally concerned getting the job done right the first time. I did not care if employees were sick, because the work still had to be done. I had my own problems and I didn't want to hear theirs. Besides, I thought that most problems were excuses; excuses were for losers.

This was my attitude and sometimes (unfortunately), it still is. But it is a problem that I recognize and am willing to try to continually improve upon. I have recognized the need to address abuse in the workplace. Addressing this abuse started with addressing my own abuse. Where else could it start? Robert Greenleaf relates the following story in his book, *Servant Leadership:*[1]

> A king once asked Confucius' advice on what to do about the large number of thieves. Confucius answered, "If you, sir, were not covetous, although you should reward them to do it, they would not steal." This advice places an enormous burden on those who are favored by the rules, and it establishes how old is the notion that the servant views any problem in the world as in here, inside oneself, not out there. And if a flaw in the world is to be remedied, to the servant, the process of change starts in here, in the servant, not out there. This is a difficult concept for that busybody modern man.

I have no illusions that I am an expert in the process that Greenleaf refers to. So, I am somewhat reluctant to provide any suggestions on how you should start your journey. Each person's journey will be different. I do believe it will be the most important journey you will ever take in your life. It is the long, never-ending journey to become a "Total Quality Person." It was the most difficult journey that I have ever started and I have been working on it for over fourteen years now. Since attending that first abuse group session, I have made an effort to continually improve myself personally. Just as with an organizational process, the goal of Total Quality is continuous improvement. For this to happen, the journey must be changed from an event focus (going to a seminar or attending a course) into a process focus. A process has no absolute beginning or end; it is ongoing. So is your personal journey.

My personal journey includes regular family meetings, professional counseling, self-help books, a men's support group, an annual three-day silent retreat, and other such periodic challenges as Lifesprings training and New Warriors' training. My counselor helps me to see myself objectively and is someone who can challenge me to reflect on my life. I frequently discuss situations with my counselor when I do not feel that I have handled myself well or when I left a situation feeling uncomfortable with the outcome. Over the years, the sessions have helped me to deal with some very difficult situations.

Socrates said that the unexamined life is not worth living. Each year, for ten years now, I have attended a three-day silent retreat where I can reflect on my life and goals and decide if I am living my life consistent with my values. I look forward each year to three full days of being able to examine and reflect on my life. I feel totally energized after each retreat. Beyond these efforts, I try to attend at least one major event each year that is concerned with personal growth, rather than a professional subject such as quality or management issues. This has included attending Lifesprings training, New Warrior training, and also contracting with a professional group to interview my peers and conduct a series of role-playing exercises with me on videotape to help strengthen my interpersonal skills. Of course, just getting the candid, uncensored responses back from my peers was invaluable in helping me to see areas where I needed to improve.

For those of you who really want to start a personal change program, I highly recommend using a modified version of the Alcoholics Anonymous 12-Step process. This process has proven successful in helping people overcome alcoholism as well as many other types of addictions, and believe me, abuse is an addiction. It is a form of control that we get hooked on because it helps us to manipulate people, to make them do what we want them to do. Of course, as with all addictions, we ignore the long-term consequences and the side effects of the addiction. The long-term problems of abusing people are manifested in distrust, skepticism, apathy, lack of creativity, and outright hostility. The short-term responses are increased fear in the workplace, lower employee morale, higher job turnover, increased employee grievances, and lawsuits. Remember, "What goes around comes around." Rest assured that if you are abusive and controlling, the ramifications of that will one day come home to roost.

If you are at all motivated to start a personal quality journey, I recommend the following modified version of the 12-step process for all of you who really desire to overcome abuse, to let go of control, and to pursue personal quality in the workplace. There are many different personal quality journeys. This may be a path for some of you, while others may need to follow a different path.

- **Step 1**   Admit that we all have a need to control others and that we are continually trying to figure out how to get others to do what we want them to do. Admit that this need leads to abuse in the workplace.
- **Step 2**   Come to understand that we are not alone in this problem and that there are many others out there who are abusive and share our need to let go of control.
- **Step 3**   Let go of stubborn self-reliance and the belief that we don't need help from anyone else, that we can do it all by ourselves.
- **Step 4**   Make an honest, fearless inventory of our strengths and weaknesses and their impacts on other people. How does our need to control affect our peers, employees, customers, families, and friends?
- **Step 5**   Admit our problems to ourselves and to others without shame or guilt. Let people know that we accept the responsibility for personal change and why.
- **Step 6**   Accept that the road to change is not a straight line. Give up the expectation that it needs to be done perfectly or not at all. Don't use a failure as an excuse to stop trying. Begin again.
- **Step 7**   Don't compare ourselves to others; we are no better or worse than anyone else, and we need others to help us make the journey. We are all in this together or not at all.
- **Step 8**   Make a list of all the people that we try to control in our lives and talk to them about how we can deal with them differently.
- **Step 9**   Whenever we backslide, we must be willing to make amends to the people we hurt and do so directly. Too often, we fail to make direct apologies or to admit that we have made a mistake and say we are sorry.
- **Step 10**  Continue to take personal inventory of our actions and their effects on others and admit when our actions have

abused or hurt someone. This is a never-ending journey.
You don't do it once and think that you are done with it.
It is a process, not a program.
- Step 11   Develop a higher spirituality by living a life that is consistent with your values and principles. We should all
carry a card with our personal mission on one side and
our personal values on the other side.
- Step 12   Reach out to others and help them make the journey
that we are making. We have the responsibility to help
others to end abuse and to create joy in the workplace.
We have the responsibility to end racism, sexism, dis-
crimination, and fear in society.

The 12-step process has worked for millions of people. If you are
serious about becoming a Total Quality Person and you are abusive
or controlling, I suggest you try following this process. You will
only be kidding yourself if you think that you can have a Total
Quality Organization without having Total Quality People in the
organization.

A number of years ago, our consulting firm worked with a very
large government organization. The head of this organization would
regularly yell at and verbally abuse employees in meetings. He told
us that his first boss had praised his aggressive behavior and that for
his entire career he had viewed such behavior as an asset and the
primary reason for his career success. We told him that while this
might be true, times have changed. In the past, such forms of abuse,
if not legal, were tolerated. But the world is now very different.
Physical abuse has been illegal for some time and this now includes
sexual abuse as well. We further explained that while verbal abuse
might not yet be illegal, we did not think that he would want to be
the test case for a lawsuit. He agreed with our reasoning and promised to make an effort to change his management and leadership
style, particularly in how he led meetings.

The potential for lawsuits and other litigation is here already. It is
hard to pick up the paper without finding some instance of sexual
harassment or abusive workplace behavior that is not the object of a
lawsuit. Women, minorities, the disabled, the elderly, jobless white
males, and others have all been able to successfully prove abusive

behavior in the workplace. In most cases, these forms of abuse were not physical or verbal, but emotional. In the past, many cases dealt with unfair promotions or hiring, verbal abuse, sexual harassment, or physical harassment. Today, we increasingly see cases that do not fit in any of these categories except the category of emotional abuse.

For instance, the hotly debated ninety-day plant closing law would have been considered ridiculous a few years ago. Today, more and more people believe that organizations need to give ample warning to workers of impending layoffs and plant closings. This warning is designed to take some of the economic stress out of job displacements. However, in a large sense, it appeals to employees because it demonstrates a form of emotional respect for their problems and lives. Employees believe that they are entitled to be treated as human beings, not just some type of disposable capital or merchandise. In the future, managers will be liable for all forms of abuse in the workplace. It will be their responsibility to end abuse.

Continuous improvement impels managers to go further. They must not only take the problems out of the system, they must continually improve. This means that managers will need to (as Dr. Deming advised) create joy in the workplace. The first step toward this journey begins within ourselves. If you have not started, what are you waiting for? Do you think it is someone else's responsibility?

## REFERENCE NOTE

1. Greenleaf, Robert K. *Servant Leadership.* New York: Paulist Press, 1977.

# Chapter 14

# The New Role of the CEO

The CEO, or organizational leader, is arguably the individual with the most influence in developing the values needed in the twenty-first-century organization. Almost every quality expert has emphasized that the involvement and support of the senior organizational leader is critical to the success of any change effort. Furthermore, studies done by several different consulting firms and academic institutions have all shown that the "lack of involvement" of the organizational leader is the most important reason for the failure of change to take hold. Organizations that succeed do not succeed only because the CEO is involved. However, without the involvement and total commitment of the CEO, it is very unlikely that any major change effort can be successful. Therefore, the role of the CEO is a necessary but not a sufficient condition for success in guiding an organization toward a new set of values.

There are four major tasks that the CEO must perform in his/her role as the leader of an organization that embraces the new organizational values:

1. Be a role model.
2. Provide the time and resources for a major change effort.
3. Demonstrate commitment to continuous education and learning.
4. Champion the effort with all stakeholders, stockholders, customers, boards, etc.

## *BE A ROLE MODEL*

Organizations need to adopt an entirely new set of values, practices, and policies that will help make them competitive in a new economic era. This is an era that is characterized by high-speed and high-volume information fueling an intense global competition. As organizations must change in order to survive, so must their organizational leaders. Much of the skills, knowledge, behaviors, and attitudes that were conducive to success in the outgoing era are insufficient for success in the era that we are entering. The leader who cannot or will not change endangers not only his/her success, but the success of his/her entire organization. There are several behaviors that are critical to the successful change effort. These are behaviors and skills in which traditional leaders are often notoriously weak. They fall into the following categories:

- Listening and communication skills
- Data and information usage in decision making
- Creativity and long-term planning
- Celebration and inclusiveness
- Self-awareness

### Listening and Communication Skills

Most leaders are used to telling, authorizing, delegating, demanding, or dictating. Many leaders have a difficult time listening to others and trying to solicit ideas from people who do not agree with them or who see the world differently. This myopia is a critical weakness in a multilingual and multicultural global economy. The leader of the future will have to spend more time working with people to solicit their ideas and opinions, and less time trying to figure out the answer by himself/herself. It will be increasingly important for future leaders to know how to facilitate consensus in a team environment. The era is over when an organization could succeed by only using the brainpower of a few managers or leaders.

### Data and Information Usage in Decision Making

In the past, it was possible to make decisions by intuition or experience and rely on the ratio of success that these processes generated. However, the increased competition in this new era means that the leader who has the best and most up-to-date information sources will have an edge over his/her competitors, all other factors being nearly equal. Leaders must learn to be experts at identifying, retrieving, and analyzing data, and they must have the expertise to use the tools that will help them in this task.

Statistical analysis is one of the most important tools for helping organizations sift through the vast amount of information available. Statistics can help a leader make sense out of the stacks of data and reports that he/she sees daily. It is an excellent tool for translating data into something that is meaningful, not just measurable. The entire organization must be trained in the proper use of statistics so everyone can make sense out of the data. The CEO must also learn and use such methods.

### *Creativity and Long-Term Planning*

Very few North American organizations do a good job of long-term planning. One common joke is that the Japanese plan for centuries, the Europeans for decades and the Americans for weeks. Many experts have attributed the American short-term planning horizon to its financial system and Wall Street's pressure for short-term profits and results. However, as organizations change (e.g., Ford is now basing executive bonuses on five-year results rather than yearly results), the skills of leaders in the organization must change. The skills for short-term planning are not the same skills needed for long-term planning. As organizations increasingly emphasize long-term planning, leaders must develop the skills to facilitate such planning.

For the most part, short-term planning is a very linear, rational process. In the short term, it is possible to predict with some degree of accuracy what the future will bring. This is not true in the long term. In the long term, there is only one way to predict the future, and that is to form a vision of what you want it to look like and then to "create" it. The skills to accomplish this task require a high level of creativity and imagination. These are not the same skills required for rational, logical planning. The new leader must at times be able to suspend logic and rational thought and engage in highly creative thought processes where the outcome is not predictable. This is very difficult for leaders who are used to everything having a predictable outcome or who are used to project-management-type tasks where everything can be laid out logically and sequentially. By its very nature, creativity is not logical, predictable, or neatly defined.

### Celebration and Inclusiveness

The organization of the future will need to be a place where people can look forward to coming to work. Noted labor leader Bob Killeen has said that "work should be fun." It should be a place where people can enjoy their jobs and take time to celebrate and recognize success. In reality, few organizations take the time to understand why something was successful or to give employees regular recognition for their daily efforts.

The organization of the future must have high levels of team-work, with people from diverse social, ethnic, racial, and economic backgrounds working closely together. Such an organization will need to foster respect for a wide diversity of human differences. It will be an organization where an atmosphere of inclusiveness pre-vails and where there is fundamental respect for the differences among people. Too often, differences are labeled by the dominant culture as bad or as deficiencies rather than as potential strengths. In the inclusive organization, there will be no room for bigotry, dis-crimination, or prejudice of any kind.

Leaders of the future will have to be able to model the kind of respect, tolerance, and recognition that is critical in a workplace where differences and diversity are seen as assets, not deficits. Leaders who have no time to spend with their employees, who cannot work as part of a team, or who are themselves bigoted and prejudiced, will not survive in the coming economic era. Further-more, it is the responsibility of the leader to ensure that no forms of discrimination or other barriers exist to establishing this kind of an organization. The leader has the primary responsibility for identify-ing barriers that do exist and then allocating the resources and time to remove such barriers.

### Self-Awareness

Socrates said, "The unexamined life is not worth living." Many historical studies have pointed out that one downfall of leaders can be traced to their inability to get an accurate reading of reality. Subordinates have a tendency to paint a rosy picture of reality for their bosses (thus avoiding the "dead messenger" syndrome). Leaders who court agreement with their own opinion or who surround themselves with sycophants gradually lose touch with what is happening around them. This can play a strong role in a leader's downfall.

Too many layers of managers between the front line and the CEO is another way that reality is obscured. In the past, the role of the leader was out in front where he or she could see for himself/herself what was going on. Modern technology has relegated the role of many leaders to the back where they must rely on getting an undistorted view from either their subordinates or data systems.

Everyone has a natural need for ego gratification; however the leader who lacks self-awareness can become an ego gratification addict if he/she is not careful. This habit will be fed by many willing people who are anxious to achieve the favors that a leader can bestow. One antidote to this addiction is self-awareness. Self-awareness helps us to perceive ourselves as we really are and to have the courage to find people who challenge our belief systems and our pictures of reality. The leader who thinks that he/she is a kind and benevolent leader cannot really know unless there is an objective opinion to confirm or disprove this hypothesis. Many leaders are not willing to seek such information if it means disproving an image or belief that they hold dear. Leaders will need to overcome such fears and seek "truth tellers" who are willing to say that the "emperor has no clothes." An unwillingness to look for such people can create a fatal myopia. The willingness to challenge sacred cows and cherished pictures of reality will distinguish the successful organizational leaders of the future.

## PROVIDE THE TIME AND RESOURCES
## FOR A MAJOR CHANGE EFFORT

The leader is responsible for providing the time and resources for the change effort. Many leaders err by believing that merely providing a budget or more training is enough. Such leaders fail to recognize that systemic change is highly dependent on the active involvement of everyone in the organization. Even more substantial than the budget that is involved is the time that employees and managers must put into the effort if it is to succeed. You cannot buy a transformation program or a transformed organization. You must create it step-by-step. The very nature of continuous improvement, as opposed to the "if it ain't broke, don't fix it" concept, means that a continuous and steady amount of time and energy must go into studying processes and systems to determine how they can be changed. This is not a one-time effort, but the ongoing core of developing an organization that will meet the challenges of the global economy.

A second error that many leaders make is trying to do it all by themselves. Some leaders believe that they can simply copy other organizations or that they can manage the transformation without relying on any "external" help. Such thinking is penny-wise and pound-foolish. Just as smart doctors and lawyers don't take themselves as clients, the wise leader will look for qualified, objective help in managing the change effort. This help could come from consultants, academicians, or professional organizations, but it should come from someone who is not invested in the current organizational paradigm. Many leaders abhor the thought of bringing in consultants or other "outsiders" for fear that the leaders themselves will lose control of their organization or that they will lose some degree of power. Paradoxically, it is this overconcern with power and control which marks the organization that probably is in most need of help. The resources for such help are essential components of the change effort and the leader that tries to save a buck by shaving corners will only increase the odds against success.

## DEMONSTRATE COMMITMENT TO CONTINUOUS EDUCATION AND LEARNING

Education and learning fuel continuous improvement. Many leaders feel that they can delegate the responsibility for this part of the change effort to others or to the consultant. Often, a leader feels the "new" training classes are for other leaders, that he/she doesn't need any of this training. While this may be partly true, it misses the point in respect to the role of the leader. By being first in line for training and education, the leader sends a strong message to the people in the organization that continuous learning and training is highly valued and essential to the success of the organization.

The successful organization of the future will be characterized by high levels of education and emphasis on the continued acquisition of knowledge in many different forms and varieties. It is no coincidence that we are experiencing an explosion of high-tech devices to manage and facilitate data and information transfer, since data and information, along with experience, are the major ingredients of knowledge. Widespread use of devices and utilities such as computers, e-mail, group mail, fax machines, modems, cellular phones, telecommunications, etc., is arising out of a need to better manage and exchange information between customers and suppliers.

The leader who fails to appreciate the need for continuous education and learning is usually highly evident in most organizations. Such leaders will probably be computer illiterate, will have a phobia for high-tech communication devices, and will seldom, if ever, take educational classes in areas that may be somewhat removed from a direct relationship with their job. These attitudes will have to change if the leader wants his/her organization to be open to change and flexible in dealing with the demands of a global economy. Every leader in the organization must have an ongoing plan for personal development and continuous improvement. This is what is meant by modeling leadership.

## CHAMPION THE EFFORT WITH ALL STAKEHOLDERS, STOCKHOLDERS, CUSTOMERS, ETC.

Employees often do not realize that the "boss" has a boss or, more likely, several bosses. This higher boss may take many forms, including a board of directors, customers, citizen groups, or government regulatory agencies. All such "stakeholders" will have an impact on the change effort. If the relationship between the organization and these stakeholders is not managed well, the impact can be negative. More than one change effort has been aborted because the boss's boss did not see the benefits in continuing the effort or did not appreciate the magnitude of changes needed.

The leader needs to ensure that interfaces between the organization and external stakeholders are managed. The skills to do this are persuasive and political as well as communicative and inclusive. The wise leader will follow a policy of "no surprises" with key stakeholders and will ensure that he/she has ongoing communication in as much depth as needed to gain the commitment of these stakeholders.

## *THE ROLE OF THE UNION LEADER IN THE EFFORT*

The role of the union leadership is, in many respects, identical to the role of the organizational leader. Certainly, the union leader must role model the new leadership skills, provide time and resources (albeit union time and resources), demonstrate commitment to life-long learning and education, and champion the effort with her/his stakeholders. Many of the skills that were identified as critical for new leadership are also critical for the union leaders involved in an organizational change effort, whether it is their own union organization they are trying to change or the organization in which they represent the employees.

There are also some key differences in the role of the organizational leader and the role of the union leader. While the role of the union leader is equally important to any change effort, the process that must be managed by both leaders is, in many respects, different. Whereas the organizational leader is hired, promoted, or appointed, the union leadership is elected. This difference in how the two leaders obtain their jobs does not mean a different set of skills is needed, but it does mean that each leader has a different agenda.

In the short term, the organizational leader usually leads with one eye on the external customer and one eye on the bottom line. In the short term, the union leader usually leads with one eye on the membership and one eye on reelection. Because of their different focuses, the actions undertaken by each leader will be considerably different. The organizational leadership must first and foremost satisfy the stockholders or owners, while the union leadership must first and foremost satisfy his/her membership. In the long term, any effort to maximize either position will only lead to an overall suboptimization of the system. No organization can survive long term unless the needs of stakeholders, including employees and customers, are met. The organizational leader and the union leader must find a way to obtain an optimal balance between the needs of employees, stakeholders, and customers. This means that short-term objectives must always be balanced with long-term objectives.

The role of the union leadership will be a critical variable for a successful change effort. Just as the roles and skills of the organizational leader must change to meet the emerging needs of a new economic era, so must the roles and skills of the union leadership change. If unions and management are to work together to achieve success, there must be equal effort on the part of both leaderships to make the needed changes.

# PART V:
# INCENTIVES

Incentives shape the goals and motivations that guide people in organizations. While people do not always do what they are rewarded for doing, they will usually move toward a greater expectancy of rewards. Incentives are like the glue that holds the ship together. A coherent package of incentives will help the ship move toward its destination. But incentives that lack coherence in terms of the mission and values of the organization are barriers to success, and can create forces in the organization that are dysfunctional enough to pull the organization apart and help it sink. The purpose of incentives has changed dramatically in the new global market. Incentives and rewards (in the form of salaries, wages, bonuses, and commissions) have always shaped the goals and purpose of the organization. However, there is now a greater recognition that incentives can inhibit organizational success. Today, managers are more conscious than ever before of the new values that are needed in organizations and of the role that incentives can play in inspiring these new values. It is this increased consciousness which is fundamentally altering and shaping a new purpose and role for incentives.

In the past, the key role of incentives was to help the organization get as much as it could by paying as little as it could. Incentives were often viewed simply as a form of exchange. The laborer exchanged effort for pay–an honest day's work for an honest day's pay. A worker was "entitled" to no more and no less. A worker had no right to know what others were paid or to be concerned with whether the organization was profitable or not. If the organization was profitable, the worker would be paid. If the organization was not profitable, the worker would be laid off or fired. Pay was pay. It was not a reward and it was not an incentive. A person worked because he or she would starve if not working.

Today, the employee has more choices. Few workers, even the most uneducated, feel as though they would starve if they did not have work. Indeed, many people are now opting to work for themselves because they do not want to put up with the many demands and petty politics that organizations place on employees. Whether working for themselves or an organization, the vast majority of people today want more than merely a salary or wage. They want a satisfying job in a healthy work environment, a chance for growth, a place for camaraderie, and a sense of fulfilling a higher mission or purpose. Incentives are viewed by many people as part and parcel of these new expectations.

Employees today feel entitled to benefit more if the organization is successful. They feel entitled to know what others are paid, how wages and salaries are determined, how profitable the organization is, and whether or not they can expect some form of recognition for work well done. Incentives are a new organizational value because they are based on an entirely new belief system. Incentives may include an "atta boy" as well as a year-end profit sharing bonus. In an inclusive organization, there is a sense of "all for one and one for all." Thus, if managers and owners are rewarded because the organization is having a good year, then employees now feel that they are entitled to some form of reward and recognition. After all, the organization would not have been successful without the help of all employees.

Furthermore, in the past, workers were only selling labor. The old contract between employees and owners was based on an exchange of labor for pay. Today, a new contract is being formed that is based on exchange of both knowledge and labor for incentives, rewards, recognition, and pay. The expectation is that "If you want my brain, I need to feel as though I am part of this organization. I will only feel included in this organization if the incentive systems make me feel included rather than excluded." Private cafeterias and private parking for managers are incentives that reflect the old organizational value of exclusion. New incentives must be developed that support the new values described in this book. Organizations that adopt incentives as a new value will be in a better position to consciously guide the goals and mission of the organization and to create the necessary conditions for success.

# Chapter 15

# Incentives for Change, or "What's in it for Me?"

One of the frequently asked questions of professionals involved in organizational change is "What's in it for me?" Answers have included the succinct, "Your job"; the patient, "We are all on the same team"; the altruistic, "Profit sharing"; and the desperate, "Survival." Many organizations attempt to answer this question through the use of motivational strategies that include profit sharing, gain sharing, Pay for Performance, Employee Stock Ownership Programs (ESOPs), Pay for Knowledge, and many other techniques designed to provide incentives and motivation for employees to help make major changes.

Dr. W. E. Deming always said that people are self-motivated. According to Deming, what managers need to do is to find ways to take the demotivators or barriers out of the system. If management can do this, then employees will do the best job they can within the limits of the system. Deming's Red Bead experiment was a dramatic representation of this theory. In this well-known experiment, Deming demonstrated that employees could not be expected to perform greater than the system would allow. In the experiment, various incentives and inducements were tried on the volunteers in an effort to obtain greater performance. At times, participants in the experiment thought that they were increasing performance or sometimes getting worse, and some thought that they were beating the system. Finally, when the experiment was over, Deming would show that all the increases and decreases were merely a result of the natural variation in the process. None of the participants did any better or any worse than the others. The differences were statistically insignificant and due to normal chance. Most participants in the Red

Bead experiment went away with their eyes opened to a different view of performance management systems.

Alfie Kohn, in his book *Punished by Rewards*, writes about the contrary effect that many systems designed to motivate employees have on the employees. Piecework systems (e.g., pay for the number of widgets produced or valves ground), bonus systems (e.g., if billable hours are up, extra pay is awarded), and other pay-for-performance systems (some well-known ones reward employees for new clients or new contracts obtained) do not usually increase performance of the overall system. More often, they lead to suboptimization of the system. This is due to the fact that individuals in the system attempt to maximize their personal earnings regardless of the effect on the overall system. There is a great deal of basic experience available to show that most piecework and bonus systems are counterproductive.

The supply department at a major naval station was selected for a university study on incentives due to the large number of invoices and transactions the naval supply department handled. The university researchers wanted to show that incentives could increase the output of the department. During the study, a small incentive was paid out for each invoice that was processed. Upon reaching a certain level, the incentives would increase. It was basically a piecework system. A few weeks into the study, the head of the supply department was asked how it was going and replied, "Well, the employees love it. They are making more money than ever before. But it is ruining the department. They don't want to work on anything else except these invoices and there are many other things that need to get done to keep the department running." This response was not surprising. There is much evidence of the damage that can be done by well-intentioned but misguided and misapplied performance and incentive systems.

Many enlightened practitioners cite another reason, other than recognizing individuals, for looking at innovative reward and compensation systems—to create a sense of community within the organization. This is a much better reason, but it is not without its pitfalls. Often, it is easy to create a system that we think recognizes outstanding performance when such performance is actually within the system, not the individual. For example, "employee of the month" programs sound like a good way to recognize outstanding effort. However, in many cases, such effort is very difficult to distinguish from normal performance. When the employee of the month is selected, the recipient is not sure what he or she did to earn it and other employees are resentful because they feel that they did the same work, but did not get recognized. Like Deming's Red Bead experiment, we must know whether behavior which is deemed outstanding is really exceptional or if it is just normal. Failure to make such a distinction carries with it the risk of unfairly rewarding a few individuals and ignoring the vast majority of workers.

It is much more effective to reward people for the work that they do on a regular basis. Employees often complain that they are always told when they do something wrong but seldom told when they do something right. When managers worry excessively about recognizing "outstanding" performance, they can easily forget about the rest of the "average" employees within the system. Such selective treatment will not create a feeling of community and teamwork within the organization.

There is a revolution going on in terms of employee responsibilities. We are seeing the values of inclusiveness and cooperation replace the values of exclusion and win-lose competition. The value of innovation is replacing the value of "it if isn't broke, don't fix it." Many attempts to deal with "new style" rewards and incentives do not address this fundamental value shift. Many "innovative" reward systems merely amount to tampering with the system. Tampering with a system, without understanding the system, will generally make things worse. Fundamental improvements require an understanding of the revolution affecting the role of workers in organizations.

The role of workers has already (in many organizations) changed from that of "Worker as Doer" to that of "Worker as Process Owner." Furthermore, the role of workers is still changing. Employees at every level of the organization are given, and expected to take, more responsibility and accountability than ever before. The basic global and competitive forces acting on business and government will continue to drive this revolution and to force changes in worker responsibilities. Workers will be required to progress up a scale of successively more demanding and responsible job roles. We have called this the "Scale of Empowerment and Responsibilities." The path of employee responsibilities seems to be headed up this scale. The oldest and lowest rung on the ladder was "Worker as Doer" and the highest and most progressive and demanding rung on the ladder is "Worker as Co-Owner." The other rungs reflect levels of responsibility and accountability between doer and co-owner.

### Scale of Empowerment and Responsibilities

Worker as Co-Owner
Worker as Manager
Worker as Supervisor
Worker as Process Owner
Worker as Doer

Some organizations have progressed from "Worker as Doer" to "Worker as Process Owner." Some have even gone as far as "Worker as Co-Owner." Most organizations are still struggling to make the transition from "Worker as Doer" to "Worker as Process Owner." As employees progress from "Worker as Doer" to "Worker as Co-Owner," the level of responsibilities increases as well as the information needs at each level. At each stage, there are fundamental organizational changes in policies, procedures, and structures that must be made for the changes to be effective.

### WORKER AS DOER

In the past, it was said that employees were hired from the neck down. Managers did the thinking and workers did as they were told. Using the Taylor System of Scientific Management, each job could be described in detail, including how long each task should take. If every worker did what they were "supposed to," maximum productivity would be achieved. Any problems in the system should be taken care of by one of the layers of management. With the advantage of hindsight, it is easy to see that this system could not begin to tap the full productivity of the workforce. The Taylor System of Scientific Management completely ignored any concept of innovation or creativity on the part of both workers and management. It not only took power away from employees, it also took power and decision making away from managers. A manager's job no longer had anything to do with strategy; instead, the manager was a fire-fighter whose job was to deal with parts of the system that periodically broke down. For instance, if a worker called in sick, management's job would be to scurry around as quickly as possible to find a replacement so that work could go on as normal.

Theoretically, under Taylor's concept of scientific management, it would be easy to pay employees a fair wage, since it was already established precisely how much each employee should be able to produce. Basically, it would be piecework pay. This sounded very fair since employees would get paid for what they produced. If the employees achieved what they were expected to, they would earn their full day's pay. If they achieved less, they would earn less. On the face of it, what could be fairer and more equitable? When you produced more, you got paid more.

Unfortunately for the workers, Taylor did not understand the concept of "normal variation." The Taylor Scientific Management System does not address the fact that in any group of people, there will be a normal distribution (bell-shaped curve) of abilities. By establishing an average, we are effectively setting a target that is easy for nearly 50 percent of all employees and perhaps impossible for the other 50 percent. How do people react when faced with an impossible task? They may circumvent procedures by taking short-cuts, compromise on quality, or resort to outright cheating. In almost all cases, long-term productivity will suffer.

One case that demonstrates the negative example of the Taylor System of Scientific Management is of an ore mining company that had just hired some "productivity experts" to do a Taylor-style efficiency study. Employees admitted, "Whenever we see one of those guys with a stopwatch, we go half as fast as we can." When one of the "efficiency" experts heard what the employees said, she laughed and replied, "Oh, we take that into consideration. I always double the figures that my studies report to compensate for such loafing."

The "Worker as Doer" philosophy disrespects the motivation and brainpower of people. It assumes that employees are either stupid or lazy and must be constantly watched by management or inspectors. It ignores the contributions that employees could potentially make to the system, instead creating a class of specialists who erroneously assume that it knows more about the processes than the people who do the work. No company can afford such a system today. However, as the Taylor System is thrown out, so must the rewards and recognition efforts that were a part of his system be discarded. They will not fit in with the emerging role of employees in the workforce.

## *WORKER AS PROCESS OWNER*

Total Quality Management has made everyone aware of the importance of having a basic understanding of process. Statistical Process Control methods are now taught in most organizations to help employees chart, control, and improve the processes for which they are responsible. Since the worker in the process generally has the most knowledge about the process, it makes sense to turn control of the process over to the worker on a real-time basis. This trend has led to the concept of "Worker as Process Owner."

When a worker becomes a process owner, he or she is responsible for controlling and correcting errors in the process on a real-time basis. Many workers chart critical process variables and use the appropriate controls to see that they stay within correct limits. This was probably a role that was formerly delegated to quality assurance personnel. Often, groups of workers responsible for similar processes will work on a process improvement team to find ways to improve the process. Such improvements may entail making fundamental changes in the process that go beyond merely controlling the stability of the process. Workers on these teams, or working on their own, assume many of the responsibilities that were once delegated to first-line supervisors. In addition, end-of-process inspection is often decreased or even eliminated as the process owner finds ways to prevent defects and rejections from occurring. The "Worker as Process Owner" now owns part of the role that was once delegated exclusively to supervisors, inspectors, and quality assurance people.

The "What's in it for me?" question becomes very important to employees when they are expected to become process owners, a role that once belonged to someone else. Keep in mind that in most organizations supervisors, inspectors, and quality assurance people are paid more than the hourly people. These same hourly people are now being asked to handle more responsibilities and may even be displacing "white collar" staff, often with no corresponding pay increase. It is a well-known fact that middle managers are experiencing a disproportionate share of job cuts in most organizations. Some of this is no doubt due to the increased use of information systems, but another reason is that workers are assuming responsibilities formerly reserved for staff and management people.

## WORKER AS SUPERVISOR

The next level of responsibility up the scale is "Worker as Supervisor." In organizations with a very flat structure or self-managed work teams, or in some high-empowerment organizations, workers are already assuming this role. The "Worker as Supervisor" may set daily production goals, decide on maintenance and repair schedules, call for shut downs when needed to solve process problems, develop his/her own education plan, and even work with suppliers and customers to ensure needed quality levels. All of the responsibilities of "Worker as Process Owner" are also assumed by the "Worker as Supervisor."

This is a significant empowerment step for most employees. It brings with it opportunities for much greater job autonomy, creativity, and job satisfaction. However, many employees do not see it this way. One union leader said, "Most of my members just want to work nine to five and don't want the hassles of a manager's job." Other employees have indicated that they did not sign on for such an expanded job role and just want to do the job they were hired for. As organizations expand the responsibilities for workers, the role of rewards and recognition systems will need to evolve to match these responsibilities.

The type of reward-and-recognition system that exists in a workplace where employees are characterized as "Worker as Process Owners" will need to be different from that where the predominant role is "Worker as Supervisor." In a "Worker as Supervisor" system, the distinction between hourly workers and management and between hourly workers and salaried staff will no longer have any valid meaning. This will have an impact on pay systems, minimum wage systems, time off, and leave policies. Where the pay system now institutionalizes the distinction between hourly workers and salaried (or exempt and nonexempt), there will no longer be a way to make such distinctions in a system where "Workers are Supervisors." Thus, as employees progress up the scale of responsibility, the rewards and recognition systems in the organization will need to be adapted.

## WORKER AS MANAGER

When workers become managers, they may literally have the keys to the building. Workers will have a budget and will be responsible for new product development, research and development, and sales and marketing. All of these tasks will be part and parcel of the responsibilities of all employees. There will no longer be a department for each of these areas where so-called specialists exist apart from the normal daily business of the organization. There may be system coordinators or facilitators in some of these areas, but the organization can be infinitely more productive when all employees share such responsibilities.

In his book, *Maverick*, Ricardo Semler describes an organization where workers have many of the responsibilities of management. Semler is CEO of a company in Brazil called Semco. Semco is a manufacturer of industrial equipment that employs several hundred people. Since Semler took over, the company has gone from fifty-sixth to fourth place in its industry in terms of size and sales. Semler describes a very unorthodox approach to management. "Imagine," Semler's book jacket says, "a place where employees can choose to work at home, study, and discuss the company's financial statements, make corporate decisions, start their own business with company assets, redesign corporate products, and set their own work hours and salaries." Semco's last job posting generated 1400 responses. Twenty percent of all college students in Brazil said they wanted to work for Semco when they graduated. Is Semco the wave of the future or a mere statistical anomaly? It may be too early to tell, but we believe that Semco is on the right path.

In an organization where everyone is a manager and where even the traditional role of the manager has been greatly expanded, what will the role of rewards and incentives look like? The majority of rewards will be nonfinancial. Most people simply want to know how they are doing and whether or not others respect them and feel they are doing a good job. Perks that are currently reserved for managers will either be nonexistent or, perhaps better yet, will exist for all employees. Imagine each employee having a company car complete with a cellular phone and a set of impressively printed business cards. Imagine every employee with an oak-paneled office, a large walnut desk, and the latest microcomputer. This probably sounds ridiculous, but it is not so. Keep in mind that every employee will have duties that now are only done by staff specialists. In the future, an employee will meet with customers, suppliers, and even competitors. In this vastly expanded role, employees will need a much greater range of information than they currently have access to.

## WORKER AS CO-OWNER

One of the biggest complaints that many business owners and senior managers have is that employees don't appreciate what it costs to run a business. They take for granted the paper clips, rubber bands, and other small necessities that can add up to thousands of dollars, and feel they deserve a salary or wage increase regardless of employee productivity or other cost factors. Owners are absolutely right. Most employees, and this includes a large portion of all managers, don't appreciate the cost of running a business. There are several good reasons for this.

In some organizations, neither managers nor employees actually see profit-and-loss reports or other company financial statements. Many divisions of large corporations are not responsible for marketing and sales, only for producing a certain number of widgets per month. The responsibility for what is to be produced and who it will be sold to is reserved for corporate experts. In organizations such as this, if managers do not really have business responsibilities, is it any wonder that workers are almost totally removed from the realities of the business world?

In other organizations, strict secrecy surrounds most business and financial information. The hierarchy designates who has access to certain information based on the military "need to know" model. Those who allegedly have no "need to know" are denied access to information available to others. This creates "information haves" and "information have-nots." Again, is it any wonder that many employees are not in touch with the realities and actual costs of doing business?

During a workshop on SPC (Statistical Process Control) for some production employees, I mentioned that standard of living had to be tied to productivity, that none of us deserved a raise, and that society could not afford wage increases to industries where there were no productivity gains. The reaction was a sea of blank faces. After more questioning, the employees were asked if they understood the linkage between wages and productivity. No hands went up to answer, but several participants asked me to explain it. After the explanation, one older man raised his hand and asked, "Why didn't they teach this kind of stuff in school?" It was a good question; it still is.

Another reason for the lack of understanding of the costs of doing business comes from the way finances are managed in most organizations. How many employees have to pay for the paper clips they use or the rubber bands they take? How many employees even really know what such items cost? Many workers only hear about the costs when it comes time to negotiate contracts or during salary reviews. This leads employees to think, "I am not responsible for costs, only management is." In such organizations, workers take costs for granted because they see no connection between their neglect or wastefulness and the overall impact on the bottom line. There is a great deal of merit in creating a system (open book management) where the costs of doing business are not only transparent, but are felt and appreciated by all employees, perhaps by giving all employees a budget and attendant responsibilities.

In a system with "Workers as Co-Owners," the responsibilities, liabilities, and costs of doing business will be shared by all employees. In addition, the profits and gains of doing business will also be shared to a much greater extent than is now the case with current profit-sharing plans. In the twenty-first-century organization, employees will have a greater stake in the success or failure of the organization. People are committed to what they are involved in. If you want employees to be committed to the enterprise, then you must involve them in all aspects of the enterprise. There are at least two barriers to doing this. The first is providing the requisite level of training needed to handle increased responsibilities. The second is finding a way to provide employees with the additional information that they will need to handle the new responsibilities. These two conditions can determine the success or failure of organizations as they attempt to flatten the organization pyramid and empower employees.

## INFORMATION AND TRAINING

As employees move up the scale from "Worker as Doer" to "Worker as Co-Owner," the organization will have to see to it that employees are given the training and information to handle the new responsibilities. Imagine, if you will, the employee who must lock up the office when she/he leaves, but is not told where the key is (lack of information) or given the needed training to turn on the security system (lack of training). It is impossible to move up the scale of responsibilities without a large increase in both training and information. Organizations will have to double or triple their present training budgets to fuel this revolution. Most studies of American businesses find that less than 1 percent of payroll is spent on training. It is estimated that world-class organizations are spending in the neighborhood of 4 percent on training and many are anticipating that figure will need to go to at least 8 percent in order to stay competitive. However, it will take more than just training to create "Workers as Co-Owners."

Organizations are going to have to develop strategies to break down the barriers surrounding information in the organization. This is scary to many managers and staff people. Information is power. As we move from "Worker as Doer" to "Worker as Co-Owner," we are taking the power and responsibilities away from managers and staff people and distributing them more equitably across the organization. There will be many who will resist this. It will not be an easy task to find new roles for these employees and to help them see the benefits of change. The commonly heard question, "What's in it for me?" is being asked not only by lower-level workers, but by many of those in management and staff positions. It will be critical that this question be answered for them as well.

# Chapter 16

# New Style Incentives

There are two initial tasks we must complete in order to understand the role of incentives in an organization. Webster's dictionary defines the term "incentive" as "Something that incites or has a tendency to incite to determination or action." Incentives can be viewed as having a broader capacity to incite to action than either rewards or recognition. Incentives include self-generated motivation such as wanting to get home on time or feeling good when a job is done well. The concept of incentives does not have the narrowness of scope that one commonly attributes to the idea of rewards and recognition. This is because most rewards and recognition are traditionally generated by "others" who are in supervisory positions. Furthermore, rewards have become associated with financial remuneration to a great degree. Thus, we view rewards and recognition as a subset or a subcategory of incentives.

Another important subcategory of incentives includes "disincentives." Most so-called "motivation" or "morale" problems are produced by the "disincentives" that are pervasive in many organizations. For instance, the familiar syndrome of "shooting the messenger" is a strong "disincentive" to being open and candid with management about problems that are recognized by employees. Dr. Deming always maintained that 94 percent of the problems in an organization were system problems and only 6 percent were people related. He believed that the issue was not how to motivate employees or how to provide incentives to get more work out of employees, but how to take the "disincentives" or "demotivators" out of the system. Dr. Deming repeatedly argued that most such disincentives were part of the system and were not intrinsic to the employees. Programs dealing with such issues as conflict management, morale, empowerment, and motivation often miss the mark because the implementers of the programs assume that employees need "motivating" when actually what employees need is less "demotivating."

Another reason we prefer to think of organizational incentives versus rewards and recognition is that the broader concept allows us to apply the category to other stakeholders in the organization. Until the onset of the Total Quality movement, most organizations saw their priority as maximizing shareholder assets. In other words, maximizing profits and dividends. The major incentives or rewards in most American corporations were for the stockholders, a subset of stakeholders. Stakeholders can be defined as "Anyone who has a vested interest in what the organization achieves." A broad set of stakeholders for a corporation would include stockholders, owners, investors, customers, suppliers, managers, employees, the government, the community, and labor organizations. Customers, suppliers, and society may also have a fair claim to incentives, as well as the stockholders and management. In terms of "inciting" to action, we most certainly want to incite suppliers and customers to be committed to our organizations. It seems reasonable that we should examine the incentives for these groups as well as for employees and the traditional groups that are usually associated with incentives.

In America, we have traditionally done everything we could to satisfy our stockholders and, until the advent of Total Quality, we virtually ignored the customers and other stakeholders. By way of contrast, the Japanese have made a religion out of satisfying customers, but often ignored the needs of other stakeholders. Akio Morita, founder and former CEO of Sony Corporation stated that "Japan's competitiveness has been achieved by keeping margins and prices low over a long time in a constant search for volume to provide cash flow. This has meant skimping other stakeholders in favor of the customer. Japan must fashion a new corporate attitude, rebalancing stakeholder interests and going some way to meet the West."

The secret of organizational success is to *optimize* the needs of stakeholders and the needs of customers. System optimization is a concept that deals with the need to fine tune a system by adjusting multiple variables which impact success. Systems theory provides ample evidence that maximizing (ignoring the concept of multiple factors in favor of one single factor) any one variable in a complex system will lead to the overall suboptimization or poor performance of the entire system. In a simple system where only one factor is important to success, it is permissible to attempt to maximize this factor. However, in a complex system (where more than one variable impacts success), any effort to maximize one variable (whether employee satisfaction, morale, turnover, ROI, etc.) can only lead to suboptimization of the overall system.

Managing an organization means that we have to take a systems view to the effort. We cannot ignore the fact that success is a multifactor phenomenon. No one factor can guarantee success. Maximizing strategies (cutting costs, cutting employees, downsizing, etc.) often ignores this principle and leads to systems that either perform worse than before or nowhere near their overall capability. Maximization strategies create systems that are out of balance and lack any possibility of synergy. Many managers do not understand why "maximizing profits" will lead to inadequate system performance. These managers fail to see that as they scrimp on research, training, employee development, quality, innovation, and customer service, they are sowing the seeds of their future demise. As the Japanese have found out, even a preoccupation with customers can lead to suboptimal performance.

## DISINCENTIVES

Incentives are the primary mechanism for balancing and addressing both stakeholders' and customers' needs. Disincentives are the means for frustrating either stakeholders' or customers' needs. It will do no good to provide countless incentives if the disincentives are not removed from the system. One example is a hotel that routinely sponsors free giveaways based on the number of nights its customers stay. The hotel's service is mediocre, but it spends lots of money on its promotions. This is a waste of time, money, and effort. Most business travelers care very little about hotel giveaways. They care about service, quality, and convenience. If another hotel in the area provides these, the hotel offering the giveaways will probably lose much of its business. If there is no competitor nearby, the giveaways are a waste of money in the first place. Giveaways would only be a useful differentiating factor if the competition was equally mediocre. It is sad to reflect that many service organizations tolerate mediocre service and quality. Too often, establishments such as this hotel look for new and unique incentives, but ignore the fundamental disincentives that are part of its overall system.

It is important for organizations to identify and understand the disincentives that exist in their systems. This is not an easy task because disincentives are often invisible to the employees and management inside the system. Dr. Deming provided one list of disincentives that exist in many, if not most, organizations. He called these the "Seven Deadly Diseases." They included the following:

1. Lack of planning and purpose
2. Emphasis on short-term profits
3. Performance evaluations that ranked people
4. Mobility of management
5. Management by visible figures alone
6. Excessive medical costs
7. Excessive costs of liability

Deming's list provides a starting point to look for disincentives, but does not go far enough. There are many other disincentives besides the ones he has identified. In every organization, there are disincentives that are unique to that organization. The Malcolm Baldrige National Quality Award criteria can be used to help ferret out some of these disincentives. Some of the Baldrige Award categories apply to customers, some to employees, some to stockholders, some to suppliers, and some more to owners. Each of the seven categories can help to identify the disincentives that exist in an organization for one or more of the appropriate stakeholder groups.

For example, Category Two (Information) of the Baldrige Award criteria can help to identify the disincentives that confront many employees. Do employees get the information they need to do their jobs? Do they feel they understand the mission and goals of the organization? Do they have the data to improve their processes? Do they get enough information to help customers if the need arises? Do they have adequate ability to bring up problems and get timely answers to problems?

With respect to addressing the needs or disincentives that face suppliers to your organization, you might ask the following questions: Are there regular information and problem exchanges between suppliers and the organization? Do any kinds of meetings take place where suppliers are able to contribute their ideas on improvement? Can the suppliers get information needed from the organization? Is there a sense of openness and honesty that exists in transactions between the organization and its suppliers?

Category Two can also be used for identifying disincentives that confront managers in your organization. Do managers have access to information needed for long-range planning? Do they understand the needs of their customers? Are they involved in long-term planning and goal setting for the organization? Do they get information from employees on how well they are managing? Are there regular means of information exchanges between employees and managers that deal with continuous improvement, product quality, innovation, safety, etc.? Do the stockholders and owners keep the managers well informed as to future directions and anticipated changes?

By looking at how each category of the Baldrige Award relates to all stakeholders and customers, a large number of problem areas can be identified. For instance, in Category Four of the Baldrige Award criteria (Human Resource Development and Management), there are many issues which, if not addressed, could create major disincentives for employees and managers, as well as customers. The elimination of such problems as part of a systematic effort will contribute more toward ensuring the success of your organization than giveaway schemes or short-term rewards such as the annual Thanksgiving turkey or the annual supplier recognition dinner. Even the stockholders will feel more confident knowing that the dividend checks they receive will continue for many years and perhaps get bigger and bigger.

## *INCENTIVES*

When most managers think about incentives, they usually want to know how they can motivate employees to higher levels of performance or increased productivity. Dr. Deming consolidated his ideas on management into what he called his "System of Profound

Knowledge." Deming argued that there were four essential elements to managing, and that all managers should be well versed in these elements: Knowledge of Variation; Appreciation for a System; Knowledge of People, or psychology; and Theory of Knowledge. Each of these elements plays a role in the ability of organizational incentives to affect the productivity of an organization. Without this knowledge, a new incentive system is just a random exercise and may even make things worse.

We are all aware of complaints about unfair employee compensation systems, gain-sharing plans and profit-sharing plans that are inequitable and demotivate rather than motivate, suggestion programs that get labeled as "bitch boxes," and bonus systems that decrease employee morale rather than increase it. One of the funniest problems is probably the traditional company "Thanksgiving turkey." In many organizations, the turkey is just one more avenue for employee complaints and grievances. Managers wonder how something as seemingly innocuous as a turkey could cause such problems and headaches. The best way to avoid these problems is by understanding how the four elements of Deming's System of Profound Knowledge affect the way that incentive systems will be viewed by organizational stakeholders.

## APPRECIATION FOR A SYSTEM

A great deal of time and effort has been spent finding schemes to "motivate" employees. We hear about "Alternative Reward and Recognition" schemes, "Gain-sharing Plans," "Profit-sharing Plans," "Pay-for-Performance" systems, "ESOP Plans," "Hay System for Compensation," and "Pay-for-Suggestion Plans." The schemes and the zeal with which they are promoted can easily confuse and hide what really makes an organization successful. The criteria for evaluating the success of these schemes are often one-dimensional or ignore other key organizational success factors. Thus, the accounts receivable clerk may double the amount of forms he/she processes under the new Pay-for-Performance or Gain-Sharing System, but the overall organization suffers because she/he ignores other work that is not part of the compensation scheme. In one organization that I worked with, a new single source contract with one supplier resulted in lower costs on some key materials. However, it was later noted that the supplier compensated for this loss by raising the prices for other items that were sold to the organization through another contract. These were charged to another department which ended up paying higher prices than it could have gotten from another local vendor. It could easily be said that the purchasing agent was too eager to go to single sourcing and should have been more careful. However, the key point here is that many strategies and schemes opt for maximization over optimization. People maximize the desired variables (costs, output, etc.), but while this may benefit one area, it has the net effect of lowering the overall productivity of the organization instead of raising it.

Before establishing any kind of an incentive system, the overall system and the factors impacting the system, as well as interactions, must be adequately understood. It is okay to suboptimize a system when it is clearly understood what the trade-offs will be and you are willing to live with them. For instance, if costs are too high, you may have to cut advertising or marketing budgets, but you should be clear on how much sales and revenue may be reduced. If you can live with lower overall revenues and increased profits, this might be a good trade-off. It is very dangerous when you either do not understand the negative effects or you cannot live with them. For example, if you wanted to increase the number of telephone transactions with customers, you might put in incentives to encourage speedier phone transactions or institute a toll-free 800 number. Here, the key variable is the number of transactions versus other factors such as costs, customer satisfaction, etc. Of course, the trade-off might mean either lower customer satisfaction or increased costs.

Incentive systems cannot be separated from the overall system and that includes the external system. Any scheme that attempts to improve individual productivity and ignores the interactions that exist among people, methods, technology, materials, environment, and information is almost certain to lead to suboptimal performance somewhere in the organization. Hence, the importance of having an "appreciation for a system." The importance of such knowledge and what it means for managing the organization cannot be overstated.

## *KNOWLEDGE OF PEOPLE, OR PSYCHOLOGY*

There have been many schemes to increase organizational productivity which have been based on an understanding of the psychology of people. Herzberg's Motivation Theory, Skinner's Behavior Theory, and Maslow's Pyramid have been studied by almost all human resource development practitioners at one time or another. Such theories give a good understanding of the psychology of motivation. They can tell us how lottery schemes or slot machines work (how they are based on different payback principles). They can help us understand why something motivates one person but not another. These theories can also help us understand that as people mature, their needs and aspirations can change over time. The theories can teach us the difference between intrinsic and extrinsic motivators and why some are more powerful than others. It is important to understand all of these concepts, but it is not sufficient. A knowledge of psychology is a necessary, but not a sufficient condition for understanding how incentives will be viewed by stakeholders and whether or not incentives will make a positive contribution to organizational performance.

Many incentive schemes go wrong because they are based on an overly simplistic view of human nature. Some schemes (e.g., piecework plans) basically assume that people are greedy. Others (pay-for-performance schemes and gain-sharing schemes) fail to examine the nature of cooperation and teamwork that are fundamental to organizational productivity. Such schemes are generally based on the concept of competition or individualism rather than cooperation. In one plant, where seamstresses were paid for each garment produced, one employee always exceeded all others in output. Her compensation was nearly double that of the next closest employee. She said that she had a "secret," but would not share it because the organization would then adjust the piecework schedule and she would lose wages. The company even went so far as to install a TV monitor, but the worker was too canny to be observed. So her secret, which could have doubled overall productivity, remained a secret because most piecework schemes reward competition over cooperation.

In other organizations, managers seem to be more concerned with compensating "star performers" than recognizing the daily "average" contributions of the majority of their employees. Most employees could be fit around a bell-shaped curve and about 86 percent of them will qualify as "normal" or average employees. Worrying only about compensating the "stars" might mean missing a great deal of other effort that contributes to the success of an organization. Recently, some organizations have become aware of the importance of team cooperation, diversity, shared knowledge and meaning, and internal customers. Such elements require a different incentive system than one based on the assumption that the entire organization will benefit if Joe or Mary produces more widgets per hour or if the "employee of the month" can be rewarded with a special parking spot and an engraved plaque.

The basic premise of most programs is that it is better to give a few people a great deal of money than many people a little money each. In American organizations, suggestion system managers agonize over how much a suggestion is worth because employees are usually paid for their ideas on the basis of the savings or productivity increases the ideas generate. Given the unknown variables that go into trying to figure it all out, it is probably an exercise in fantasy at best. Nevertheless, in several organizations, the calculations have been cause for grievances.

The Japanese worry less about what the savings from a particular idea will be and more about making sure that lots of ideas get submitted. Generally, this means that it is better to reward or recognize an employee for every idea submitted and worry less about the cost savings or benefits. The difference between the American system and the Japanese system is similar to the difference between the lottery payback system and the slot machine payback system. In America, we seem to favor the lottery system (few winners, but big paybacks). The Japanese favor the slot machine system (many winners, but less payback). The result is that in Japan, the savings from ideas exceeds that of the United States by almost ten to one.

There is little doubt that lotteries motivate people to buy tickets. But again, basing organizational incentive systems on a lottery (e.g., employee of the month, manager of the year, salesperson of the week, etc.) also ignores the important element that teamwork and cooperation play in the success of any one individual. One IBM plant disbanded its suggestion incentive system after many employees refused to submit ideas while part of a team. One employee submitted an idea to the suggestion program and received a very large cash reward, causing other employees to think, "Why share my ideas for free with a team, when I can submit them to the suggestion program and get paid a great deal of money?" If we are too narrow and restrictive in our understanding of how human nature relates to our incentive systems, we will likely cause little increase in productivity and performance and may even cause a decrease in many elements needed for long-term success.

## KNOWLEDGE OF VARIATION

Dr. Deming's Red Bead experiment is the single best example of the negative impact that failing to understand variation can have on an organization or individual. Not only is the organization suboptimized by this failure, but the spirits of individuals are often destroyed. Many other examples of the knowledge of variation can be used to demonstrate how a failure to understand variation can only produce destructive incentive systems. Generally, when individuals are rewarded or punished for something that is out of their control, they, and others, are confused. Such rewards will either lead to an overall loss of morale or a feeling by employees that "success" is a random event.

In any system of employees, performance will generally follow a bell-shaped curve. Less than 1.5 percent of the employees are either star performers or really bad performers. Natural and normal variation accounts for the rest of the differences between individuals. Understanding this creates an entirely new perspective on how one approaches incentive systems. Zytec (a winner of the Malcolm Baldrige National Quality Award) applied this theory to its annual performance appraisal system and its system for increasing salaries. Instead of calling the 97 percent "average performers" (which always has a pejorative connotation), Zytec called them "Quality Performers." This was not just an exercise in semantics; the company also adjusted the quality performers' salaries and compensation systems accordingly to reflect this concept. Zytec still gave bonuses to "above average" employees, and the company still had to deal with substandard performance. However, the company no longer confused poor performance caused by the system with individual or "motivation" problems.

Zytec recognized that it was just as important to provide incentives for the "Quality Performers" as it was for the "Stars." Contrast this kind of knowledge with the fundamental ignorance exhibited by organizations that break down performance curves into five or more levels. It is statistically invalid and a pragmatic impossibility to draw this many distinctions between employees. Thus, such systems create the following paradox: While statistically, 97 percent of the employees are average, in terms of incentives, the system will respond as though anywhere from 0 to 50 percent of employees are either above average or below average. This, of course, results in the well-known "creep" or escalation effect whereby, in a few years, all or most employees are rated as above average, another statistical impossibility. Is it any wonder that organizations frequently change performance appraisal and compensation schemes? Most of these schemes demonstrate little or no understanding of the principles of statistics and normal variation. Frequent changes in such performance appraisal systems do more to create an illusion of progress than to create any fundamental improvements or insights on the part of employees as to how to perform better.

## THEORY OF KNOWLEDGE

Dr. Deming always believed that theory could not be divorced from practice. If you wanted to understand something, you had to create a theory and then test it. He repeatedly reminded us during his seminars on Methods for Management of Productivity and Quality that "There is no substitute for knowledge. Whatever it is that you do, you must understand how and why something works. You must have theory. You must test your theory. Management's job is prediction and theory testing." One such theory was created by John Rawls, author of *Theory of Justice,* who explained that there are many different elements of justice, and understanding them helps all of society become more equitable. Chaos theory (most simply described by Margaret Wheatley in her book, *Leadership and the New Science*) is a theory created to explain the behavior of elements in a nonlinear system. Theorists such as Wheatley have shown how managers can use this theory to better explain the changes and transformations that their organizations are undergoing. Such theories support the contention of Kurt Lewin that "There is nothing so practical as a good theory." In this light, it makes sense to have a "Theory of Incentives" that can guide us in developing and applying incentives within an organization. Without some theory, efforts to improve organizational incentives are destined to be helter-skelter events.

Several elements seem essential to a theory of incentives. Some of these elements have been "common sense" in many organizations for years. The first, and probably the most important element, is *fairness*. Incentives must seem fair and equitable to the employees or recipients. Fairness means that there is a reasonable relationship between the effort and the reward. This principle is well acknowledged, if not practiced, by most organizations. In addition to this element, several additional elements should be part of a theory of incentives, including inclusiveness, accessibility, excitement, affirmation, constructiveness, respect, and purpose. A few of these elements are used implicitly in some organizations. A good system of incentives would attempt to optimize these elements but not emphasize any single one of them.

*Inclusiveness* means that employees receive incentives that make them feel a part of and committed to the organization. Incentives that are inclusive would break down barriers between managers and employees, as well as those between departments and different "classes" of employees. *Accessibility* is the ease by which employees can receive incentives. Incentives should not be established that are unattainable or beyond the reach of individuals. *Excitement* means that the incentive should be unique, interesting, and challenging. All incentives get stale with the passing of time. *Affirmation* means that the incentives should reward people for being the best that they can be and are trying to be. It means that one employee is not elevated or "recognized" at the expense of another employee or by destroying morale and teamwork. *Constructiveness* means the system of incentives promotes the value and norms of the organization. There should be an alignment among the organizational culture, norms, and incentives. *Respect* means that the system takes into account individual differences in people and acknowledges diversity in the workforce. Incentives must not only respect diversity but, ideally, should promote it. *Purpose* means that the system of incentives works toward some larger aim. The aim should be aligned with the goals and objectives of the organization. The incentives should not lead to system suboptimization.

The elements described could be used to create a rating scale which an organization would use to evaluate its incentive systems. This would help create a database that could be used for continually improving the system of incentives that exists in the organization. For instance, if employees rated the incentive system low on inclusiveness, this would indicate that more ways need to be found to help employees feel that they are part of the organization, or more efforts are needed to promote teamwork. A low rating on respect might indicate that you are not doing enough to recognize cultural differences in the organization or to support a culture of innovation and diversity within the organization. Each of these elements are indicative of the quality of a good incentive system and should be reviewed.

A rating scale (such as that described above) could also be adapted to examine the impact and value of incentives as seen by other stakeholders and customers. The concept of customer incentives, in the broadest sense, directly relates to the ability of an organization to provide added value to the customer. However, there is a value to the customer in doing business with your organization that is above and beyond anything he/she expects to receive or purchase. One way to measure this additional value is through the concept of incentives. In other words, what motivates or incites the customer to come to your organization? We are not talking about giveaways to customers. Such thinking is analogous to the idea that carrots on sticks are essential to "motivate" employees. This is naive and simplistic thinking at best.

Software companies are a good example. There are several excellent software programs on the market. But customer support for some of these is either grossly lacking or nonexistent. Some companies do not have toll-free 800 numbers, forcing the customer to incur significant costs while waiting for a technician to help them. When customers do call, some technicians do not seem to even understand their own programs and are often quite anxious to blame any problems on the customer's hardware or operating system. Even when a company has technically excellent service (toll-free 800 numbers, available twenty-four hours a day, seven days a week), it often wants to apply a formula to the customer's problem and pay little attention to whether it's the right answer to the specific problem. There is little or no consideration given to what it is costing the customer in terms of time and money. I have yet to find a company that offers me any kind of incentive to mitigate my headaches and frustration even when the problem is in that company's software. Calling this support "customer service" oversimplifies the concept of incentives that the organization provides to keep its customers. But for the astute software company, there is a great marketing opportunity that lies virtually unexploited. When this is added to the frequent upgrades and version fixes (which often have new glitches), it is easy for customers to start asking, "Why upgrade? What is the incentive to change from version 95.119 to version 95.121? What is the incentive to try new software from these companies?"

Establishing a great incentive system is a good deal more complex than merely handing out cash awards, giveaways, or "attaboys." Incentive systems need to address a much broader range of organizational issues than are typically looked at. Without good incentive systems, how can an organization reinforce the goals that it wants to achieve? Instead, the disincentives built into most systems will work to oppose any new directions, changes, or goals the organization hopes to accomplish.

# Chapter 17

# Ideas, Yes. Suggestion Boxes, No.

At the first Deming seminar I attended, I met a senior human resource manager from Tectronics Corporation. During a coffee break, we were discussing Dr. Deming's thoughts on his "Seven Deadly Diseases" when my new acquaintance commented that he knew what the "eighth deadly disease" was–the corporate suggestion box. I was surprised by his remark. I had never paid too much attention to the suggestion boxes that had been used at my previous places of employment, so I didn't have strong feelings about them one way or the other. In fact, taken at face value, I would have thought they were a great idea. What could be better than soliciting ideas from employees on how to improve the workplace? Certainly, this shows at least a willingness by management to listen to the ideas of employees and to try to put some value on employee contributions. In many organizations, employees are even rewarded for the cost savings generated by their ideas. Theoretically, this should create a direct incentive for employees to help the organization as well as benefit themselves. While these thoughts were going through my head, I wondered why anyone would criticize the use of suggestion boxes to the point of labeling the practice as the "Eighth Deadly Disease."

I did not question his reasons at the time, but I put his comment on suggestion boxes somewhere in the back of my mind. I was just starting my career as a consultant and I had many more important issues to ponder. Nevertheless, I never forgot his comment and, eventually, time and experience proved the manager from Tectronics correct. Over the years, I have seen so many examples of the problems created by suggestion systems that I would now advise organizations to do away with what I call the "old style suggestion system."

I became more interested in suggestion boxes and the harm they cause shortly after visiting Ron Schmidt, CEO of Zytec Corporation. My visit to Zytec was about two years before the company won the Malcolm Baldrige National Quality Award. I talked with Ron about his company's quality improvement effort. Ron told me that Zytec had just been audited by a group of Japanese consultants who cited Zytec as being weak in terms of methods for obtaining individual ideas from employees.

Ron assumed that the Japanese consultants wanted a suggestion system for employees and challenged them on this because he was well aware of the dangers of "suggestion systems." The Japanese consultants argued that a good program for obtaining ideas from employees could be developed that did not have the drawbacks of the traditional suggestion system. Ron then began to research how suggestion programs are handled in Japan and found some surprising differences between Japanese and American suggestion programs. As he shared his new knowledge, I gained a better understanding of the problems in the traditional American suggestion programs. The opportunity to compare Japanese programs with American programs soon arose.

In 1991, as a member of Process Management International's Executive Study Tour to Japan, cosponsored by Komatsu Career Development Enterprises, I studied some of the leading Japanese TQM practitioners, including some of the organizations that had won the Deming Prize, the Japanese prize for quality. Everywhere we went, our hosts were more than happy to answer our questions. We toured each organization, then spent two to four hours in debriefing sessions where we asked many questions. Often the debriefing was preceded by a formal presentation outlining the TQM strategies of each organization. I used every opportunity to question and research the different suggestion systems that were described at these award-winning organizations. Following this tour, I conducted nearly a year of research into suggestion programs in the United States, including a literature search and extensive consultations with managers of suggestion systems.

In many respects, the flaws underlying the traditional American suggestion programs are the same flaws underlying the traditional American management system. They are based on assumptions that sound plausible–until you really study them. Then it becomes clear how dangerous and false these assumptions are. Once you understand these assumptions and why they are false, it is very simple to design a suggestion system that will generate thousands of excellent employee ideas. In fact, when we suggested these ideas to one manager, her response was, "We can't do that. We would be overwhelmed with ideas on how to improve things!" She was still stuck in the old system where managers were the ones who actually did all the improvement work. So she equated more suggestions with more work. It was no wonder she didn't want to listen.

## THE TRADITIONAL SUGGESTION BOX

Many organizations have requisite forms to fill out if you have a problem or a solution to a problem. The usual procedure is for the employee to fill out a form, put it in a locked box and wait . . . and wait . . . and wait. The suggestion system box is eventually opened by a supervisor or manager and ideas are sent to the "central suggestion system processing" person. Generally, each organization has a suggestion system coordinator who is responsible for monitoring ideas, providing forms, helping to decide which ideas are accepted, and how much cost savings have resulted. In some organizations, if an employee's idea is accepted and any cost savings result, the employee often receives a share of the projected or actual cost savings. In other organizations, employees are recognized at an annual dinner or with a certificate of recognition.

The traditional system is viewed by many managers as a "pain in the butt" or as the "bitch box on the wall." It is often seen as a place where more work is made for managers and where many unjustified complaints are dumped by disgruntled employees. Managers do not see their role as one of getting ideas, but rather one of weeding out ideas.

One organization I worked with had nearly 8000 employees, but at the end of the fiscal year, had received and reviewed only 287 ideas. Two full-time employees and one half-time employee were assigned to the suggestion system program. I commented (somewhat facetiously) that if the company had received five ideas per employee per year (40,000 ideas submitted), it would have needed a staff of nearly 350 employees to approve or disapprove ideas. The company called its program the "Beneficial Suggestion System" program. The employees called it the "Benny Sucks" program because they felt it was so biased and bureaucratic.

Another organization I worked with took an average of 400 days to approve or disapprove a suggestion. The company's leaders wanted to carefully scrutinize ideas because they had received many complaints from employees that rewards were not in line with cost savings. Employees had even filed union grievances over the issue. Most employees saw the suggestion box as a sort of "black hole" where submitted ideas were never seen again. They assumed management was stealing employees' ideas and did not want to give the employees credit. Actually, management would have just liked to see the whole system disappear, but there was some pressure in the system to have a means for obtaining employee ideas. Senior management assumed that any system was better than no system. In reality, a bad system is worse than no system.

## MANAGEMENT VERSUS WORKER RESPONSIBILITY

The organizations described above had traditional suggestion systems that were clearly not meeting the goals and objectives of the sponsors. The number of suggested ideas per employee was low, the response times were long, and the percentage of ideas accepted was also low (usually less than 20 percent of ideas were approved). In the eyes of most managers, these "problems" are okay because management already has enough work to do. The manager just sees more ideas as more work that will be put on his/her plate. Herein lies the fault with the traditional system.

In the traditional system, the manager is empowered, but the worker is not. Thus, it is the manager's responsibility to implement suggestions, not the employee's. The employee sees his/her role as pointing out to management what is wrong and expecting management to fix it. Sometimes the suggestions deal with productivity issues, but often they deal with "hygiene" problems that are a low priority for many managers. Still other suggestions would clearly bankrupt many organizations. I have seen suggestions such as, "The parking lot needs to be paved," "We need a new printing press," to

"A covered bike path is needed during winter months." Managers who are comfortable with firefighting are often overwhelmed by the ideas that come out of the traditional suggestion system box. Management deems many of these ideas as cost prohibitive, frivolous, irrelevant, or impossible to implement under any circumstances.

The single most important assumption that must be changed is that it is management's job to approve and implement suggestions and it is the worker's job to simply complain or suggest what must be improved. Such a system sets up an adversarial relationship between management and labor that will never be able to handle more than a few suggestions per year. Management effectively acts as a bottleneck when ideas are sent up the traditional organizational pyramid.

In the new style system, the roles of management and workers are very different. The worker is given responsibility for implementing, not just suggesting. The manager is given the role of coordinator and solicitor of ideas. In addition, the supervisor is expected to help facilitate the implementation of ideas. The responsibility for approving ideas is kept as low as possible in the traditional organization chart in order to prevent the bottlenecking and lengthy time delays typical in the traditional system. In the new style system, workers are given access to information that previously has been known only to management. Access to more information and greater resources are essential for the new style system to work.

If workers are empowered to implement suggestions, it is important that they be clear on what is a good suggestion. Many authorities advise that any idea is appropriate. The argument has been made that suggestions should not be limited to an employee's job or work area. This argument presupposes that a work process can cut across many work areas and that many good ideas would be lost with such a restriction. One criteria that is essential for any suggestion concerns the ability of the person (perhaps with fellow employees or local supervision) to implement the suggestion. An employee can easily find fault with someone else's work but he/she cannot know everyone else's processes well enough to understand how they can be fixed. We often think we can do someone else's job better than he/she can, but a criteria for a suggestion must be whether responsibility can be placed or assumed by the suggester for implementation.

There is nothing wrong with making suggestions to improve someone else's work processes if the other party is a coproducer of the suggestion.

Another important criteria for the new style suggestion program concerns the need for small incremental improvements versus looking for the giant breakthrough. There may be a time when a new printing press is actually needed, but there may also be hundreds of little ideas that will get greater productivity out of the current press. In the new style system, employees need to look for base hits, not home runs or grand slams. If the system is set up to get the base hits, then the home runs will be inevitable. The old style system seemed to value only those suggestions that were major breakthroughs or "home runs" in scope. As a result, many employees did not feel that their ideas were worth consideration and did not bother to contribute them.

In Japan, the overall employee participation rate is about nineteen suggestions per employee per year. In the United States, it is about .05 ideas per employee per year. A Japanese company with 7,000 employees would have about 133,000 suggestions approved per year while a typical U.S. company with the same number of employees might have about 350 ideas approved per year. With this many suggestions, home runs are not necessary. The Japanese typically have a much lower rate of return (monetary savings) per suggestion than in the United States, but with the greater number of suggestions submitted and approved, the overall cost savings is considerably higher than in the United States. At the Fuji Xerox plant I visited in Japan, the annual cost savings from their suggestion program was nearly 21 million dollars a year. The company's budget for the maintenance and administration of the program was nearly three million dollars, including rewards and payouts to suggesters.

The average employee knows how to improve his/her job. Encouraging and empowering the employee to do so can result in staggering cost savings. One caution is to avoid thinking that any single system will solve all of the problems in an organization. Possessing a hammer does not mean that every problem is a nail. No suggestion system, no matter how effective, can either reveal or solve all of an organization's problems and improvement needs.

## FINANCIAL REWARDS

The traditional suggestion system bases rewards on a formula that usually allocates potential (sometimes actual) cost savings to each suggestion. The employee may get a percentage of the cost savings. The basic underlying assumption in the traditional system is that the dollars paid out will provide an incentive for employees, assuming that when they see other employees receiving financial rewards, they will also be motivated to put in suggestions. There are serious problems with this assumption. Most payback formulas are very problematic. Many good ideas can't be quantified in terms of dollars and cents, and even for ideas where it is generally acknowledged that there will be cost savings, it is very difficult to project the actual amount. Management often wants to underestimate the savings since it will have to pay out based on the projections. To the employees, it appears that management is trying to "cheat" them. Actually, it is more a case of fiscal conservatism than cheating. Management will have paid out the money before it is possible to actually determine what the savings will be, thus management's tendency is to be conservative in projecting actual savings.

Yet another problem with the formula system is exemplified by what happened at one IBM plant. An unusually large payout to an individual employee created negative impacts on all of the team improvement efforts that were also going on in the plant. Many employees, seeing the sizable payout, felt they would be better off submitting their ideas to the suggestion program instead of contributing them within their process improvement team efforts. Team-based improvements did not offer the magnitude of the payout offered by the individual suggestion program. This is a typical example of what could be called the "Grand Lottery" effect. Everyone sees the winner with the six million dollar check and runs out to buy a lottery ticket. Few people stop to consider the odds against winning. It is a heart over head response. Employees saw the big payout at the IBM plant and all wanted in on the pot.

In the new style system, the incentive effect is more like that of a slot machine. It is based on what the behaviorists call "small continuous reinforcement principles." Thus, each time you play, you receive some sort of a payback. The paybacks are kept small and are not tied to any cost-benefit savings formula. The purpose of this system is basically to recognize the contributions of individuals with some tangible rewards. Managers often ask if the rewards need to be extrinsic, intrinsic, or if a letter from the president will do. One employee answered for many when she said that she would rather have the tenth dollar bill (assuming she received one dollar for each suggestion) than the tenth letter from the president. Furthermore, can you imagine a company president sending out hundreds or even thousands of letters each year? She/he would do nothing but write boring repetitive letters thanking employees for their suggestions.

Extrinsic rewards do not need to be added directly to employee paychecks. They could be gift certificates, free tickets to a movie, coupons to McDonald's, or some other small token that can be exchanged for something the person wants. Many organizations use a catalog of products and when a sufficient number of points are reached, the individual can redeem his/her points for a gift in the catalog. In this system, an employee accrues points for each suggestion and can save and redeem those points at any prize level he/she chooses. Another idea is for points to be granted to employees for each idea received, with time off given when a sufficient number of points are obtained.

Many organizations find that they need to periodically change the rewards or come up with innovative ideas as the old ones get stale. One hospital had a team of employees which coordinated its suggestion system program. The team was responsible for handling the budget for the program and for deciding on rewards and incentives for participation. It was also responsible for dealing with the measurement and monitoring of the system's effectiveness as well as efforts to continually improve the system.

## CONTINUOUS IMPROVEMENT OF THE SYSTEM

Measurements of the suggestion systems must be used for the purpose of continuous improvement. Measurements should include the time it takes to process suggestions, the number of suggestions implemented, the percentage of suggestions rejected, the cost savings per suggestion, and the cost payout per suggestion. The system must be committed to continually improving each of these performance parameters. Furthermore, the system needs to challenge itself to continually set and achieve new goals. I challenged one organization to create a suggestion system that could achieve the following goals:

1. It would create an average of ten suggestions per employee per year.
2. It would take no more then fourteen days for a suggestion to be approved or disapproved.
3. Over 90 percent of all suggestions would be approved and implemented.
4. Over 75 percent of all employees would participate in the system.
5. Each employee would receive some kind of an extrinsic reward for each idea that was implemented.
6. There would be no bureaucracy created to measure, monitor or facilitate the suggestion system.
7. Forms for submission of ideas would be simple, easy to use, and no more than two pages.
8. Data kept on the system would be used for continuously improving the system.

Whatever the system does today, the data must be used to find out how to improve it even more tomorrow. For instance, it is important to find even more ideas per employee and to continually increase the percentage of ideas approved. Customers of the system can be periodically polled to find out if it is providing a reliable means for employees to contribute ideas and be involved in continuously improving the organization. Employees should feel that the system helps make their jobs and their work better. It is also important to be sure that employees feel the system is successful in terms of providing rewards for people who submit and implement ideas.

Organizations that embrace these new assumptions will move away from the static old style suggestion box to dynamic new style suggestion systems (some have called them "Enhanced Employee Involvement Systems" or "Innovative Idea Systems") that are continuously evolving and changing to meet the needs of employees and benefit the organization.

# PART VI:
# INFORMATION

We are all surrounded by a virtual avalanche of information. We no sooner dig out when we're blanketed again. In fact, many of us never get out from under the first one before the second, third, and fourth ones hit us. The amount of information that we are exposed to on a daily basis is beyond comprehension. We hear "information" on the radio, cellular phones, home phones, office phones, and in endless conversations. We see information on our e-mail, Internet boards, postal mail, fax letters, VCRs, television, print media, and in movies. We even smell "information" on the streets, in the office, at home, on the bus, in restaurants, and in tear-off ads in many magazines. We touch "information" on our keyboards, in elevators, as our bodies age, and when we buy new products and services. Even our "taste" for "information" is accelerating as new cuisines are continually being introduced into the marketplace. Not too long ago, Chinese food was exotic for Minnesota; now my local meat market carries Cajun smoked wild boar jerky.

Of course, we have all been promised that the new "high-tech, super-fast, user-friendly, and ergonomically designed workstations" (also call desktop computers) would take care of our information overload. So far, if you are like me, it has probably only seemed to add to your workload. I now have to lug a laptop computer through the airport in addition to my cellular phone, beeper, and briefcase. The salvation promised by the new information technology seems to be more of a living hell. There is no respite from the ceaseless rings, beeps, hums, tweeps, and jiggles that signal more information is on the way, another message is waiting, or a decision is expected—right now!

If there was ever a new value forced on organizations, it is information. Most of us dream of a vacation spot where there are no phones, computers, faxes, beepers, or answering machines. Information has become a new value because there is no hiding from it, no escaping it. You must deal with the avalanche the best you can or you will soon find that things get even worse. Yes, they can get even worse. If you ignore all the information that surrounds you and put your head in the sand, you will become obsolete in a shorter period of time than it takes to send a letter via the U.S. Postal Service (or, more likely, Federal Express) to your aging aunt.

Like it or not, you must find a way to handle information. Since the amount, if not the type, of information is exponentially and qualitatively different than it has ever been in any time in history, we must find new ways to handle information. It is not enough to try to do more reading, scan messages faster, subscribe to abstract services, etc. Doing more of the same things that worked in the past does not help when the fundamental paradigm shifts. As Joel Barker reminds us, what makes you successful in the old system will not guarantee you success when the system shifts. You must approach the problem in a fundamentally different way. The following chapters are designed to help you think about information in a new way. They are not an antidote to your beeper or cellular phone, but they will help you to gain a better understanding of the new information value and how you can manage it, rather than let the avalanche overwhelm you.

# Chapter 18

# Information as a Concept

For several years now, numerous business periodicals have heralded the end of the Industrial age and the emergence of the Information age. We read everywhere that information has replaced labor and capital as the principal determinant of business success. Organizations loudly proclaim that their new goal is to become "learning" organizations where risk taking and innovation will become the norm. Innovation will be fed by apparently vast amounts of data and information that will be turned into knowledge. If you are skeptical of this "vision," you are in good company. To date, there is little evidence that managers use information any differently than before, despite such magnanimous propositions. Little progress has been made in most organizations to systematically integrate the study and analysis of information with the overall strategic operations of the business. Few managers treat information with the same degree of importance as other critical process and product factors; seldom is information recognized and explicitly regarded as either a major input to, or product of, specific organizational functions and activities. Even less often is information regarded as being a process in and of itself. Peter Drucker has noted that there are many managed information systems (MIS) managers but few information managers.

Past work in organizational mapping,[1] information quality analysis,[2] cognitive mapping for information requirements analysis,[3] critical success factors,[4] and information systems technology[5] have all made substantial advancements in identifying specific organizational sources and requirements for information. Nevertheless, such methodologies do not go far enough since they consistently fail to examine the intricacies and complexity of information theory and process in an organization.

Information systems still seem to be controlled by "technical" people that are more enamored of the hardware and software than they are of the idea of creating "shared meaning" out of the morass of data they have available. Information is often restricted or available only to a privileged few in the organization. The concept of measuring the usefulness of information and the ability of the organization to translate information into useful products, services, and competitive advantage is virtually unheard of. There are very few organizations which have a system for acquiring information, disseminating it, creating a shared meaning around it, and then measuring how effectively the system works so that it can be continually improved.

By default, information has become associated with high technology. In most organizations, the science of information analysis remains the exclusive domain of computer specialists and/or data processing specialists. Adequate information processing becomes equated with the existence and utilization of databases or other computerized information services in the organization. This proliferation of information services can easily lead to the meaning and value of the information being lost to the organization. Tools such as benchmarking can become just another exercise in collecting "meaningless" or "unused" data. The proper utilization of data in an organization can only take place if managers are willing to take the time to understand the basic principles of information and then to use these principles to translate data into information, information into knowledge, and knowledge into meaningful activity.

There are two major dimensions of information: structure and process. Each is composed of a number of elements. In one sense, information is somewhat analogous to the old model of an atom, where an atom has both structure and process. The structure was understood by examining the protons, electrons, and neutrons which comprised the atom, but the atom's process could only be understood in a wider context by understanding how the atom behaved as it interacted with its environment and with other elements. Thus, a single atom of hydrogen would not have much meaning to anyone. However, when the atom is combined with oxygen and another hydrogen atom, we have water, which is very meaningful and very useful.

The disciplines of information systems management and organizational communications have each developed some potentially important models and tools to help managers better understand information. However, neither discipline has integrated its various perspectives into a unified theory of information. This failure to develop a unified theory of information has led to a fragmentation of approaches at managing information in organizations. Without a decent theory of information, it is understandable that managers have not been better able to organize and effectively use information. The following description of information provides a starting point for developing a unified theory of information. As with any model, each shows only a partial reflection of reality.

## *INFORMATION STRUCTURE*

Information has a structure which is separate and distinct from the character of the information user. This structure can affect the meaning and interpretation of the message. If a message was sent in Greek to an individual who only understood German, then the message would probably be ignored. The structure of any message can be informative or confusing. In some cases (for instance, coded messages), the message is deliberately confusing. The meaning of information is also determined by how the message is carried, who carried the message, the context within which the message is delivered, the noise present in the system upon delivery, and the timeliness of the information. All of these elements will affect how the information is perceived and understood. These factors affect its overall value and usefulness.

"Usefulness" can only be determined by the customer. The characteristics that affect information structure can be broken down into seven elements: domains, classes, scope, mediums, sources, transfer, and criteria. It is important to keep in mind that the structure of information cannot be defined by any single one of these elements. The character of the information is defined by the nature and interaction of all seven elements.

## 1. Domains

The Department of Labor's *Dictionary of Occupational Titles* breaks information about jobs into three categories: information about people, information about things, and information about ideas. A fourth category could be information about events. Trends and fads, as well as new world orders, can arise out of the consequences of new things, new ideas, new events, and the actions that people take. The amount of information that organizations typically collect in respect to these four domains varies widely. The greatest amount of information is usually collected about things. Most organizations have vast databases of information about material and financial assets, but somewhat less about new technologies. These are all in the "thing" category.

The lack of information about people (notwithstanding the Information Privacy Act) reflects the lower value placed on human resources compared to material and financial resources. Despite the fact that employees are often noted in company mission statements as being an organization's most valuable asset, in many organizations, no one could tell you the unique skills and abilities of even 10 percent of the workforce. Often, employees get passed over for promotions and unique career opportunities as employers go outside for the talent. At the same time, employers do not have the slightest bit of data as to the intellectual and psychological abilities of their current employees. Even organizations that have Human Resource Information Systems (HRIS) often cannot determine the level, type, or amount of education of the organization's management employees, never mind its hourly employees. Establishing these systems should not be an exercise in quantity of information as much as in quality of information. This would require organizations to establish end objectives and goals before setting up an information system to collect personal data.

Information about ideas is even less adequate in most organizations. Few organizations seem to place a very high value on ideas. There is often very little time spent in any organization solely on the generation of new and useful ideas for making operations more effective. Research and development (R&D) groups have generally been delegated the task of coming up with new technology and monitoring technological developments. Seldom do R&D groups monitor or develop new concepts.

The general lack of commitment to research and development seems underscored by the fact that when finances get tight, R&D funds are often some of the first units to be cut. In some organizations, the primary function of the R&D group seems to be to put out fires that have been started elsewhere in the organization. Generating and monitoring new knowledge is not even a peripheral exercise for most R&D departments. The talent that is wasted in these departments is tragic, but even worse is the fact that organizations have "compartmentalized" the whole idea of creating new knowledge and research. Organizations need to ask every employee to accept responsibility for R&D. Research departments should consist of one person who is called the "research coordinator." His/her job should be to harness the brainpower of the entire organization in one massive research and development effort.

Some organizations are afraid of new ideas. These organizations work to restrict the amount of information collected or new ideas considered. This is accomplished by requiring blind obedience to work standards and procedures, by restricting information to certain groups in the organization, by treating hourly employees as though their ideas are inferior, by insisting that everybody stay busy and thereby have no time to think, by proclamations that the company's historical way of doing business is the only way and, perhaps most devastating of all, by the common tendency for managers to want to hear only good news and to punish the bearers of bad news.

Organizations need to collect data about ideas, people, things, and events on a systematic, regular basis. If the organization can't afford to do this, it should hire a think tank or trend group that will do the data collection for the organization. Regardless of how the organization generates the data, the key is to have systems in place within the organization to disseminate the data and help generate a shared meaning concerning significant data and information. While data and information may seem synonymous, data itself is not information until meaning is associated with it.

Each of these four domains of information is essential to the successful operation of a business or service in a highly dynamic environment. Organizations need to allocate resources for identifying the characteristics of people, things, ideas, and events which are potentially important to each business function. Information on these essential characteristics must be systematically collected and disseminated to potential users.

## 2. Classes

There are two broad classes of information: information that deals with analytic problems and information that deals with enumerative problems. These two classes of information are adapted from concepts proposed by W. E. Deming. At a conference in 1987, Brian Joiner differentiated the two by explaining that the number of bears in Yosemite National Park and the fiscal year-end inventory of General Motors are both examples of enumerative information, while studying rainfall patterns to decide whether to irrigate or not is an example of analytic information.

It is essential to recognize the differences between the two classes of information, since confusing them is a major cause of poor decision making. Simply having numerical data, regardless of the volume, cannot adequately explain what should be done in the future. Nor will such data say anything about the underlying cause system which produced the data. For instance, the percentage of part-time workers has been rising in most developed countries for the past ten years. This is an interesting and potentially useful fact, but knowing this fact does not help us to understand why it is true or what is causing it to happen. The ability to make decisions based on accurate data is essential to good management, but it is not enough.

The solution to many problems depends as much on analytic information as on enumerative. In many cases, one must make conclusions or draw inferences which will go beyond the scope of existing data. Much of the talk about data in continuous improvement totally ignores the concepts of implicit and intuitive knowledge. This is a major error since many, if not most, of the great organizations in the world owe their success as much to intuitive skills as to logical, rational planning skills. Enumerative data alone would be adequate if one lived only in the past. But we live in a present which continually demands decisions about the future. Which products should we market? Which programs should we try? Which employees should we hire? If the nature and limitations of the data upon which such decisions are based is not clearly understood, it is impossible to assess the probabilities for the "accuracy" or effectiveness of a given decision. Many managers think that just having vast amounts of data will take the error out of decision making. This supposition leads to paralysis by analysis or to faulty judgments buttressed by a great deal of data.

## 3. Scope

Scope refers to the breadth and depth of information. For instance, in terms of breadth, information in an organization could involve one's immediate job, department, division, company, conglomerate, industry, or competitors. Depth can be defined by analyzing the degree of detail that is involved in the information. Examples include a job application that lists many positions held by the applicant (breadth) or details about the responsibilities and accomplishments that the applicant achieved in his/her last job. The latter could be called information depth versus breadth. The depth and breadth of the information relate to its complexity. Complexity of information is always relative to the user and will be discussed in more detail in the discussion on information process.

The scope of information is an essential concept for understanding how organizations use data and information. Most organizations collect a great deal of information about their internal operations, but ignore large areas outside this scope. Such areas are often extremely important for the decision-making operations of the business. The scope of broad information generally allows managers to look at issues of strategic importance and areas that fall into the realm of effectiveness issues. Effectiveness has been defined as "doing the right things" versus efficiency, which is "doing things right." Reflecting on the poor use of "broad" information by organizations, G. L. Parsons noted that most executives could not articulate the strategic importance of "information technology" and even fewer could explain its importance for the future.[6] Competitors' position, government regulations, trends in technology, and even environmental changes all play an important role in an organization's success or failure, yet little data is collected by most MIS systems on issues and trends outside the organization. The recent interest and attention to benchmarking by many organizations may denote a trend toward more outward-looking strategies and fewer inward-looking strategies.

A study done by Great Britain's National Economic Development ment Office found that "winning" companies studied their competitors intensely and continuously, and also closely monitored and exploited new technology.[7] J. M. McGrane stated, "Virtually every corporate management function is becoming more dependent upon tracking changes in the competitive environment."[8] Richard N. Foster, in his book *Innovation: The Attacker's Advantage*, observed that the failure to anticipate the emergence of a new key technology is the leading cause of corporate failure.[9] It seems apparent that unless organizations review both the breadth and depth of their information, they will not be able to survive in a competitive marketplace.

### 4. Mediums

There are three major mediums or channels through which information is absorbed or assimilated by a user: print, sound, and visual. Print mediums include books, newspapers, telefax, electronic paper copiers, and any other type of manuscript relying on printed characters to convey information. Sound mediums would include direct and indirect communication, as well as electronic devices for carrying sound, such as telephones, radios, and tape recorders. Visual mediums include any method for transmitting information that is meant to be observed, not relying on the printed character to convey information. This would include work demonstrations and sit-down strikes, as well as images formed by electromechanical devices such as computer terminals, televisions, photographs, and VCRs. A carrier such as the Internet would allow for passage of information on all three channels. An Internet user can access information that is in visual, print, or sound mediums. Television is limited to visual and sound while radios are primarily a channel that conveys information through the use of sound.

The mediums described are all methods for sending information to either sight or sound sensors. Mediums for transmitting information to touch, smell, and taste sensors are less defined, but perhaps provide yet another important avenue upon which to devise new methods for transmitting information. Few such mediums have been explored to date. I remember once going to a movie that was billed as "smell-a-rama." During the movie, smells associated with images were somehow piped into the theater. Apparently, "smell-a-rama" did not quite succeed. Any channel of information or information carrier is subject to both noise and distortion. This means that the information transmitted is dependent upon limitations built into the medium. It also means that the medium profoundly influences the intended message. M. McLuhan[10] noted that "every medium of communication is a unique art form which gives salience to one set of human possibilities at the expense of another set. Each medium of expression profoundly modifies human sensibility in many unconscious and unpredictable ways."

It is important for organizations to develop an understanding of the ways in which they transmit information. Each medium of transmission has its own potential advantages and disadvantages. The various mediums of information transmission will, in all likelihood, be interpreted differently by each individual and will have a different impact. Furthermore, with the advent of machine-to-machine communication, i.e., direct electronic feedback mechanisms, communication systems between computer networks, etc., managers need to give even more attention to the potential impact that a particular medium may have on the way that information is used, shared, and in which meaning is attached to the information by organizational members. One of the most commonly stated problems in organizations is communication. Many organizations adopt the simplistic solution to publish and begin some type of in-house newsletter assuming that this will improve communication. Usually, such efforts are only a drop in the bucket. Information needs to be transmitted through multiple mediums in order to be effective. An organization can publish, dictate, and utilize mediums to provide information, but none of this will improve communication unless there is a chance for real dialogue and the building of shared meanings around the information and data.

## 5. Sources

Sources include the originator or bearer of the information, as opposed to how the information is transmitted. For instance, a manager gives an employee a series of verbal instructions for a work procedure that needs to be done. In this case, the source is the manager and the medium is spoken or verbal. The source is an important part of the information. If the same instructions were given in the same medium (verbally) by a lower ranking member of the organization, those instructions would very likely not carry the same significance for the receiver. Sources of information can be either human or material. A machine can be a source of information and can transmit information through a variety of mediums. We have fax machines that transmit printed material, e-mail boxes which give us visual information, and voice mail systems that give us information in sound format.

If the source of information can have a profound impact on the information (for instance, when your boss tells you to do something), it is important to be sure the senders and receivers are adequately matched in order for the information to carry appropriate emphasis. Organizations should try to understand how and from whom employees receive information and the impact of the source on the receiver. This is true both for sources internal to the organization and for sources external to the organization. Internal sources may transmit information externally and external sources will communicate to the organization through a number of different interfaces. Thus, do customers get listened to? Do suppliers and other key stakeholders get listened to? What does it take for a crisis to get "listened" to by an organization? How do organizations "hear" the competition?

It is important to examine the impact of all sources of information on receivers both inside and outside of the organization. In any organization, a great deal of information is directed to customers, stockholders, investors, and other stakeholders. The impact of information on those outside the organization can have profound influences on the success of an organization. Many customers have received the "wrong" message from actions and statements transmitted to them by the organization. Misunderstandings from improperly translated information has led to lawsuits and numerous cases of lost customers. Nestle products were boycotted for many years, primarily due to the impact that the company's marketing practices and advertisements had on the external community. As the war between Nestle and the boycotters escalated, neither side was willing to listen to reason or to try to find potential win-win solutions to the problem.

It must also be determined if a source of information needs to transmit analytic or evaluative information. Without this knowledge, the source of the information often produces information that is meaningless. We have been in many meetings where endless debates occurred around agenda items that were merely informational. At other times, quick decisions were made about key issues with little or no discussion and absolutely no data or supportive information. We advise committees to label items on agendas as "information," "discussion," or "decision." This helps distinguish whether the speaker merely wants to convey some information, initiate a discussion in which no decision is needed, or whether a decision must be reached. This method helps the members to make a practical (even if they might not realize it) distinction between enumerative versus analytic issues and problems. Managers who expect employees to react to enumerative information ("I sent you the process data, wasn't it clear what you should do with it?") as though it were analytic ("How come I'm the only one that makes decisions around here?") cause much resentment among employees ("Well, if I had only known that you wanted me to do something . . .").

### 6. Transfer

Information is transferred within an organization, vertically and horizontally. Transfer may take place into, out of, and within the organization. It may be transferred between groups, individuals, or any combination thereof. Information that is transferred vertically may go bottom upwards or top downwards. The most common transfer of information in an organization is top down.

Traditional models of organization structure and hierarchy tend to restrict information transfer under the outmoded military dictum of "need to know." Thus, hourly employees (being lowest on the hierarchy) are often assumed to have the least need to know. The structure of most organizations is also a major impediment to the adequate flow and utilization of information. Each level in an organization represents a vertical barrier to information, and each functional area represents a horizontal barrier. If we multiply the number of functional staff areas by the number of vertical levels we may find a number generally ranging from 100 to 400. Now multiply this by the number of employee categories (managers, staff, executive, hourly, part-time, etc.) and you come up with the number of structural roadblocks to information that exist in many organizations. It is little surprise that communication is the biggest problem in most organizations. Indeed, it seems almost a miracle that any transfer of information is even possible.

A systematic regulated flow of information throughout the organization may be compared to the flow of blood through a human organism. It is essential to have a steady blood flow to every cell in the body. Unless this occurs, those cells deprived of blood will die. Similarly, in an organization, death of a sort occurs when members do not have access to the information they need to make important decisions. This results in a form of institutionalized "death" for many employees. Without adequate knowledge or means of transmitting knowledge, they become cut off and alienated from the ebb and flow of organizational life. The organization dies slowly from within as employees become cynical and apathetic.

Organizations need to identify patterns of information transfer and whether such patterns are consistent with the goals and objectives of the organization. Managers must give up outdated ideas of information restriction in favor of a broader view of information. Within this broader view, all members of the organization have a "need" to know. The question must become not whether they have the need to know, but whether they "want" to know. If an organization legitimizes the right of its employees to know, then it must identify "blockages" in the current transfer patterns of information and work to eliminate such blockages. In many cases, this will require a restructuring or redesign of the organization, along with major changes in job descriptions.

## 7. Criteria

The criteria for judging the quality of information content or structure must depend on the customers' requirements. It is not possible to judge the quality of information without knowledge of what the customer expects and needs. In some cases, the customer will not be able to articulate these requirements. The customer of information could be a computer or robot as easily as it could be a human being. Four categories can be identified which broadly address the needs of all customers: efficiency, effectiveness, timeliness, and quantity.

The efficiency of information can be defined as how economical the information is in terms of its ability to satisfy the requirements of the user. The cost of information is a major factor in the generation and distribution of knowledge. The price of computer time, books, electronic transmittal, person-to-person meetings, etc., have all risen rapidly in the last few years. Furthermore, there is no evidence that quality is related to cost in respect to information. Thus, the supplier and customer for information must deal with a very nebulous transaction.

Organizations must begin to track the actual and potential costs of information, as well as relate these figures to their accounting procedures. Information should be a budget item in all organizations, but traditional accounting procedures are inadequate in measuring knowledge transfer and information costs. Some of the new accounting procedures that capture "activity costs," knowledge capital, and environmental costs may have some potential for providing a cost system for information. Nevertheless, the difficulty of measuring things as nebulous as value, meaning, knowledge, and wisdom will require the development of entirely new systems and procedures, if not concepts of value and evidence. This is a subject that is currently being looked into by many of the leading accounting firms and business schools in North America.

It is difficult to evaluate the effectiveness of information for either an individual or an organization. By "effectiveness," we mean primarily how well the information relates to the needs of the customer. For example, how much did it help to solve the problem, increase productivity, generate new ideas, produce more revenue, etc.? Did it help the user make the right decisions? Was it the right information, and was it conveyed so that it was effective to use? In trying to analyze this criteria, there are many intangible factors which prevent a valid and final conclusion, at least in respect to the evaluation of information exchanges between individuals.

Nevertheless, if cost or efficiency of information is important, then it is equally important to develop measures for establishing the effectiveness of information. The effectiveness of information could potentially be judged by recourse to various types of "soft" analysis. Satisfaction to the customer, expected versus actual return to the organization per unit cost, and problem-solving utility are some of the more obvious measures for determining the effectiveness of information. In addition, one could look at effects of information on the process as well as the outcomes.

When dealing with information exchanges between machines (e.g., a bottling machine feeding into an automated boxing machine), or machines and people (e.g., a software program written for a welding robot), the outlook for developing measures of information effectiveness is much more positive. For instance, the effectiveness of a new program for a robot welder could easily be evaluated on a number of criteria such as the number of defect-free welds, time per weld, strength per weld, and the number of welds produced. The nature of information exchanges between machines and, to some extent, between machines and people, renders these exchanges more susceptible to an analysis in terms of information effectiveness. The fact that "accuracy" is much more critical to an information exchange between machines, or machines and people, means that this aspect of information effectiveness may be more readily quantified and measured.

Timeliness, as a criteria of information quality, is critical because of the fact that outdated information and late information can seriously affect the quality of any organizational or strategic effort. The importance of the timeliness or datedness of the information will depend on the nature of the problem being studied and on the time constraints that affect the intended customer. Information can be 250 years old and neither be too late nor out of date. Conversely, it can be two minutes old and be much too late. Information has a definite life span; it is futile to spend enormous amounts of time collecting data that will be obsolete before the data collection is finished. Customer surveys often measure the past, not the present; by the time the organization gets around to measuring customer satisfaction, many things have changed in the customer's life or the customer no longer has any feelings or thoughts about the product or service that was purchased.

Finally, the quantity of information is important since an organization may have too much or too little information. Information overload occurs, for instance, when too many people try to speak at the same time, when a company has too many meetings, or when data is generated without a systematic model to analyze it or a set of priorities to regulate its production. It is very easy to hook into the Internet and to experience information overload in a very short period of time. A friend recently noted that information management today means knowing when to disconnect rather than when to connect.

Conversely, information-poor environments are characterized by a shortage of information. In some companies, resources such as books, computers, meetings, training, policies, procedures, etc., are considered to be "luxuries" that are ill afforded or that are limited to a privileged elite. Only managers go to training, only certain people need computers, information is restricted on a need-to-know basis, etc.

In a world where information has replaced capital and labor, and where managing it properly will spell the difference between survival and obsolescence, managers must understand that the value and utilization of information in a company needs to be measured like any other organizational factor of production. Managers can begin to develop a system for more effective use of information by creating a set of expectations for how information is handled in their organizations. These expectations should address each of the seven elements of information structure described in this chapter. This set of criteria or expectations can help managers design more efficient and effective networks for the production, exchange, and utilization of information in their companies. However, we have only described the structure of information. It is equally important to understand the process of information. By "process" we mean the manner in which meaning and usefulness are attached to the information which the customer receives. Some might call this the "knowledge creation process."

## *INFORMATION PROCESS*

Information process is the second key dimension of information. It is proposed that there is no useful information unless data can be translated into some type of meaningful and useful activity. It is assumed that this transformation has a basic process much as does any process. A process is characterized by inputs, transformative actions, and outputs. In the information process, the input is the raw data and the output is the final action or decision consummated as a result of the data. The steps in the information process are listed here:

DATA → KNOWLEDGE → DECISION → ACTION → RESULTS

Data is the input. The major transformation processes involve converting the data to knowledge and converting the knowledge to a decision. The process outcome is the action taken. Results assume that for every action, there is a reaction or consequence. The two major actions that happen to the data during the transformation process are associated either with cognitive processes or electro-mechanical processes that attach meaning and utility to the raw data.

Managers and information specialists must have an understanding of the process by which data is transformed into meaningful, useful activity. Sahrmann has noted, "Information, when used correctly, can lead to significant improvements in quality and productivity."[11] He observed:

> A disproportionately large amount of money and time is spent on turning data into information. The remaining steps of turning information into action and action into data should receive similar attention. . . . Organizational changes are required to increase the probability of turning information into action. (p. 569)

If managers can develop a greater understanding of the process by which meaning and utility are attached to data, they will be in a better position to see that data is used to generate positive results for the organization. Issues associated with this problem will be addressed in greater detail in Chapter 19.

## REFERENCE NOTES

1. Madlin, N. "Remapping the Corporation." *Management Review,* Vol. 76, No. 5, pp. 60-61, 1987.
2. Vacca, J. "Information Quality Analysis." *Infosystems,* Vol. 32, No. 11, pp. 60-61, 1987.

3. Montazemi, A.R. and Conrath, D.W. "The Use of Cognitive Mapping for Information Requirements." *MIS Quarterly,* Vol. 4, No. 4, pp. 45-55, 1980.

4. Munro, M.C. and Wheeler, B.R. "Planning, Critical Success Factors, and Management's Information Requirements." *MIS Quarterly,* Vol. 4, No. 4, pp. 27-38, 1980.

5. McKenny, J.L. and McFarlan, F.W. "The Information Archipelago–Maps and Bridges." *Harvard Business Review,* Vol. 60, No. 5, pp. 109-119, 1982.

6. Parsons, G.L. "Information Technology: A New Competitive Weapon." *California Management Review,* Vol. 25, No. 1, pp. 1-13, 1983.

7. Pilditch, J. *How Winning Companies Create the Products We All Want to Buy.* New York: Harper and Row, 1987.

8. McGrane, J.M. "Going On Line for Planning and Competitive Intelligence." *Management Review,* Vol. 76, No. 10, pp. 55-56, 1987.

9. Foster, B.L. *Innovation: The Attacker's Advantage.* New York: Summit Books, 1986.

10. *McLuhan: Hot and Cold.* Edited by G.E. Stearn. New York: Signet Books, 1967.

11. Sahrmann, J.F. "Information: The Key to Process Improvement." In: *Quality: The Universal Equation for Excellence.* Proceedings of the 41st Annual Quality Congress, pp. 569-573; Milwaukee: American Society for Quality Control, 1987.

# Chapter 19

# Information and Action

Employees and managers must translate information and data into positive results for the organization. The information process is incomplete unless data is transferred into some type of meaningful, useful activity. This transformation has a basic process much like any other human endeavor, with input, transformative actions, and output. In any process, something is taken in and transformed to something which is new and unique. In an information process, the input is the raw data and the output is the final action or decision consummated as a result of the data. The steps in an information process are listed here:

DATA→ INFORMATION→ KNOWLEDGE→ DECISION→ ACTION→ RESULTS

The major transformation processes involve converting data (the main process input) into knowledge, and knowledge into a decision. The process outcome is the action taken, with results stemming from the actions taken.

For every action, there is a reaction or consequence. For instance, during the Vietnam war, the CIA amassed a great deal of data concerning the troop strength of the North Vietnamese. Based on these erroneous estimates, the U.S. military undertook a disastrous series of military actions that stemmed from wrong assumptions and wrong decisions. The assumptions and the decisions were wrong because the CIA's data and information were wrong. With correct data, it would still have been possible to reach incorrect decisions and to take incorrect actions. However, with incorrect data, the U.S. military could only rely on luck and chance. Only with luck and good fortune can correct decisions be made on the basis of incorrect data. A brief review of the above six steps is in order before looking at the fundamental conditions that must be present before these six steps can happen.

## DATA

Data was once commonly defined as "Basic facts and figures . . . descriptive rather than evaluative"[1] Today, this definition must be expanded to include any form of input that can be translated into information, either by humans or machines. An expanded definition would include sensory impulses, electronic impulses, mechanical impulses, chemical impulses, and impulses generated on a sub-atomic scale, such as magnetic or gravitational impulses. The input to today's information processes have been greatly expanded by our knowledge of electronics and other methods of transmitting data.

Remus and Kottemann stated, "Making a good decision starts with having or gathering the right information upon which to base a decision."[2] This conclusion is only partially right. It would be more accurate to state that it starts with gathering the right data. Data itself is not information. The letters in the alphabet, a series of numbers, or a set of electronic impulses are all forms of data. Data itself does not tell you anything. Humans must associate some meaning with data before it is any more than a pile of numbers and impulses. One of the major problems with most "information systems" is that they gather huge amounts of data that are irrelevant or immaterial. We know of vice presidents who receive reports every morning that are absolutely meaningless to them. They have no idea what the implications of the reports are. Part of the problem lies in the way that the data is translated and displayed. Another part is that there is no perceived importance or value to the data.

## INFORMATION

There are several definitions of information. Some of these are in mathematical terms, some in behavioral science terms, and others in information science terminology. Le Roux cautioned that it is easy to get lost in the numerous, and often conflicting, definitions. He summed up the difference between data, information, and knowledge as follows:

> Data consist of loose, unconnected, and unprocessed facts; information is that which is conveyed in a state of having been processed, while knowledge is the result of the process which manifests itself in the human mind: that is to say, when the information has been processed and has been made one's own, it becomes knowledge.[3]

According to Meltzer, the U.S. Department of Commerce defined information as data that has been organized and communicated. Meltzer (1981) defined information as "the result of the analysis, synthesis, and evaluation based on available data."[4] Reviewing the various definitions of information, one finds that common to all is the concept of organization. Numbers, impulses, letters, etc., have been organized in some manner that facilitates the attribution of meaning and utilization of the original data. Thus, we can define information as "organized data." However, organization alone does not beget knowledge. Deming once said that a dictionary is full of information but not knowledge. The dictionary is, however, full of organized bits of data.

## KNOWLEDGE

The process of transforming information to knowledge starts when the data is organized into information that can be understood by the customer. However, the creation of knowledge involves a great deal more than just organizing data. Even the best organized data (information) will have no value to the customer if it cannot be converted into knowledge. Knowledge is created when the customer is able to attach meaning and utility to the information or data received. The customers (the receivers of the information) must perceive some value in the information. Generally, this means that they are able (or at least think they will be able) to use the data to perform some activity (either cognitive or physical).

In organizations, knowledge is created when information is shared with other employees in such a manner that all employees are also able to attach meaning and utility to the data. The concept of the "Learning Organization"[5] is based on the possibility of organizations developing shared meaning around new ideas and concepts. When information is shared with others on a regular basis, and when there is ample dialogue and discussion around the meaning and definition of the information, organizations have established some of the basic conditions needed to become a "Learning" organization. Nonaka and Takeuchi[6] note that this dialogue "can involve considerable conflict and disagreement, but it is precisely such conflict that pushes employees to question existing premises and to make sense of their experience in a new way. This kind of dynamic interaction facilitates the transformation of personal knowledge into organizational knowledge."[7]

## DECISION

The next step in the information process occurs when the individual forms a decision on what knowledge will be used and how the knowledge will be used. These decisions can be latent or actual and, in many cases, may consist of a nondecision. When the individual decides to do nothing with what he/she knows, which is a decision of sorts, it could perhaps be said to lead to a "nonaction," where the individual does nothing. So-called "nonactions," such as the example of Emperor Nero playing the fiddle while Rome burned, can have major impacts.

## ACTION

Actions are outcomes of decisions made on the basis of interpreting a set of initial facts or opinions concerning some activity that needed to be addressed by the organization. Actions can be positive or negative, independent of their outcome or results. For example, illegal actions could have positive results for the organization, at least in the short run. The values that an organization espouses (either implicitly or explicitly) form the boundaries for those actions that employees in the organization can feel safe pursuing. If an organization values creativity and risk taking, employees will pursue a different course of action than they would in an organization that values conformity and tradition.

## RESULTS

All actions create reactions or results. Results are both the hardest and the easiest things to measure in an organization. Some results are easy to measure, but it's often difficult to link specific results to specific data or even actions. Nevertheless, all organizations must develop a process for measuring, evaluating, and using results data to continually improve their processes. There are two big mistakes that most organizations make in this area. The first is to collect results data on too restricted a field of inquiry. For example, most organizations only look at financial data (particularly profit-and-loss statements) while ignoring areas that might have long-term company or societal implications. Corporations such as General Motors, Tectronics, Harley-Davidson, and U.S. Steel ignored the trend for quality until well after each company's overall market share had substantially declined.

The second mistake most organizations make is ignoring positive results and not exploring the underlying factors that created desirable outcomes. Most organizations would rather firefight than study processes or events that seem to be going right. We often read of the "best" companies to work for or the "top" corporations, only to read a few years later that those companies have suffered disastrous market turndowns. In the late 1980s, IBM topped many lists as the best company to work for. A few years later, IBM was fighting for survival.

Many organizations become so engrossed in their "success" that they become myopic to those very factors that made them successful in the first place. Once the decline starts, they become caught up in survival and have no time to study "success" factors. All they do is try to find ways to stop the ship from sinking. As Dr. Deming often said in his seminiars, "Putting out a fire does not improve the hotel." Organizations must systematically create a balanced study of results, looking at both the positive and negative results. Success comes from understanding both what you have done right and what you are now doing wrong. It is quite possible that, as times change, what was once right is now a prescription for failure.

## KEY CONDITIONS FOR SUCCESS

Human beings will quite naturally move from data to results if the necessary conditions for success are available. The following six key conditions must be present if employees and managers are going to be able to use information successfully.

1. A felt need must exist in the organization.
2. The source of the information or data must be credible.
3. The data/information must be comprehensible to the customer.
4. A shared meaning must be created in terms of knowledge.
5. Priority for action must be assigned.
6. A frame of solutions must exist.

Surveys, safety statistics, department budgets, evaluations, audits, financial results, performance indicators, and even weather reports do not guarantee that any actions will actually be taken. Whether or not action will be undertaken and results achieved depends upon the dynamics among the six conditions identified above. These conditions do not guarantee successful results, but they do guarantee that some action will be taken. The structure of the information (those characteristics described in Chapter 18) has a direct bearing on whether the results will be positive or negative. Those with a good understanding of information structure will have a better chance of achieving positive results.

### 1. A felt need must exist.

An individual must have either a need, a problem, a goal, or an issue that is important and salient before he/she will perceive any use from certain data or facts. When a felt need is present, the potential exists for data to be transformed into information. As information, the data has some meaning to the individual, though it still may not have any importance. Regardless of whether it is important or not, the individual must be receptive to hearing the data before anything can happen with it. In communication theory, we would say that the channels must be open and the noise level low enough so that the primary signal is not unduly distorted. The most important factor in determining whether the channels will be open concerns the condition of felt need. When General Motors and the rest of the American automobile industry were making money hand over foot, they had no need for SPC, benchmarking, or Total Quality Management. But as soon as a "felt need" arose, in the form of Japanese imports and Japanese competition, the channels of the American automobile makers became wide open and the companies' receptivity to new ideas increased exponentially.

There is a sort of paradox involved in creating a "felt need." Dr. Deming used to say, "How would they know?" meaning that if company leaders are unaware that a crisis or problem exists, they will not perceive a felt need. Dr. Kano said in 1991, "A crisis state of mind is fundamental for continuous improvement." By crisis, Kano meant a state of mind that was always seeking and searching for new opportunities and that regarded standing still as a potential disaster waiting to happen. Many managers regard education and learning as "extra" activities that are needed only when some problem or goal must be addressed. Few managers attend educational sessions or read books in areas outside their expertise. Even fewer regularly scan research or global activities that might affect their businesses. Most organizations are like ships without radar or other sophisticated navigational equipment that are caught in a storm. The purpose of such "scanning" equipment is to prevent, or at least anticipate, pending disasters in order for crews to plan and be better prepared for them.

Fundamental to creating a "felt need" is the issue of awareness. Organizations must find ways to create awareness and attention before crises occur. Most organizations have very poor systems for helping individuals attend to issues and to create the basic awareness that leads to "felt needs." Awareness begins when something or someone has obtained the attention of the employee. The employee then becomes open and receptive to the introduction of new information. It is very difficult for such conditions to exist in organizations that are hierarchically structured or that have strict rules and protocols about who needs to know what, and who has access to certain information and who does not. Furthermore, in organizations where only the top managers are responsible for long-term or strategic planning, it is very difficult for employees to attach meaning to events which are out of their control or frame of reference. Many employees at General Motors were buying Japanese automobiles without attaching any significance to their purchase. This trend was happening long before GM finally accepted that the Japanese were a major threat to its market dominance. Better communication with its employees might have alerted all to the crisis long before top management finally decided to act.

There are an infinite number of possibilities for creating awareness, but they are not all equally effective. For instance, if a manager calls a worker into his/her office to tell the worker something, the worker is much more likely to pay more attention to the manager's information than to information overheard in the cafeteria. It is easier for managers to obtain the attention of their employees than it is for employees to obtain the attention of their superiors. This is a barrier of hierarchy. Creating awareness and meaning can also be complicated by other barriers in the organization. "Sacred cows," traditions, status, turf, and political issues pose basic problems to creating awareness. These are major components in the communication problems that plague organizations. Some of these problems can be overcome by a greater sensitivity to the communication preferences of the customer. But many of these problems can only be addressed by a fundamental restructuring and rethinking of the organization.

A system for creating awareness starts by identifying the needs of the customer. Since every employee in an organization is a potential customer for information, it is necessary for organizations to carry out systematic information audits or information requirements analyses. In other words, who needs to know, or wants to know, what, when, and how. Creating such audits should be a fundamental job for the Information Systems Department. Any analyses must address the needs of the customers in terms of what data or information the customers feel is required to help them reach their goals and objectives.

Information audits should be used to establish visible, measurable links between the goals of the organization and the needs and expectations of external customers. The priorities of the organization must address the needs and wants of its external customers, and these priorities must be communicated to, and well understood by, all employees. Employee goals and objectives must be linked to the goals and objectives of external customers via the priorities that the organization sets. It is critical that all employees be aware of, and understand, the priorities and needs of the external customers and the organization. However, creating awareness must be a two-way street. The priorities and needs of employees, as well as the organization, must be clear and understood.

### 2. The source of the information or data must be credible.

Individuals tend to subconsciously assign probability ratios to different facts and data. The weather announcers make a conscious declaration of this process when they report, "On Sunday there is a 40 percent chance of rain." If they tried to tell us that there was a 100 percent chance of rain, very few would believe them. Weather forecasters' data is given more credibility by assignment of what we think are realistic probabilities. In addition, most of us also assign our own probabilities to the weather report depending on our experience and other factors. For some of us, the probabilities will be influenced by our arthritis. For others, the *Farmer's Almanac* will influence their belief in the accuracy of the weather forecast. The credibility of your weather sources ultimately determines the probability that you assign to any weather forecasts. Unless you feel that your weather forecasting sources are credible, you are unlikely to take any actions on it. So, in this case, knowledge will not be translated into action if the end user does not feel that the sources of knowledge are credible and that there is some probability of inaccuracy and unreliability to the data.

Who presents the data to employees also affects the credibility process. If a manager tells employees something about a medical problem, it will not be given as much credibility as if would if the information came from a physician or, vice versa, if the physician told the employee something about a production problem, it would probably not be given as much significance as it would if it came from the production manager. Similarly, the Human Resource manager's opinion on a labor issue would probably carry more weight than the opinion of the Quality Assurance manager. The credibility of the source is a significant determinant in whether the customer attaches any importance to the information and, hence, whether or not any decisions or actions are taken around the information.

If information and data are going to be used, they must be matched to the customer's expectations. A good information system should identify what information suppliers or sources are credible to any potential information users. The organization should look at how credible its present sources of information are and what impacts these sources have on the willingness of customers to use the data in a meaningful way. Without addressing such issues, it is little wonder that organizations continually complain about "communication" problems, and are forced to deal with them.

### 3. The data/information must be comprehensible to the customer.

Comprehensibility is a measure of the ability of the individual to make sense out of the information that is presented. The more complex the data, the more difficult it is for the individual to translate it into information. It must be possible for the customer to correctly perceive the meaning of the data before the user can know if the data has any importance. This is where the distinction between data and information becomes important. The way that the data is organized may make it easier for the customer to understand. For instance, control charts often show data in a manner that is much easier for some people to understand. The greater the degree of understanding, the more likely that information will become useful knowledge. If data cannot be understood, for instance, if a person receives a message in Greek, but he/she doesn't understand Greek, he/she will have little understanding of the message's meaning. With little understanding of the message's meaning, he/she is not likely to attach importance to the message and, hence, it is unlikely that any knowledge, decisions, or actions will occur (unless the credibility of the sender is such that the receiver knows that the message must be important).

Part of the translation from information to knowledge depends on the particular cognitive skills and abilities of the user. Every individual has both innate and learned abilities with which to relate information to some cognitive schema or theory. Deming was fond of saying that experience without theory teaches nothing. He correctly implied that an individual must have some theory or schema that allows him/her to translate the information into a set of assumptions or expectations concerning potential outcomes. Thus, a physician has one set of assumptions about the world and an engineer another. Each of us will put our own meaning onto the same information because of our own experiences and backgrounds, and the meaning could be quite different from someone else's. One of the most common mistakes made in organizations is to assume that all people "hear" information the same way or draw the same assumptions from information.

Our individual experiences and assumptions define how information is changed and shaped into knowledge. We first receive information and then (if it is understood and important) change this information into knowledge. With the knowledge obtained, each of us then makes a decision or a set of decisions. The new knowledge changes and reshapes our existing belief systems and expectations. These new belief systems lead to a new set of decision possibilities. Whether or not these possibilities are acted on, the new knowledge becomes the basis for establishing future actions. Without an ongoing flow of data and information, the creation of new knowledge is impossible. Knowledge is essential to prediction. Deming often said that the main responsibility of managers is prediction. Prediction is part of the cycle of both organizational and individual learning. Prediction helps us by allowing us to test the accuracy and validity of the assumptions and expectations that we draw from our information and knowledge. Without testing theories, it is possible to assume that all knowledge and data are equal. If one believes this, then decisions will invariably be made on the basis of instinct and gut feelings.

### 4. A shared meaning must be created.

Slater and Narver state, "The final stage of knowledge development is shared interpretation of the information. Without a consensus on what the information means and its implications for the business, organizational learning has not occurred."[7] Slater and Narver present a model of organizational learning that includes three components: information acquisition, information dissemination, and shared interpretation of the information. Slater and Narver also distinguish organizational learning from individual learning and believe that this distinction happens primarily through the dissemination and sharing of knowledge. While Slater and Narver oversimplify the creation of knowledge from data, it is true that no organizational learning occurs unless a shared meaning is created. Furthermore, there is little likelihood that significant actions will be taken unless a shared meaning is created.

Creating a shared meaning with the larger organization leads to a felt need on the part of the organization. This means that one must get the attention of the organization, synthesize the data so that it is meaningful to others, and have enough credibility within the organization so that others will listen. Some people might call this a political process. In effect, one is trying to mobilize a critical mass that will help to generate a priority for meaningful action and results. Unless there is some felt need by the organization, it is unlikely that a decision to act or a priority for actions will be developed.

### 5. Priority for action must be assigned.

The prioritization of potential decisions is a critical step in the transformation of information into actions. If the organization attributes a high degree of priority to the issues, it will more likely be receptive to completing the process. A continuum exists along which priorities can be established. On one end is information highly related to a current issue or concern of the organization, while on the other end is information totally unrelated to any perceived problems or needs. Information that is directly related to a current problem will receive a much higher prioritization than information that is not.

When we have set a priority to act, we have, in effect, made a decision to do something. There is a big difference between being aware of something and choosing to take action about something. Many people confuse these two concepts. Managers who say that they are committed to a program such as Total Quality Management are merely indicating that they are aware of the possible benefits from a total quality effort. This is not a commitment to quality. Commitment is not sincerity, beliefs, knowledge, or even wisdom. Commitment is action—what one does, not what one says one will do.

Commitment to action means assigning accountability, responsibility, resources, people, deadlines, and methods for assessing results. Organizations collect a great deal of data, make mountains of information from the data, involve employees in endless meetings and numerous seminars, and still fail to make the fundamental changes needed to be successful. There may be many excuses for this failure, but the only real and compelling reason is the lack of a priority and commitment to act.

Managers often say that they believe in this or that program, but they just don't have the time to work on it. This is nothing more than a statement that the managers have other priorities which they believe are more important. Priorities must be established for change to take place. Indeed, if change is not a priority, then all things will remain as they have been. This may be okay in a static world, but in a dynamic environment, maintaining the status quo is a prescription for obsolescence. Organizations need to be clear about their priorities. Unless priorities are established, no amount of learning and information will create either a learning organization or a knowledge organization. True learning and knowledge creation must result in meaningful, useful activities.

### 6. A frame of solutions must exist.

The final condition that is necessary for data to be translated into meaningful and potentially successful results has to do with the potential solutions that exist. All of the other conditions can be present, but if no solution can be found, then no successful actions can be taken. Research and study merely build a foundation for the subsequent breakthroughs that are needed to solve today's problems. Unfortunately, many problems that exist today are probably unsolvable, given our present knowledge and technology.

Recognizing the limitations noted above does not constitute an excuse for doing nothing. There is a great deal of value in moving anyplace along the information process that has been described. If new knowledge is created but the problem cannot be solved with it, that's all right. Perhaps someone else will also create a new bit of knowledge that, when put with the other knowledge, will lead to a useful and successful result. The biggest threat to success is not to try at all. Organizations that foster fear, use rigid hierarchies to control employees, hide information from employees, and stifle innovation and creativity through paperwork and bureaucracy are doomed to failure. It was mentioned earlier that information and knowledge are the vital lifeblood for the twenty-first-century organization. Any organization that restricts the flow of these vital elements is doomed to failure. The task for all organizations is to create the conditions for constantly acquiring new knowledge and ensuring that it is translated into successful results.

## REFERENCE NOTES

1. Meltzer, M.F. *Information: The Ultimate Management Resource.* New York: AMACOM, 1981.

2. Remus, W.E. and Kottemann, J. E. "Toward Intelligent Decision Support Systems: An Artificially Intelligent Statistician." *MIS Quarterly,* Vol. 10, No. 4, pp. 403-419, 1986.

3. Le Roux, H.S. "A Managerially Based Framework for the Role and Contribution of an Information Service in a Production Organization." *Information Services and Use,* Vol. 5, No. 3, pp. 143-156, 1985.

4. Meltzer, 1981.

5. Based on ideas made popular by P. Senge's book, *The Fifth Discipline.* New York: Doubleday, 1990.

6. Nonaka, I. and Takeuchi, H. *The Knowledge-Creating Company.* New York: Oxford University Press, 1995.

7. Slater, F.S. and Narver, J.C. "Market Oriented Isn't Enough: Build a Learning Organization." Cambridge, MA: Market Science Institute, Reports 94-103, 1994.

# Chapter 20

# Measuring Progress, Measuring Success

There are many change efforts being undertaken by organizations today and the question on everyone's mind is, "How will I know they are making a difference?" Most people think the solution is to find a way to measure what they are doing. They think that if a good "yardstick" can be devised, then it should be possible to determine if the changes being made are worth the effort. The hunt for "best" measurements, benchmarks, performance measures, and key indicators has spawned numerous workshops on measurement and data collection.

Many of these seminars ignore W. E. Deming's admonition that "The most important figures for management are unknown and unknowable." Managers believe that certain measures are essential for their change efforts (whether those measures are reengineering, total quality management, or something else) and diligently search for a list of measurements that will let them know whether they are on track and how successful their efforts have been. Some of this trust in measurements is misguided and can lead managers to ignore other factors that are equally important to running a business or other type of organization.

There is a tendency to look for simplistic measures without taking the time to understand the underlying implications and assumptions around the process of measurement. It is almost like the drunk looking for his/her keys under the street light. When asked where the keys were lost, the drunk replied, "Down the block, but the light is better over here." Too often the measures that are studied are like this story, they are convenient and easy to collect, but they have little bearing on the real organizational issues. What is seldom understood, according to W.E. Deming (mentioned at many of his seminars), is that "[t]here are no absolute values of anything. It all depends on how something is measured." It is impossible to collect measures that will be useful unless one is willing to study the process itself.

However, studying the process of measurement is viewed as too theoretical and conceptual by those who are unwilling to take the time and effort. They do not realize that a failure to understand the basic concepts of measurement can lead to the collection of useless data. In the worst case, it can even lead to completely erroneous assumptions and predictions based on incorrect data and measurements. In the information process model discussed in Chapters 18 and 19, the first step was data. If the data is wrong or unreliable, the entire process is bad from the start.

In the past, managers were doers, not thinkers; however, in the twenty-first-century organization, the real value added by managers will be as innovators, entrepreneurs, and conceptual modelers who can help find new ideas that add value for their customers and the organization. Managers must learn to be comfortable with theory building and with handling abstract concepts. If the leadership in a company is not comfortable with theory building, where will the new ideas come from? Eventually, new ideas must come from everyone, but it is the job of leaders and managers to chart the course and to be role models for the new skills and behaviors desired. As more workers are empowered, it will free many supervisors and middle managers from their former roles as overseers and inspectors. A new role for them can be to help create new ideas and information. Supervisors and middle managers will not be able to fulfill this function if they allow a search for short-term results and simplistic measures to get in the way of working with process and concepts that are ambiguous and ill defined.

When I was on a trip to visit leading Japanese companies, the plant manager at Fuji Xerox told the following story to my group: Professors from Harvard had visited the previous year, and had given a picture, the Harvard Crest, as a gift. The crest showed a man studying a book. A short time after the Harvard professors' visit, a group of MIT professors came to visit. They, too, left a picture (the MIT crest) commenting that theirs was "better" because it had two men on the crest, one with a hammer and one with a book. The MIT professors explained to the plant manager that this emphasized the value of practice as well as theory.

The Fuji Xerox manager told us that he thought both Harvard's and MIT's crests were interesting, but incomplete. He said, "For my plant, what I would like is a crest with one man on it. In one hand is a book and in the other is a hammer. This emphasizes that unlike MIT or Harvard, we want to have a well-rounded workforce." This illustrates the forward thinking views of a senior Japanese manager who does not ridicule theory, but sees it as an important component in the success of an organization.

## CONCEPTS

Concepts are the building blocks of all progress. Leaders must realize that creating, studying, and applying concepts to their work will be their key tasks in the twenty-first century. Edward de Bono, in his book, *Sur Petition*, gives the following definition of a concept: "A concept is a way of doing something which achieves a purpose and provides value."[1] Whether or not we define concepts apart from ideas, theories, models, metaphors, and analogies is less important than the ability to think conceptually and to foster conceptual dialogues in an organization. For instance, what is the difference between accountability and responsibility? This is not a trivial question, since as we move into an era of empowerment, cluster organizations, and self-managed work teams, the ability to provide leadership and see results is directly related to accountability and responsibility. Few managers would be able to provide a good definition of these two concepts. It is doubtful if a discussion around these concepts has been on the agenda of many organizational meetings. If leaders spent more time trying to develop a shared meaning around such concepts, organizations might be much further along in terms of knowing why they are succeeding or failing in the marketplace.

De Bono states, "In the future, concept development is going to be every bit as important as technical development. . . . Even if you adopt a me-too strategy and simply wait for others to develop a concept before following with the same concept, you will need some concepts of your own to follow successfully."[2] R. Stacy, in his book *Managing the Unknowable*, professes the belief that traditional strategic planning does not work because it is based on flawed concepts about the nature of systems and system stability. He believes that because of erroneous concepts and assumptions, most visions, missions, objectives, and action plans are a waste of time. He sees these concepts primarily as a means to keep people quiet and to produce a false sense of security in the organization. This false sense of security is, of course, ruinous to the organization. The antidote he offers is to foster "strategic thinking, using analogies and qualitative similarities to develop creative new ideas in the here and now, not vainly trying to predict the unknowable."[3]

## THEORY OF KNOWLEDGE

Most organizations really do not understand the reasons for their failures or their successes. (Evidence for this statement can be seen in the number of companies that quickly fall off the *Fortune 500* list and the rapid obsolescence of "Best Companies" lists.) Dr. Joseph Juran once said that 80 percent of American businesses did not understand their processes. At first, this statement sounded ludicrous to us, but over the years we have come to realize that he was right. Too much of management is an art, not a science. While there will always be an art to leadership and success, there is a need to create a balance between the art of leadership and the science of success. Such a balance is essential to understanding the successes and failures of an organization.

W. Edwards Deming was propounding a theory shortly before he died that attempted to integrate the different types of knowledge that leaders will need in the twenty-first century. He called his model "A Theory of Profound Knowledge." Deming's theory of "Profound Knowledge" had four parts: Knowledge of People, Knowledge of Variation, Theory of Knowledge, and Appreciation for a System. Each of these parts was dependent and interactive with the other parts. Before TQM became popular, such management theorists as Peter Drucker, Frederick Herzberg, Rensis Likert, and Abraham Maslow had already convinced managers of the need to understand people and to increase employee development within their organizations.

Total Quality Management (TQM) helped managers to understand the important effects that variation had on processes and quality. The major contribution of the quality movement to American business just might be its introduction of variation as a key concept in the toolbox of organizational leaders. An understanding of variation has become essential to managing product and service quality and to reducing waste and rework. The importance of systems thinking has been spotlighted by Peter Senge in his book, *The Fifth Discipline*, and by the efforts of those promoting Business Process Reengineering, Sociotechnical Systems, and Organizational Redesign.

With an acceptance of the first three parts of Deming's Profound Knowledge well underway, it only remains for managers to recognize the importance of a theory of knowledge and the role that conceptual thinking plays in such a theory. However, to date, few managers have tried to incorporate theory building and a theory of knowledge into their works. A theory of knowledge is essential for understanding success and failure. As Deming said, "Experience without theory teaches nothing."[4] Many believe that the reverse is equally true. A "theory of knowledge" is at least as important to an organization as understanding financial reports and profit-and-loss statements.

The following questions might help you to start building a theory of knowledge. How do you promote conceptual thinking in your organization? Do you allow time for people to do such thinking? How does your Concept R&D stack up against those of your competitors? Is the development of new ideas the function of only one group, one part of your organization, or do you have systems in place to encourage everyone to get involved in creating new ideas? What are the barriers to creativity and innovation in your organization? Do you have a plan to reduce such barriers? If so, how successful is your plan? Do you promote the development of a theory of knowledge in your organization? How? What are your theories?

## *MEASUREMENTS*

Just as many people confuse information with knowledge (Deming taught that a dictionary contains information but not knowledge), many confuse measurements with information. Unless one understands the differences between these concepts, one is sure to either measure the wrong things, draw the wrong conclusions from the measurements, or both. Thus, we return to Deming's remark cited earlier: "There are no absolute values of anything, it all depends on how you measure it."

A brief example will illustrate Deming's comment. My office thermometer says it is seventy-two degrees in the office. This sounds like a fairly absolute, unambiguous, and incontrovertible measurement. However, I recently purchased a thermometer watch. It measures and records the present air temperature. It will store twenty-four measures and compare each hour during a 24-hour period. Several mornings, I noticed that there was always variation in the room temperature during any 24-hour time period, regardless of the thermostat setting. Furthermore, even during the same hour, the measurements would vary depending upon where the watch was placed in the room. Given this revelation, I developed a deeper respect for Deming's admonition about the relationship of process to measurement. So, if you ask me what the temperature is in the room, I would now ask you to tell me when I should measure it and where in the room you want it measured. (We will assume that the same measurement device is used every time and that it is an extremely reliable and accurate one, which in reality is never the case). Thus, you will find that it is impossible to define an absolute value for the room temperature independent of the measuring system. When and where it is measured will affect the temperature reading by several degrees. The fact that there are no absolute values has very serious implications for any efforts undertaken to measure success and failure in organizations.

Let us apply this concept to the measurement systems in organizations. Using Total Quality Management (TQM) as an example, it is well known that many organizations that have undertaken a TQM effort have not been "successful." Critics state this is because TQM does not focus on results or that it is too process oriented. However, most of the critics either do not understand TQM or do not understand measurement and data analysis. It cannot be a question of process over results since continuous improvement (in the quality sense) cannot happen if process and results are separated. A reading of any TQM book will show that Deming, Juran, Ishikawa, and others have all noted that both process factors and result factors must be identified and understood in order for continuous improvement to take place. These factors are analogous to what in scientific experiments are called independent variables (process factors) and dependent variables (result factors).

As any scientist will tell you, it is not enough to merely identify the key variables, it is equally important to identify the correlation between the variables. For instance, if you work in a medical setting, you might want to know if a vaccine (the process) really has an impact on medical recovery (the result). You would know that this is important, but that it has often been shown that placebos can have the same result (and cost a great deal less). Failure to understand the "placebo" effect on our measurements has led to many superstitious beliefs by managers. Despite ample evidence to the contrary, managers continue to believe in the power of individual incentives and bonus systems as tools to increase organizational effectiveness. Most such superstitions could be dispelled by correlating process measurements with bottom line results. Correlations would not prove a strict cause and effect between such measures, but they do suggest that a relationship may exist.

Many people get confused because they think in terms of either/or; process factors and results factors cannot be put into such a box. In fact, they can be both, depending on the context. Something that is a process factor may also be a result factor and vice versa. This is due to the fact that each one can only be defined relative to a place in a larger process. For example, the room temperature may be the result or outcome of a number of process factors. On the other hand, if the humidifier kicks on at a certain temperature, then the temperature becomes part of the process factors relative to the humidity in the room. The humidity then becomes the result or outcome factor and the temperature is one factor affecting our measurement of this outcome. Similarly, in any organization, performance measures cannot be identified as process factors or result factors independent of the larger process and context in which they are studied. Hence, to say that TQM is not concerned with results and only looks at process is a ridiculous assertion since this is a physical impossibility. If we are studying process, then we must also be studying results at some level. It is much more accurate to say that many of the TQM critics do not understand the measurement process.

A good measurement process is essential for a successful organization. However, measures that are put in place just to be able to say that something is being measured or, worse, to check up on employees, will quickly become detriments to quality and productivity. For instance, telephone operators, travel agents, ticket takers, and telemarketers may all be monitored by measurement systems which look at the number of people served, tickets written, orders written, etc. If success and quality are only judged by the numbers, then it is fairly certain that some aspects of quality (such as customer service) will suffer in such a system. Measurement systems cannot be designed that do not have trade-offs in terms of what they promote or in terms of accuracy and reliability. It is essential that managers recognize these facts. The following list of caveats can help guide anyone who is concerned with using measures in his/her organization.

1. Be sure all measures are guides to help focus efforts and that the achievement of measures does not become an end in itself. Beware of using fear to gain a result; it will usually produce the result but at a net loss to the larger system. It will result in answers and data that are not accurate, answers and data that have been "tweaked" to give somebody the information that he/she desired.

2. Do not attempt to set numerical goals without an understanding of the process and overall process capability. To do otherwise is to engage in absolute fantasy or suboptimization of the organization. Stretch goals can usually be accomplished, but they often have detrimental effects on the rest of the organization. The ability of the system must be understood as well as the underlying goal-setting process.

3. Be sure that your understanding of process capability includes the ability to distinguish statistically between special versus common causes. Most government rules and regulations are established as though everything was a unique event (special cause), and the resulting cost to the system is overwhelming. Most of the system becomes caught up in extraordinary costs designed to prevent unique occurrences from ever happening again.

4. Understand the strengths and weaknesses of any procedures that are used to generate measures. Remember that how we measure something is as important as what we measure.

5. Be sure that the measurement process itself is subject to continual improvement. It might sound ridiculous, but measures need to be continually improved and their reliability and validity continually checked. A system should be in place to do this.

6. Recognize that (at best) your measures are mere approximations of reality. Just as there are no absolute models of reality, there are no absolute measures. Some measures are more useful than others but, as Deming notes, "The most important figures are unknown and unknowable." Your measurement system should examine the value of any measures used and indicate the pros and cons in an objective and realistic manner.

7. Be sure that your measurement system is focused on the long term as well as the short term. Financial measures, productivity measures, etc., often look only at short-term results and ignore the long-term results. This can be dangerous because the future success of the organization can be sacrificed for short-term success.

8. Use valid statistical procedures in your measurement system. You should be concerned about the validity and reliability of all measures that you produce. All measures have validity and reliability. These should be examined and published so that everyone is aware of the "dependability" of the measures.

9. Since you will probably get what you measure, you should be very sure that it is what you really want. Furthermore, if you are getting this, you will not be getting something else. Be sure you understand and can live with the trade-offs. It has been said that what gets measured gets managed, so you need to decide if what you are measuring is really what you are concerned with managing.

10. Data costs money. Don't collect it unless you are really going to use it; otherwise, you are just wasting money, time, and other people's efforts. Know what you want to use the data for before you collect it. It is important to be sure that data is tied to actions and results.

## *MINDLESSNESS*

The following are typically listed as the most common reasons for the failure of such efforts as TQM and reengineering:

1. Lack of senior management leadership
2. Improper training
3. Poor communications with key stakeholders
4. Failure to empower employees

While these are the most often cited reasons, several other reasons have been given for the failure of TQM efforts, including poor measurement systems, not focusing on results, too much focus on improvement and not enough on innovation, the need to restructure the organization, not scheduling time for TQM, not budgeting funds for TQM, lack of financial incentives for change, and disincentives with the organization.

Years of experience with successful and unsuccessful efforts have taught us that these reasons only explain part of the problem. If we dig a little deeper, we find a recurrent tendency on the part of many managers to simply want to copy others. Managers want to copy the Japanese, to benchmark the "Best in Class," or to religiously follow the latest and hottest guru or best-selling author. Pundits call this the MBS approach, Management by Best-Seller. *The International Quality Study*, conducted by Ernst and Young and the American Quality Foundation, noted the following in its Best Practices Report:

> We found that the hypothesis of universally beneficial practices is not supported by the [International Quality Study] evidence and analysis. Practices that are beneficial at one level of organizational performance show no association—or even a negative association—with performance at other levels. . . . As a result, a number of organizations are expending a tremendous amount of resources and energy on practices that have little or no impact for them.[5]

Deming was fond of saying that "You cannot copy. You must understand why something works." It would seem that the real reason for poor performance is an almost insane desire by managers to copy without understanding why something works. There is some merit to this belief. It has been attributed as evolving from an American predilection for instant results and action over reflection. Nevertheless, deeper analysis finds an even more interesting and compelling reason for the failures of not only major change efforts but even organizations. E. J. Langer calls it "mindlessness." She states that "Mindlessness sets in when we rely too rigidly on categories and distinctions created in the past. . . . We build our own and our shared realities and then we become victims to them—blind to the fact that they are constructs, ideas."[6] In other words, much like the emperor with no clothes, we let our hopes and desires blind us to the truth around us.

We believe that transformational efforts do not fail because "leaders do not lead" or "communication is poor." Transformational efforts fail because organizations blind themselves to the changes and new assumptions that are needed to become successful when the marketplace has changed. IBM floundered because it believed hardware was the future of computing. The railroads declined because railroad companies ignored the impact of the automobile and highways. Many unions have failed to anticipate or heed the changes taking place in the American workforce. The Swiss nearly lost their stronghold on the watch industry because they ignored the impact of the quartz watch, which they themselves invented.

Looking at Langer's theory in more depth, we see that theory building, itself, must proceed with caution. If not, we can easily get blinded to the fact that our theories and concepts are only limited pictures of reality at one point in time. W. T. Grant failed to realize that the principles for his stores' success were no longer valid in a new economic climate. Grant's, Zayre's Woolworth's, and Sears suffered dramatic loss of market share at a time when Wal-Mart was experiencing unprecedented growth. Similarly, Microsoft was growing while others in the computer industry, such as Control Data, Sperry Unisys, and Honeywell were experiencing downsizing and significant market loss. No one can attribute these declines to the unwillingness of the American consumer to buy. It was the companies' insistence on applying outdated principles that led each of these major companies to decline and/or to declare bankruptcy.

Mindlessness embraces a multitude of sins, all of which can be fatal. When we become mindless, we copy without understanding why something worked for someone or the context in which it worked. We lose sight of the end and confuse means with ends. Thus, teams, critical success factors, core competencies, visions, missions, SPC, quality function deployment, process redesign, strategic planning, TQM, reengineering, and the "learning" organization become ends unto themselves. The organization loses sight of what it was pursuing in the first place. Managers fail to realize that all of these concepts are merely tools to help the organization add value for its customers. The organization expends its energy on fruitless efforts to get everyone to believe in self-managed work teams (SMWT) or on arguments over whether it should do SMWTs in the first place, as though SMWTs were an end in themselves. I once saw an article titled, "Self-Managed Work Teams or Total Quality Management" as though the two were mutually exclusive possibilities. With the recent fervor over reengineering and the "learning" organization, we have seen many concepts and gurus take on an almost religious aura as though they were sacred and should not be questioned. Consultants and academicians galore are out there selling concepts as though each one was the panacea for the end of the world. Mindlessness can set in when we do any of the following:

1. Copy without understanding why something works
2. Focus on techniques, not the larger process
3. Assume that there is one best way for all time
4. Proceed without any theory or hypothesis which can be tested
5. Cite tradition and push on
6. Attempt to create an unquestionable consensus
7. Avoid conflict and disagreement for the sake of harmony
8. Rely on proven recipes and formulas
9. Stake your life on a model or theory
10. Benchmark mindlessly

Four principles or guidelines can help to avoid mindlessness and also help to begin applying a knowledge of theory. When you confront a new strategy or idea, you should ask, "What are the underlying concepts?" For instance, "What are the key concepts behind quality circles in Japan?" "What are the underlying principles or concepts behind reengineering or the "learning" organization? Second, we should try to find a theory that explains why something gives value and what limitations exist in terms of its ability to offer value. For instance, "Why did quality circles help the Japanese? What made quality circles successful in Japan?" Third, after determining why quality circles worked in Japan, try to pose a theory stating under what conditions quality circles might work in your organization, wherever it may be. Finally, you should look for a natural balance in all things. When someone says that all variation is bad, look for counterexamples of where variation might be helpful. For instance, variation in art, music, literature, ideas, and people makes life interesting and challenging. If teams are being exalted as the only way to do business, you should look for examples of when and where individuals could do things more effectively.

These four principles or guidelines could be applied to any of the current business vogues. These principles could be applied to such ideas as core competencies, critical success factors, business process reengineering, etc. Doing so will teach you a great deal about these techniques and strategies. The main point is to not let anything become mindless. When you do that, you are reduced to being a mere copier.

The theme that runs through this chapter is that we must think about what we are doing and we must have a theory that helps us to make predictions about what we are doing. The theory itself must not become a religion because it will need to be continually refined and parts of it rejected. Eventually, entirely new facts will arise that will no doubt force us to discard the entire theory. Thus, theory building, theory testing, theory refinement, and theory rejection are all part of one continuous process that gradually helps to build up knowledge about ourselves, our organizations, and our environment. Measurements are attempts to apply some objectivity to the process, but measurements themselves are a synthetic abstraction of reality. If we get blinded by the numbers and measures that we generate and do not fully appreciate the measurement process, we will surely lose sight of reality. When we lose sight of reality, we become mindless and copy from others rather than trying to understand why and how something works. Copying and mindlessness are prescriptions for failure.

## REFERENCE NOTES

1. de Bono, E. *Sur Petition.* New York: HarperCollins Publishers, Inc., 1992.

2. de Bono, 1992.

3. Stacy, R.D. *Managing the Unknowable Boundaries Between Order and Chaos in Organziations.* New York: Jossey-Bass, n.d.

4. Deming, W.E. *Out of the Crisis.* Cambridge, MA: Massachusetts Institute of Technology, 1982.

5. *International Quality Study. Top-Line Findings.* A joint project by Ernst & Young and the American Quality Foundation. Cleveland, OH, 1991.

6. Langer, E.J. *Mindfulness.* Reading, MA: Addison-Wesley Publishing Co., 1989.

# Bibliography

Ackoff, R.L. *Creating the Corporate Future*. New York: John Wiley and Sons, 1981.

Akao, Y. *Hoshin Kanri: Policy Deployment for Successful TQM*. Cambridge, MA: Productivity Press, 1991.

Berwick, D.M., Godfrey, A.B., and Roessner, J. *Curing Health Care*. San Francisco: Jossey-Bass, Inc., 1990.

Block, P. *Stewardship: Choosing Service over Self-Interest*. San Francisco: Berrett-Koehler Publishers, 1993.

de Bono, E. *Serious Creativity*. New York: Harper Business, 1992.

de Bono, E. *Sur Petition*. New York: HarperCollins Publishers, Inc., 1992.

De Jordy, H. *Blueprint for a Country Turnaround*. Toronto: CdC International Press Ltd., 1992.

Deming, W.E. *Deming's Methods for Management of Productivity and Quality*. Seminars sponsored by George Washington University.

Deming, W.E. *Out of the Crisis*. Cambridge, MA: Massachusetts Institute of Technology, 1982.

Deming, W.E. "The Logic of Evaluation." In: *The Handbook of Evaluation Research*, edited by E.L. Streuning and M. Guttentag, Vol. 1, pp. 53-68. Beverly Hills: Sage Publishers, 1975.

Deming, W.E. *Quality, Productivity and Competitive Position*. Seminar series.

*Dictionary of Occupational Titles*, Fourth Edition. U.S. Department of Labor, Employment, and Training Administration, 1977.

Ditz, D., Ranganathan, J.R., and Banks, R.D. (Eds.). *Green Ledgers: Case Studies in Corporate Environmental Accounting*. Baltimore: World Resources Institute Publications, 1995.

Drucker, P.F. "Managing the Information Explosion." *The Wall Street Journal*, April 10, 1980, p. 24.

*Environmental Self-Assessment Program*. Washington, DC: Global Environmental Management Initiative. 2000 L. Street N.W., Suite 710, Washington DC 20036. Call 202-296-7449 or Fax 202-296-7442 for a free copy of Environmental Self-Assessment Program.

Fairview Values Project Task Force. *Identifying and Integrating Organization Values for Fairview Hospitals and Healthcare Services*. Unpublished report, Fairview Hospitals, Minneapolis, MN: September, 1992.

Foster, R.N. *Innovation: The Attacker's Advantage*. New York: Summit Books, 1986.

Greenleaf, R. K. *Servant Leadership*. New York: Paulist Press, 1977.

Hamel, G. and Prahalad, C.K. *Competing for the Future*. Boston: Harvard Business School Press, 1994.

Hammer, M. and Champy, J. *Reengineering the Corporation*. New York: Harper Business, 1993.

Horton, T.R. "The Business of Managing Information." In: *Innovative Management for Changing Times: Tips from Thomas R. Horton, President and CEO*. New York: American Management Association, 1987.

Howe, R.J., Gaeddert, D., and Howe, M.A. *Quality On Trial*. St. Paul, MN: West Publishing Co., 1993.

Imai, M. *Kaizen*. New York: Random House Business Division, 1986.

*International Quality Study: Top-Line Findings*. A joint project by Ernst & Young and the American Quality Foundation. Cleveland, OH, 1991.

Ishikawa, K. *What Is Total Quality Control?* Translated by David J. Lu. Englewood Cliffs, NJ: Prentice-Hall, Inc., 1985.

Joiner, B.L. "Teaching Statistics to Managers." Paper Presented at the 43rd Annual Conference on Applied Statistics, Newark, NJ.

Juran, J.M. *Juran on Leadership for Quality*. New York: The Free Press, 1989.

Kanter, R.M. and Stein, B.A. "Unloading Overload." *Management Review*, Vol. 76, No. 11, pp. 22-24, 1987.

Kohn, A. *Punished by Rewards*. Boston: Houghton Mifflin Co., 1993.

Kuhn, T.S. *The Structure of Scientific Revolutions*. Chicago: University of Chicago Press, 1962.

Langer, E.J. *Mindfulness*. Reading, MA: Addison-Wesley Publishing Co., 1989.

Le Roux, H. S. "A Managerially Based Framework for the Role and Contribution of an Information Service in a Production Organization." *Information Services and Use*, Vol. 5, No. 3, pp. 143-156, 1985.

Lewin, K. *Field Theory in Social Science: Selected Theoretical Papers*, edited by D. Cartwright. New York: Harper and Row, 1951.

Lewis, C.I. *Mind and the New World Order*. Dover, England: Scribners, 1929.

Madlin, N. "Remapping the Corporation." *Management Review*, Vol. 76, No. 5, pp. 60-61, 1987.

Marchand, D.A., and Horton, F.W., Jr. *Infotrends*. New York: John Wiley and Sons, 1986.

McGrane, J.M. "Going On Line for Planning and Competitive Intelligence." *Management Review*, Vol. 76, No. 10, pp. 55-56, 1987.

McKenny, J.L. and McFarlan, F.W. "The Information Archipelago–Maps and Bridges." *Harvard Business Review*, Vol. 60, No. 5, pp. 109-119, 1982.

Meltzer, M.F. *Information: The Ultimate Management Resource*. New York: AMACOM, 1981.

Mintzberg, H. *The Rise and Fall of Strategic Planning*. New York: The Free Press, 1994.

Montazemi, A.R. and Conrath, D.W., "The Use of Cognitive Mapping for Information Requirements." *MIS Quarterly*, Vol. 4, No. 4, pp. 45-55, 1980.

Munro, M.C. and Wheeler, B.R., "Planning, Critical Success Factors, and Management's Information Requirements." *MIS Quarterly*, Vol. 4, No. 4, pp. 27-38, 1980.

Munro-Faure, L. and Munro-Faure, M. *Implementing Total Quality Management.* London: Pitman Publishing, 1992.

Nadler, D.A., Gerstein, M.S., Shaw, R.B. and Associates. *Organizational Architecture.* San Francisco: Jossey-Bass Publishers, 1992.

National Geographic Society. *Changing Geographic Perspectives.* Proceedings of the Centennial Symposium, 1988.

Nonaka, I. and Takeuchi, H. *The Knowledge Creating Company.* New York: Oxford University Press, 1995.

Olson, S.R. *Ideas and Data: The Process and Practice of Social Research.* Homewood, IL: Dorsey Press, 1976.

Parsons, G.L. "Information Technology: A New Competitive Weapon." *California Management Review*, Vol. 25, No. 1, pp. 3-13, 1983.

Perez, V.I. "Levels of Sophistication of Information Management Systems and Their Upgrading." *Information and Management*, Vol. 7, No. 1, pp. 29-36, 1984.

Persico, J. "Query: Can Quality Improvement Principles Be Applied to Crime and the Criminal Justice System?" *Judicature, the Journal of the American Judicature Society,* Vol. 73, No. 2, pp. 66-68, 1989.

Peters, T. and Waterman, R. *In Search of Excellence.* New York: HarperCollins, 1982.

Pildtich, J. *How Winning Companies Create the Products We All Want to Buy.* New York: Harper and Row, 1987.

Priesmeyer, H.R. *Organizations and Chaos.* Westport, CT: Quorum Books, 1992.

Quinn, J.B. *Intelligent Enterprise.* New York: The Free Press, 1992.

Rawls, J. *A Theory of Justice.* Boston: Harvard University Press, 1989.

"REL Consultancy Group Survey." *Quality Progress,* Vol. 28, No. 6, 1995.

Remus, W.E. and Kottemann, J.E. "Toward Intelligent Decision Support Systems: An Artificially Intelligent Statistician." *MIS Quarterly* Vol. 10, No. 4, pp. 403-419, 1986.

Sahrmann, H.F. "Information—The Key to Process Improvement." In: *Quality: The Universal Equation for Excellence.* Proceedings of the 41st Annual Quality Congress, pp. 569-573. Milwaukee: American Society for Quality Control, 1987.

Semler, R. *Maverick.* New York: Warner Books, 1993.

Senge, P. *The Fifth Discipline.* New York: Doubleday, 1990.

Shewhart, W.A. *Economic Control of Quality of Manufactured Product.* New York: Van Nostrand Co., 1931.

Slater, F.S., and Narver, J.C. "Market Oriented Isn't Enough: Build a Learning Organization." Cambridge, MA: Market Science Institute, Report #94-103, 1994.

Stacey, R.D. *Managing the Unknowable Boundaries Between Order and Chaos in Organizations.* New York: Jossey-Bass, n.d.

*State of the World.* L. R. Brown, project director. Worldwatch Institute Report on Progress Toward a Sustainable Society. New York: W.W. Norton and Co., 1993.

Stearn, G.E. (Ed.) *McLuhan: Hot and Cold.* New York: The New American Library, 1967.

Tzu, S. *The Art of War.* Translated by S. B. Griffith. New York: Oxford University Press, 1963.

Vacca, J. "Information Quality Analysis." *Infosystems*, Vol. 32, No. 11, pp. 60-61, 1987.

Von Oech, Roger. *Creative Whack Pack.* Stamford, CT: U.S. Games Systems, Inc., 1992.

Vroom, V. H. *Work and Motivation.* New York: John Wiley and Sons, 1964.

Webb, E.J., Campbell, D.T., Schwartz, R.D., and Sechrest, L. *Unobtrusive Measures: Nonreactive Research in the Social Sciences.* Chicago: Rand McNally, 1965.

Wheatley, M. J. *Leadership and the New Science.* San Francisco: Berrett-Koehler Publishers, 1992.

World Resources Institute. *Green Ledgers*, edited by D. Ditz, J. Ranganathan, and R.D. Banks. Baltimore: World Resources Institute Publications, 1995.

Zaleznik, A. *Learning Leadership.* Chicago: Bonus Books, Inc., 1993.

# Index

Page numbers followed by the letter "f" indicate figures.

# Order Your Own Copy of
# This Important Book for Your Personal Library!

## THE NEW BUSINESS VALUES FOR SUCCESS IN THE TWENTY-FIRST CENTURY

### Improvement, Innovation, Inclusion, Incentives, Information

_____ in hardbound at $49.95 (ISBN: 0-7890-0155-1)

_____ in softbound at $19.95 (ISBN: 0-7890-0239-6)

| | |
|---|---|
| COST OF BOOKS _____ | ☐ **BILL ME LATER:** ($5 service charge will be added)<br>(Bill-me option is good on US/Canada/Mexico orders only; not good to jobbers, wholesalers, or subscription agencies.) |
| OUTSIDE USA/CANADA/<br>MEXICO: ADD 20%_____ | |
| POSTAGE & HANDLING _____<br>(US: $3.00 for first book & $1.25<br>for each additional book)<br>Outside US: $4.75 for first book<br>& $1.75 for each additional book) | ☐ Check here if billing address is different from shipping address and attach purchase order and billing address information.<br><br>Signature_____ |
| SUBTOTAL _____ | ☐ **PAYMENT ENCLOSED: $** _____ |
| IN CANADA: ADD 7% GST _____ | ☐ **PLEASE CHARGE TO MY CREDIT CARD.** |
| STATE TAX _____<br>(NY, OH & MN residents, please<br>add appropriate local sales tax) | ☐ Visa    ☐ MasterCard    ☐ AmEx    ☐ Discover<br>☐ Diner's Club<br><br>Account # _____ |
| **FINAL TOTAL** _____<br>(If paying in Canadian funds,<br>convert using the current<br>exchange rate. UNESCO<br>coupons welcome.) | Exp. Date _____<br><br>Signature _____ |

Prices in US dollars and subject to change without notice.

NAME _____

INSTITUTION _____

ADDRESS _____

CITY _____

STATE/ZIP _____

COUNTRY _____ COUNTY (NY residents only) _____

TEL _____ FAX _____

E-MAIL_____
May we use your e-mail address for confirmations and other types of information? ☐ Yes    ☐ No

*Order From Your Local Bookstore or Directly From*
**The Haworth Press, Inc.**
10 Alice Street, Binghamton, New York 13904-1580 • USA
TELEPHONE: 1-800-HAWORTH (1-800-429-6784) / Outside US/Canada: (607) 722-5857
FAX: 1-800-895-0582 / Outside US/Canada: (607) 772-6362
E-mail: getinfo@haworth.com
PLEASE PHOTOCOPY THIS FORM FOR YOUR PERSONAL USE.

BOF96